THE SOCIAL WELFARE FORUM, 1978

John B. Turner

THE
SOCIAL WELFARE
FORUM, 1978

OFFICIAL PROCEEDINGS, 105TH ANNUAL FORUM

NATIONAL CONFERENCE ON SOCIAL WELFARE

LOS ANGELES, CALIFORNIA

MAY 21–MAY 24, 1978

Published 1979 for the

NATIONAL CONFERENCE ON SOCIAL WELFARE *by*

COLUMBIA UNIVERSITY PRESS *New York*

ISBN: 0-231-04702-9 clothbound
      0-231-04703-7 paperback
Library of Congress Catalog Number: 8-85377
PRINTED IN THE UNITED STATES OF AMERICA

Foreword

THE EDITORIAL COMMITTEE is happy to present this representative selection from among the thoughtful speeches and papers presented at the 105th Annual Forum. With the theme of "Social Services/Human Services, a Team Effort," the Forum explored ways to work together. President Turner opened the Forum by commending Congress and the national Administration for considering national government policies and programs to improve the quality of living for all Americans, but cautioned that responsibility for insuring a maximum social welfare impact rests with all of us.

The Forum program included a lecture in memory of Joe R. Hoffer, who died September 28, 1977; he had served as Executive Secretary for the National Conference on Social Welfare from 1948 to 1972. This stirring memorial address was delivered by the Reverend Jesse L. Jackson. The Forum also featured the Whitney M. Young, Jr., Memorial Lecture, delivered by James Farmer.

This volume includes papers on broad national policies such as welfare reform, ethical issues about distribution of resources and opportunities, and ways of helping particular groups, such as immigrants, discharged mental patients, minorities, and persons suffering from delinquent behavior and illiteracy. Space limitation prevented the inclusion of many other excellent papers; copies of all manuscripts are on file at the national office, however.

Members of the Editorial Committee were H. Frederick Brown, John J. Cardwell, Lela Costin, Bernice Harper, and Patricia W. Soyka. We also appreciate the consulation of Margaret E. Berry, Executive Director, NCSW, and John D. Moore, Columbia University Press.

We hope you will enjoy reading this volume and that it will be useful for many years. It was a pleasure to serve the members of the Conference.

JAMES E. HUDDLESTON
Chairman, Editorial Committee

National Conference on Social Welfare Distinguished Service Awards

THE NATIONAL CONFERENCE on Social Welfare Distinguished Service Awards for 1978 were awarded to the following:

COY EKLUND who, as president and Chief Executive Officer of the Equitable Assurance Society, has provided leadership demonstrating acute awareness of corporate social responsibility, as evidenced by the company's practical concern for the betterment of cities, for the housing of citizens, for the advancement of minority well-being, and for its effective affirmative action and corporate support programs; as well as by his own dedication to serving those who are less fortunate.

In both his personal and business affairs he has consistently demonstrated commitment to a better life for all, and he exemplifies leadership to be cherished in private enterprise consistent with the public interest.

VERNON E. JORDAN, JR., who, as Executive Director of the National Urban League, is providing leadership unique and admirable, vigorously calling the nation's attention to the continuing plight of black Americans, thus embracing the problems of all disadvantaged, and the unmet needs of society as a whole—employment, adequate income, housing, health, and welfare.

He has, in reality, made his struggle our struggle—exemplifying in every way all that is to be cherished in leadership by a professional in the voluntary sector.

CYNTHIA C. WEDEL for her lifetime of voluntary and tireless commitment to organizations such as the American National Red Cross, the World Council of Churches, Church Women United, the National Council of Organizations for Children and Youth, the President's Commission on the Status of Women, and countless others, which has not only contributed to the betterment of human conditions in this country and around the world, but has also provided an inspiring example to women everywhere.

She has, in reality, made the hopes and aspirations of others a mandate for herself, exemplifying in every way all that is to be cherished in the volunteer sector.

May 24, 1978   JOHN B. TURNER
105th Annual Forum   *President*
Los Angeles, California
                                                       MARGARET E. BERRY
                                                       Executive Director

NATIONAL CONFERENCE ON SOCIAL WELFARE
DISTINGUISHED SERVICE AWARDS, 1955–1978

1955   EDITH M. BAKER, Washington, D.C.
       FEDELE F. FAURI, Ann Arbor, Mich.
       ELIZABETH WICKENDEN, New York
1956   TIAC (Temporary Inter-Association Council) PLANNING COMMITTEE, New York
1957   THE REVEREND MARTIN LUTHER KING, JR., Montgomery, Ala.
       WILBUR J. COHEN, Ann Arbor, Mich.
1958   THE HONORABLE JOHN E. FOGARTY, R.I.
       LEONARD W. MAYO, New York
1959   ELISABETH SHIRLEY ENOCHS, Washington, D.C.
       OLLIE A. RANDALL, New York
1960   LOULA DUNN, Chicago
       RALPH BLANCHARD, New York
       HELEN HALL, New York
1961   THE HONORABLE AIME J. FORAND, R.I.
1962   JOSEPH P. ANDERSON, New York
       THE ATLANTA *Constitution,* Ralph McGill and Jack Nelson, Atlanta, Ga.
       CHARLOTTE TOWLE, Chicago
1963   HARRIETT M. BARTLETT, Cambridge, Mass.
       ERNEST JOHN BOHN, Cleveland
       FLORENCE G. HELLER, Glencoe, Ill.
       Special Award: Television Documentary, "The Battle of Newburgh," IRVING GITLIN and the NATIONAL BROADCASTING COMPANY, New York
       Special Citation (Posthumous): ANNA ELEANOR ROOSEVELT, "First Lady of the World"
1964   DR. ROBERT M. FELIX, Bethesda, Md.
       Special Citation (Posthumous): JOHN FITZGERALD KENNEDY, "Man of Destiny"
1965   JAMES V. BENNETT, Washington, D.C.
       SIDNEY HOLLANDER, Baltimore
       CORA KASIUS, New York

1966 REPRESENTATIVE WILBUR D. MILLS, Ark.
1967 THE HONORABLE HUBERT H. HUMPHREY, Washington, D.C.
PLANNED PARENTHOOD—WORLD POPULATION
Special Awards (Posthumous):
HOWARD F. GUSTAFSON, Indianapolis
RUTH M. WILLIAMS, New York
1968 LOMA MOYER ALLEN, Rochester, N.Y.
KENNETH BANCROFT CLARK, New York
1969 THE HONORABLE ELMER L. ANDERSEN, St. Paul, Minn.
HARRY L. LURIE, New York
IDA C. MERRIAM, Washington, D.C.
1970 No award
1971 SAM S. GRAIS, St. Paul, Minn.
DOROTHY I. HEIGHT, New York
1972 WHITNEY M. YOUNG, JR. *(Posthumous)*
1973 WINSLOW CARLTON, New York
THE HONORABLE JAMES CHARLES EVERS, Fayette, Miss.
JOE R. HOFFER, Columbus, Ohio
NATIONAL COUNCIL OF JEWISH WOMEN, New York
1974 ASSOCIATION OF AMERICAN INDIAN SOCIAL WORKERS
1975 MITCHELL I. GINSBERG, New York
1976 BERTRAM S. BROWN, M.D., Rockville, Md.
THE HONORABLE BARBARA JORDAN, Washington, D.C.
THE HONORABLE WALTER F. MONDALE, Washington, D.C.
WILLIAM A. MORRILL, Washington, D.C.
1977 ROY WILKINS, New York
1978 COY EKLUND, New York
VERNON E. JORDAN, JR., New York
CYNTHIA C. WEDEL, Washington, D.C.

In Memoriam
Joe R. Hoffer

JOE R. HOFFER, Executive Secretary of the National Conference on Social Welfare for nearly a quarter of a century, died on September 28, 1977. He had also been Secretary General of the International Council on Social Welfare for eighteen of those years. His death meant "the end of an entire era of social welfare," as Kate Katzki, ICSW Secretary General, so aptly put it, and the loss of "a true social statesman in every sense of the term," according to John Turner, NCSW President.

A man of courage and vision, dedicated to ideas and ideals, he served NCSW as Executive Secretary from 1948 until 1972, coming to it during serious financial problems and leading it successfully through those as well as subsequent crises of reorganization, priorities, civil rights, and demonstrations. He headed ICSW from 1948 to 1966, and has been called the principal force behind its development.

When he died Joe Hoffer was Chief of the Medical Assis-

tance Program of the Ohio Department of Public Welfare in
Columbus where he had been since 1974. Between his retirement from NCSW and this final post he served as a Visiting
Professor in the School of Social Work at Ohio State University, his alma mater, where he had received his Ph.D. He was
honored by the university as "one of its most distinguished
alumni" in 1970; by the American Public Welfare Association
with its Award of Special Merit in 1972; and by NCSW with
its Distinguished Service Award in 1973.

Quiet, unassuming, and calm, Joe Hoffer was a perfec-
tionist and an achiever. He was a scholar, an administrator, a
teacher, a writer, a world traveler, an athlete, and a leader in
the social welfare field. In all of these categories he per-
sonified self-discipline and excellence.

His untimely passing was mourned by many around the
globe, for, as one of his friends from overseas wrote at that
time to his widow, Mary, "The world has lost a truly dedicated international public servant."

Greetings to the Conference from President Jimmy Carter

MOST OF YOU attending the 105th Annual Forum of the National Conference on Social Welfare know that your 1978 theme is of strong personal interest to me. None of my earlier work as Governor of Georgia brought me greater satisfaction than the challenge of making a "team effort" of "social services and human services." Bringing agencies closer together in the interest of the mentally retarded and the mentally ill was one of the most rewarding of the gains we made in this critically important task.

Both Rosalynn and I continue to feel that effective community help for our most vulnerable, troubled, and distressed citizens must be among our highest priorities. As President, I have initiated many proposals toward this end, and there will be more to follow. With the support of the Congress, we have already seen considerable progress in this area. And we remain determined to persevere until we have fully realized our objectives. More than ever we look to you—the leaders in this field—to assist us in formulating sound and sensitive public policies that effectively meet the needs of our people.

May you have a most stimulating and productive session.

Contents

Contents

THE SOCIAL WELFARE FORUM, 1978

Social Services / Human Services: a Team Effort

JOHN B. TURNER

ALTHOUGH LIFE HAS improved for perhaps many Americans, a sizable number of our people continue to live in the shadow of happiness, but never with it. They are second-class citizens. The census reports that, in general, those who do live well are satisfied with their lives, except, perhaps, for the squeeze of inflation, a concern about violence and crime, about social dislocation due to busing, and occasional annoyance with television and the press.

There are, however, the private concerns about careers, children, and parents which we are more reluctant to discuss with poll-takers. Even the majority who fare well face new threats to the quality of their lives, threats which emanate from the material and physical environments, by-products of economic and technological advances in meeting our material wants and needs. Also, we face threats from the social environments which may adversely influence the ability of people to cope effectively with individual and family responsibilities.

In the area of cultural pluralism, substantial progress has been made, especially with regard to public treatment of most of the Third World minorities. But resistance to insuring socioeconomic equity for minorities melts far too slowly if at all.

In sum, one must reluctantly recognize the aptness of the phrase "two Americas" popularized in the Kerner Commis-

JOHN B. TURNER is Kenan Professor, School of Social Work, University of North Carolina, Chapel Hill, and President, National Conference on Social Welfare.

sion's report.[1] The first America consists of a majority of
people, for whom the promises of our constitution are abun-
dantly, if imperfectly, realized. The second America is comprised of those whose lives are chronically troubled and de-
meaned, in Michael Harrington's phrase, "the other
America."[2] This is the America which lives within the
shadow of happiness but seldom with it. It is to alleviate these
social ills and stresses that social welfare policies and programs are created.

THE MISSION OF SOCIAL WELFARE

A once popular and flattering view of the welfare worker was
that of a knight in shining armor, defending the poor, pro-
tecting the defenseless. The mission of social welfare is still
anchored in a conscious concern for the poor and the disadvantaged. But the expectations of social welfare programs
have shifted from a focus on survival to one on helping people to escape from their economic and social handicaps, from
a concept of benign paternalism to a focus on human rights.
Unfortunately, too many people still do not understand that
"rights" in this context refer to entitlement to equal opportunity and its results.

Along with this shift in expectations the province of social
welfare has slowly expanded to include dealing with the social hazards faced by the nonpoor. Neil Gilbert, in writing
about the "transformation of social services" during the
1960s to the present, describes this as a "drift towards universalism."[3]

The move toward universalism is not without its problems
as well as its merits. Many see it as a way of erasing stigma
long associated with social welfare clientele, and as a way of

[1] *Report of the National Advisory Commission on Civil Disorders* (New York: New York
Times Co., 1968).
[2] Michael Harrington, *The Other America: Poverty in the United States* (New York:
Macmillan Co., 1962).
[3] Neil Gilbert, "The Transformation of Social Services," *Social Service Review*, December, 1977, pp. 926–29.

increasing public understanding and support of welfare programs. While agreeing with this, others are troubled that universalism may pull already scarce financial resources and the more talented manpower away from the traditional priorities of the most needy.

THE ESSENCE OF ACCOUNTABILITY

Ten years from now, how possible is it that the major risk populations of the poor and socially disabled will not only remain undiminished in size but will contain a large proportion of the people who are presently included in those populations? For example, is there a better than even chance that with more day care programs, more community health centers, more job-training programs, we also will have more children born out of wedlock and correspondingly high infant mortality rates, the same unemployment rates for minorities, the same percentages of people living in poverty, getting divorces, being repeatedly victimized socially and physically?

I recognize some of the problems involved in trying to answer such questions, but if we go by the evidence of the past ten years, the answer is discouraging. Yes, things will be as bad or worse. Let us look briefly at poverty, unemployment, and teen-age pregnancies.

In 1969 there were 24.1 million Americans below the poverty level. By 1975 this number had increased to 25.9 million.[4]

Although more Americans are working than ever before (because there are more Americans than ever before), the unemployment rate remains about the same except for cyclical fluctuations. What is very disturbing is the chronic gap between white and minority unemployment. Black unemployment constantly remains approximately twice that of whites. Even more disturbing is the exceedingly high unem-

[4] U.S. Department of Commerce, Current Population Reports—Consumer Income: Characteristics of the Population Below the Poverty Level 1975. Series P.6 No. 106, June, 1977.

ployment rate of minority youths, currently around 39 percent to 40 percent.[5]

Teen-age pregnancies appear to be increasing, and white teen-age pregnancies exceed those of minorities. Every year, over one million teen-age girls, mostly single, some younger than fifteen, become pregnant. In 1975 the number of out-of-wedlock births to teen-agers was 233,500. In 1975 federal and state cash welfare payments to households with teen-age mothers or older women who first gave birth in their teens were reported to be $4.65 billion—half the over-all cost of the Aid to Families with Dependent Children program.[6]

These, of course, are not the only areas for comparison, and certainly we serve some people and some problems very well. However, the more worrisome problems, affecting large numbers of our citizens, show few reverses in the growth rate or in the severity of their problems. Unfortunately, the social welfare field lacks a national reporting system on results achieved with its clientele. Reports on changes in the size of risk populations are rarely provided as a function of social welfare service. To answer questions of social welfare impact, we need more and better data than are presently available.

COMMITMENT FOR THE FUTURE

The Carter Administration and the Congress are demonstrating an unusually large appetite for considering national government policies and programs to improve the quality of living for all Americans. Currently, the following social policy initiatives are on the national agenda: national health insurance; full employment and better jobs; mental health programs; urban policy; welfare reform; services for families; and tax reform. Such a response from the Administration and the Congress reflects a deep and broad and commendable concern that all Americans should fare well.

---

[5] Robert B. Hill, "The Economic Status of Black Families and Children," in *The State of Black America* (New York: National Urban League, Inc., 1978).

[6] Spencer Rich, "Teen-age Pregnancy Boom" as reprinted in San Francisco Sunday *Examiner and Chronicle*, May 14, 1978.

But the responsibility for insuring a maximum social welfare impact rests with the entire social welfare field, not just with our federal and state governments. We must be prepared to say what else is needed, in what amount, with what priority, and toward what end. We must reexamine our own priorities and technical competencies.

Economic policy action. My first suggestion for consideration by the social welfare professions is that exerting influence on national economic policy should be the central target of political and social action. Let me say parenthetically that including economic policy as a legitimate area for social welfare action means that we should seek a more active collaboration with economists, especially labor and urban economists. Martin Rein argues that "we erred in believing that we could neatly separate economics from social policies. And, more specifically that income-support programs could have sufficient redistributive force without major change in economic policy and in labor market conditions."[7] To illustrate his view, Rein points to our inability to reform programs like Aid to Families with Dependent Children to bring about a more equitable distribution of incomes.

Vernon Jordan takes a similar stand. The National Urban League opposes the proposed national tax cut because it would not contribute toward solving the problems of minorities. "There is little evidence to conclude that the job stimulation effect of the tax cut would trickle down to minorities." Chiding those critics who propose that civil rights leaders should stick to civil rights and leave national economic policy alone, Jordan observes that unemployment for whites would drop a little, but that the astronomically high rate for minorities would be largely unaffected.[8]

Rein concludes that along with fiscal, occupational, and social policy, attention must be paid to "economic policies

[7] Martin Rein, "Social Equity and Social Policy," *Social Service Review*, December, 1977, pp. 565, 569–78.

[8] Vernon E. Jordan, Jr., address delivered to the National Press Club, Washington, D.C., 1978.

such as those designed to fight inflation,"[9] the key criterion being the extent to which such policies are pro-redistributive. In short, it is necessary that marketplace policies be modified if we wish to see substantial reductions in the percentage of people, especially minorities, currently enrolled in social welfare programs. Therefore, efforts to influence economic policies in this sense not only are legitimate undertakings, but necessary actions.

Preventive programs and policies. My second suggestion concerns making a more conscious effort to shift to the prevention level the priority of outcomes that we seek in social welfare. It is obvious that we cannot begin to decrease the number of poor and socially disabled by programs and services which are primarily directed toward rehabilitation, crisis response, and maintenance. What is not so obvious is how to shift our objectives to prevention and how to develop prevention technologies.

The National Conference on Social Welfare's report on the future for social services observes that the fact that people tend to come for services after the onset of their problems, and that services are primarily geared to responding to problems after their onset, means problems become so large and so complex that alleviating them frequently requires more resources and more knowledge than we can bring to bear on such situations.[10]

The report of the President's Commission on Mental Health calls for a strategy for prevention, stating that "efforts to prevent problems before they occur are a necessary ingredient of a systematic approach to promoting mental health."[11] This comment appears to be an understatement of the importance of prevention, particularly as applied to deal-

[9] Rein, *op. cit.*, p. 568.

[10] Report of the Task Force, *The Future For Social Services in the United States* (Columbus, Ohio: National Conference on Social Welfare, 1977), pp. 45–49.

[11] *Report to the President from the President's Commission on Mental Health* (Washington, D.C.: U.S. Government Printing Office, 1978), I, 51.

ing with social disabilities which can and offtimes do relegate a person to a lifetime in the "other America."

It would help to have a federal policy with respect to social welfare funding which clearly *rewards* those programs that both seek and accomplish prevention at the primary and secondary levels. We also need increased federal support for experimental and field studies to develop the knowledge and technologies related to: changing behavior which is self-defeating; and removing risks, or providing protection from risks, which are present in the workings of social systems in which risk populations reside.

We need a system that will provide extra rewards to workers and to volunteers for achieving good results from prevention efforts with their clientele. A new priority emphasis on prevention will of necessity stress national economic policy; it will stress work with children, youth, and, especially, families; and it will systematically screen institutional policies, governmental and private, for their impact upon people and their handicaps.

Greater teamwork. Finally, I call for more effective teamwork. This too is not a new idea, but it needs a new connection if we are to realize its benefits.

Frequently, the diversity of this society is singled out for special attention. We are a nation of colorful contrasts in backgrounds, perspectives, and interests. Although some view such diversity as a source of social problems and even as a prominent source of national weakness, others see it much more as a source of cultural and social enrichment, an expanded pool of alternative ideas and creativity, a reservoir of national strength. To the objective observer, undoubtedly, diversity is both a source of difficulty and a source of strength.

On balance I believe, as I think most thoughtful Americans do, that the potential for strength and expanded alternatives far outweighs whatever difficulties may be inherently involved in diversity. Regardless of one's predilections, the na-

tion is a mosaic of diversity, bonded together, albeit trouble-
somely at times, by the overarching and dominating
purposes of our democracy.

The human service field is no exception to this pattern.
Contrasts and differences are reflected in the great multiplic-
ity of social programs; alternative patterns of sponsorship;
specialization of mission, function, clientele, and methods of
helping; and differences in manpower disciplines, training,
and uses.

The average state operates between eighty and one
hundred social service programs. The average large city has
two to three hundred governmental and voluntary, sectarian,
and nonsectarian programs. Small towns and/or counties
have a commensurate allocation of services and programs.

This conglomerate of activity is further differentiated in
terms of an array of personal and group problems, and/or
the stage of life of the clientele. Within both categories of
service organization there is a variety of assumptions about
what social and interpersonal interventions are required in
order to provide cost-effective assistance related to outcomes
desired by both the client and the public.

An additional area of diversity is found in the profile of
social welfare manpower. There are slightly more than
350,000 social service jobs alone.[12] Not only do these jobs
require personnel from different fields, but they use personnel with different levels of training; moreover many vital services are staffed with either full- or part-time volunteers.

The umbilical cord which loosely holds together this
variegated welfare system is composed of two principal
strands. One strand is comprised of common sources of public sanction: values and laws which express a humanistic concept of social justice and human rights; and concepts of majority group protection, survival, and self-interest. The
second strand is represented by an interdependence of ef-

[12] Spark Matsonaga, "Congressman Praises Social Worker Role in American Society," *NASW News,* April, 1978, p. 1.

forts stemming from both a sharing of, and competition for, clientele, and from competition for scarce resources with which to support program activities.

Diversity, however, does pose two particular threats to the goals of the human service field. First, there is the tendency to assign unequal status to diverse groups, which becomes a basis for the distribution of goods and services. Second, there is a tendency to abuse the legitimate functions of specialization or categorical interests, excluding or downplaying representation of other groups in the discussion of problems and in the negotiation and weighing of policy and action alternatives.

Social welfare is inextricably caught up in the influence of both forces. Many of the problems of a major proportion of its clientele are related to the first threat, which is a particular challenge because of the further tendency to reinforce itself by client behavior that self-fulfills the prophecy. To have an impact on social problems of this order requires that there be a unified voice from the social services and that there also be collaboration with other human service sectors, such as education, housing, health, and employment.

Abuses from specialization within social services as well as among the human service sectors can retard such collaboration both in regard to the specific help needed by an individual or group and in regard to the impact of social structure upon people. Thus, the theme for the 105th Annual Forum of the NCSW seeks to focus attention on the interdependency of programs, services, and goals and the need for more mutually advantageous ways of working together. Parenthetically, it is just this need which makes the purposes of the NCSW as relevant today as they were at the time of its founding.

There are several ways which could be used more effectively to bring about multispecialization and multidisciplinary collaboration. Perhaps the most effective way will derive from an increasingly strong expectation of outcomes which

significantly improve people's economic security without
stigma and which significantly reduce the chances of social
disability.

Americans from all walks of life are asking with greater
frequency how much we should pay to save a life. The loud-
est voices are raised about medical care, but increasingly one
hears the question: Why should we pay for the self-defeating
or self-destructive behavior of others?

Every President of NCSW for at least the last twenty years
has warned our forums of the need to protect against erosion
of life values by decisions which place a low value on human
lives, especially those that are less equal than others. Titmuss
has pointed out that the pursuit of equality is fraught with
many hazards, that the continuity of commitment to this aim
is continuously in danger of being undermined.[13]

Frederick Jackson Turner, a student of social and political
history in this country, wrote: "If mankind could once really
understand what it has done and thought in the past, is it not
possible that it would stumble along now and in the future
with more intelligence and a more conscious purpose?"

If, indeed, we are ready to walk with more intelligence—if,
indeed, we are impatient and are ready to quicken the pace
of our conscious purpose—we will, with a sense of urgency
and immediacy act to perfect our team effort in the human
services field to make economic policy more pro-redistributive, and to make our services more oriented toward prevention.

[13] Richard Titmuss, *Essays in the Welfare State* (New Haven, Conn.: Yale University
Press, 1956), as quoted in Rein, *op. cit.*, p. 566.

In Search of Alternatives to Welfare and Despair: New Challenges to Leadership

THE JOE R. HOFFER MEMORIAL LECTURE

JESSE L. JACKSON

In SEARCH OF certain alternatives to welfare and despair, new challenges to leadership, there are several premises from which I operate. The first premise is that we can save our children. Cynics do not believe that. Many professionals do not believe that, but it is possible. Secondly, we ought to save them—it is our moral responsibility. Thirdly, we must save them if we expect to save ourselves and our civilization. We can save them; we ought to; we must.

One of the things that I learned when I first went to graduate school was ways to use long words with short meanings. Dr. Tillich would say that "God is from Logos," or "God is the ground of my being"; Niebuhr, He is "nature and destiny." My Grandma would say He is "my all and all"—it meant the same thing. It meant absolutely the same thing, but they had to justify charging us to read and so they had to teach us those words.

I learned one time how we raised the "dozens" to an acceptable level. Some of us who come from a particular idiom know that the word "dozens" does not refer to eggs. When people say unkind things about another person's mama, usually it's called the "dozens." Usually when people perceive

THE REV. JESSE L. JACKSON is President, People United to Save Humanity (PUSH).

the "dozens" to be the "dozens," they join the fight, and then there is conflict over who has the most creative way of putting your mother down.

A lot of our professionals engage in a highly acceptable level of "dozens" playing. It is so smooth that people do not even get mad. That is because it has not been melted down so they can understand it. "Accumulated environmental deficit"—that means that your daddy's not home and your mama can't talk well. If you use "accumulated environmental deficit" long enough and you get bitten by it, then you need at least two professional workers to bring your check. One of them will stay and guard you; the other will stay and help you spend it. If you have "accumulated environmental deficit" in the ghetto, that means that your parents do not communicate with you. They have not figured out a word for that in the suburbs, but the same thing happens on both sides of town. Parents allow the television set to raise their children. But on one side of town they call that "accumulated environmental deficit"—I call it the "dozens." "Cultural deprivation"—that means I don't know what you know. It doesn't suggest much about what you don't know that I know, but I'm deprived because I don't know your situation.

One of the great mistakes made in the 1954 Supreme Court decision was when the social scientists rendered a rather "balanced view" of the hardships imposed upon children who must live in a nation that is "multicultured"—separated. The judges in all their wisdom used one part of that treatment. It says that black children who go to segregated schools should be desegregated. The conclusion is right: they ought to be desegregated. If they are going to live in one nation under one God, under one tax system, they ought to have one school system—that part is sound. But it gives the impression that black children who go to what are deemed academically inferior schools, because of their lack of facilities, sometimes lack inspiration and motivation and develop certain academic retardations because expectations are low and the facilities are low. It also says something about the child who is allowed to feel that he is superior to another child because of his own skin color, and develops the emotional incapacity to relate to someone else simply based on skin color and develops hatred as a defense mechanism. He engages in violence as a way to maintain his isolation. The child who is hit with a brick has skin damage. The other child, who is separated under the illusion of superiority, suffers soul damage. His soul is scarred. So the notion of cultural deprivation must be dealt with in new and different kinds of ways. Certainly if one of my children ever came to me describing his or her inability to relate to someone because of race—why he would hope that another child would be hurt or killed—I would know I had failed, no matter how high that child might score on an examination.

We talk at times of constitutional inferiority and because we do it in subtle ways every now and then these theories rise up, trying to justify our differences as being based upon the Constitution. Fundamentally, we are different not because of our genes but because of our agenda. People do best what they do most. Blacks tend to play basketball better because they practice basketball more. Some whites tend to do better in physics, art, literature, because their priority calls for it. But those blacks who make physics a priority do well in physics. And those whites who make basketball a priority do well in basketball.

This "welfare state" that many of our politicians talk about is organized by the political demagogues who talk about it. Those who put children out of school because they do not have the patience to develop the "late bloomer" and then lock them out of work—they have developed something worse than a welfare state. They have developed a permanent, hostile, subcultural welfare state that is too dangerous for any of us to live in. These are all theories to which welfare recipients are subjected. The belief is deep within the welfare structure that poverty and innate stupidity are co-partners. Unfortunately, it is difficult for me to relate to some poor people—but I try. It is difficult for me because I did not grow up poor, thank God. I did not grow up poor. We just did not have any money, but my Grandma did not tolerate that kind of talk around our house. Our dreams were wealthy, our ambitions were lofty, our ideals were noble—lack of grits and eggs does not make one poor. The presence of wall-to-wall carpeting does not make one wealthy. That is a matter largely of values.

Those who try to improve themselves often find subsidy payments reduced. There is almost no incentive to earn or learn in this system. If you try to learn more you are discouraged. If you are in the tenth grade and have to go back and finish night school and have to go to junior college you will be taken off welfare. The incentive to learn is killed. You make a dollar, they take a dollar. The incentive to earn is killed. Thus you are "locked in" that under class.

Children of welfare recipients also receive different treatment from those not on welfare—often by teachers who expect little of them. If you expect little you will get even less. A good paying job has more therapeutic value than any welfare program that I have ever heard of. A good, well-paying job is the alternative to welfare and despair. A good, well-paying job. There is no mental health solution for one who is suffering from claustrophobia other than more space. No appeal, no doling out of apples or food stamps; one who is suffering from claustrophobia needs wider space. That is the answer to that situation.

I was in Newark, New Jersey, the night that Ken Gibson won his first election. Prior to that night blacks in Newark had "central ward" on the brain. They thought that God had somehow picked them up from wherever and set them in the middle of central ward and that downtown Newark, lake front and everything, belonged to other people—whoever they were. The night that Ken Gibson won I remember young blacks coming downtown by the thousands. One could literally see them getting well. One could see mental health. One could see them simply breaking out, saying "all of Newark is my town." They got well because they went from impotence to power. From rejection to acceptance. They got well because the walls expanded.

Many people who are poor have people offering them everything they need as an antidote to poverty—everything except money. I know some rock 'n roll stars who cannot read or write, and some of them cannot see, but they have several gold records. They have butlers and maids, carpets and green grass, and flowers, and cars, and people taking orders from them—and social acceptance. No one would dare call them anything but "upright" because they have some money, which is the antidote to poverty. Money does not solve all of the problems of a poverty-stricken spirit. People who are hungry need food. People who are without money need money.

One reason the cost of our services continues to go up is because of our contempt for people who are poor. People who get money from the government because they don't plant wheat and the like get a little brown check sent directly from the Treasury Department to their house. Someone who is poor needs seven mailmen to drop it by several spots before it finally gets to his house. By and large, the water never quite trickles down.

It is hard, it seems to me, to deal with the quest for alternatives to welfare and despair without dealing with the context in which this problem is developing. First of all, we need to know that racial trauma blurs the image of what all of us are all about. There are four whites on welfare for every one black, and welfare and black are not synonymous terms. A few years ago during the Nixon Administration *Newsweek* and *Time* ran cover stories on the "Welfare Crisis." On the big bold cover *Newsweek* pictured a big black woman and about nine children with a crawling hound. On the inside they had one or two white people—social workers. *Time* tried to be a little more liberal. It had a montage of eleven pictures—nine black, one brown, and one white. But the clear impression was that black people and welfare were synonymous, and as long as we allow that to happen, we allow those people who have racial defects in their character to wipe off welfare as something that is wholly alien to our culture. For those of us who deal with this problem day in and day out our attitude must be redemptive and not punitive.

Are we going to pay to help the poor people in this society or are we going to pay because we did not help them? It is going to cost either way. If a young person goes to the University of California for four years it will cost less than $20,000. If he or she goes to the state penitentiary for four years it will cost slightly more than $60,000. If a person is in maximum security in New York it will cost $26,000 a year or $104,000 for four years. You tell Jarvis and that "tax rebellion" crowd that you are going to pay for them. You are going to pay for these children, you are going to pay for them. The only caution is, are we going to take our time and teach them to lay a brick? Or are we, through rejection and punishment, going to turn our heads and they end up throwing a brick? That will cost us more. If they are ignorant and incarcerated and can only throw a brick, and we take our time to educate and employ them so they can lay a brick, the course is clear. The choice is ours. One is an investment because we are rational. The other is money taken from us in desperation. Historically, those of us who are black have been "locked out."

There are all kinds of theories about our innate inferiority. We could not use public accommodations. We were "locked out." We did not have the right to vote—"locked out." The biologists argued that we were genetically inferior. We were "locked out." The religionist, the theologian, in Oxford, Harvard, Yale, and Columbia University, argued that God had cursed us. They gave philosophical and religious justification. We were "locked out." These fallacious theories were disproved logically and scientifically over a period of time, and they began to lose their effectiveness in world opinion.

We have a history of persons who served as "myth crashers" about our being inferior and unable to overcome. That is why the Joe Louises, the Jackie Robinsonses, the Jesse

Owenses, and the Ralph Bunches of our race will never be surpassed because they served as "myth crashers." When Marian Anderson's melodious voice with all its power became so irresistible she served as a "myth crasher." Martin Luther King, Jr., built on that foundation. His leadership symbolized a new courage, a new technique, a new determination. He was saying that no matter what our sins, the Kingdom of God is within. He had an imaginative notion that if we changed our minds about ourselves, we would rise from the "gutter most" to the "uttermost." If we changed our minds about ourselves. He said we must save our children. We can save them. We ought to save them.

It was from that leadership that we went to the opposite end. In 1954 with the Supreme Court decision, we began to "move in," and the 1964 Accommodations bill allowed us to begin to "move in." With the Voting Rights bill of 1965 we began to "move in." We "moved in" basically for our dignity—that whole struggle: people can use any hotel/motel; we can't. We fought for our dignity. People can vote; we can't. We fought for our dignity. People can sit any place on the bus; we cannot. We fought for our dignity. Now we have our dignity. But that is not enough. Dignified starvation is not enough. Dignified ignorance is not enough. Dignified and deprived are not enough.

We can rightly call that movement the Freedom Movement—"freedom" because the word officially means expanded options. We may not choose to come into this hotel now, but we have the choice to do so. That is freedom. We may not choose to vote but we have the choice. That is freedom. We may not choose to use the motel, park, or library but we can, and that is our choice. That is the freedom movement. However, our struggle now is beyond moving in, it must now move up. "Moving in" was for dignity. "Moving up" requires power. The fundamental nature of this struggle has shifted from "moving in" to "moving up." We are merely seeking dignity and freedom. Seeking equality and power. In other words, the new challenge is our share—an alternative

to welfare and despair—so we can go to the hospital as doctors, not merely as patients. We can go to the courthouse as
judges and lawyers, not merely as clients. We can go to the
store as owners, not merely as consumers. We can go to the
bank as lenders, not merely as borrowers. That is an alternative to welfare and despair.

Our challenge today is to "move up." And just as there
were elements however well-meaning that joined together to
keep us from "moving in," there are new forces that join
together to keep us from "moving up." We hear it now pronounced in *Defunis* v. *Odegaard* that they are against quotas.
Thank God I learned a little mathematics. I found one day
there was something lower than zero called −12345, and
therefore if you ever got up to zero you were beyond −50.
So historically zero has been a quota. America has believed in
quotas all of its history.

Before 1947 the baseball quota for blacks was zero. Those
blacks who now have a chance to play baseball are not worrying the social workers. Those who have the right to play foot-
ball and basketball are not worrying any social workers because opportunity without restrictions based upon race was
an alternative to welfare and despair. The broken language
of those people who earn money is tolerated. You know it is
better to say "I is rich" than "I am poor"—you know that. I
wish they would use correct English but I know that the bottom line is not subject and verb being conjugated, whether
you are in the authentic black or whether you are in the red
financially. So fundamentally we must find ourselves struggling to put our focus on how we help people move up-up-
up—an alternative to welfare and despair.

At first we said that everybody ought to be treated justly.
That was a religious concept. We found that more people
lost their religion after Sunday morning. We went beyond
that and said we ought to have equal opportunity. That was a
nice concept except they said they couldn't find any. Then
they went to the third stage and said we need affirmative action so we will have laws with claws in them. Find them—it

will cost you if you cannot find them. And then they began to find them.

The Bakke case represents a resistance to our being protected by the law. The University of California at Los Angeles, with all of its alignment of great athletes from Jackie Robinson, Kenny Robinson, Abdul Jabbar, to Willie White— all of those blacks put together—has not produced ten black doctors in its whole history—in its whole history—in its whole history.

One of the most noble expressions of protest is taking place in America just this moment. Just as blacks sat in the "hamburgers" in the 1960s, fighting for dignity, some Hispanics are sitting in UCLA this morning demanding equity and parity in education. That is their alternative to welfare and despair. If they are lawyers and doctors they can speak Spanish, and if they spend money they will be accepted, not rejected. They are at their highest and best. I am glad they are not fighting for the right to smoke pot. Fighting for the right to have their share of information as an alternative to welfare and despair—it's the only way out—their way out is not "up."

Somebody said to me the other day, "Reverend, you talk about how the kids ought to excel. How can you still be for affirmative action?" They said: "It seems like it's wrong to have reverse discrimination and to take advantage of white people." Well, if that is what is happening it would be wrong. But never has the majority culture enacted a law for the purpose of hurting whites or holding them down and it has done neither one in the last seven years, as opposed to having a hundred slots with sixteen taken away and therefore some poor old white kid, some potential president like Bakke, getting squeezed out and some blacks taking advantage of white people. On the contrary, they kept a hundred slots but then added some more for the whites—for the whites who might be made uncomfortable. The results are that there are 48 percent more whites in medical school today than there were seven years ago. There are 64 percent more whites in law school today than there were seven years ago. So blacks are not catching up at the expense of whites. As a matter of fact, blacks are not catching up and whites are not slowing down. "Well, Reverend, what is the pinch that white America feels?" The inflation that white America feels is not coming from the black middle class. That's the New York *Times* diversion. The stagnant economy is what middle-class America is feeling, and it is not coming from black America.

The steel worker's job has been lost to Japan because that government and private industry created a proposition that puts our steel companies out of business. It has affected the steel industry and also the auto industry. Those in the South who have lost textile industries are not feeling the pinch because of blacks. Those in New England who have lost the shoe industry are not feeling the pinch because of blacks. You all hear me. It is the international economic scene that has affected our lives. If we look at a white tree and miss the whole forest in which black and whites are engulfed it means we are suffering from limited vision. We are not each other's problems but we could be each other's solution if we rise above the limitations of hatred and malice and closed minds.

A reporter walked up and said, "Well, Reverend, if blacks ought to excel and if blacks ought to motivate, how can you justify leaving out some whites who have the merit?" Always use the extreme case, some white genius and some black fool. How can you take a black fool and take a slot from a white genius? Well, black fools do not take slots from black geniuses. I mean fools do not take slots from geniuses no where, no time. They take a man who was rejected by thirteen schools, including his own alma mater, who decided he wanted to become a doctor at thirty-five, and make him a genius all of a sudden. My point is that this is a legitimate question because this man was sincere. Why do blacks need special help? Why? Let me answer that. Because the record still shows that the white high school dropout still has more job options than the black high school graduate. That is a special situation caused by race.

The other groups sing the "Star Spangled Banner" and look all teary-eyed because they say they came looking for jobs and looking for religious freedom and the Statue of Liberty had her arms out wide. But we came here against our will and the Statue of Liberty turned. The lady dropped her head in shame because we came in chains, not looking for anything, but came screaming, against our will. No other group in this culture has suffered the holocaust of the loss of 60 million people, 200 years of slavery, another hundred years of legal segregation. There is no comparable situation here.

Let us observe the fact that Americans did not need a public accommodations law in 1964 because they could already use the hotel, motel, park, or library. Blacks had to have special federal laws to keep the state governments and the schools, and the churches if you will, from locking us out. Because race in this society, unfortunately, is a special situation. In 1965 all Americans had the right to vote, but blacks could not vote. They had to pass a special law. If they had not passed a special law to protect us we still could not vote. To show you how special it is even today, that law had to be renewed in 1970. The Congress still maintained the right in 1970 to take away our right to vote. Then it came up again in 1975. We had to appeal again to maintain the right to vote. And now as opposed to giving us permanent citizenship protected by law, this time they extended it seven years rather than five years—so in 1982 blacks again must fight to maintain the right to vote. Therefore we do not need special preferential treatment because we are dumb and inclined toward welfare. We need special protection of the law because we function in a hostile environment.

Those who are citizens and compassionate need to know that as we climb this mountain to survive we are climbing against an adverse wind with people standing above us putting their shoes on our fingers and challenging us to be more than we really are. We do not want to be superior but we almost have to be, just to be equal. If we are going to look for alternatives to welfare and despair we must look beyond a child's kinky hair, look beyond his stringy hair. But deep behind that black skin, that white skin, there is a soul. This little white boy, little white girl, black boy, black girl cannot be rejected. If there is any one thing I will argue to social workers across the nation today it is this: in all of your struggling don't lose your soul. It is easy over a period of time for teachers to reduce students to digits—don't lose your soul. It is easy for funeral directors to start calling their beloved ones "stiffs." It is easy to lose your soul. It is easy when you fly all day, every day, to assume that landing and flying can be taken for granted as opposed to being held up by the buoyancy of Almighty God. It is easy to lose your soul.

My argument is that we must have compassion. On the one hand, all that we are saying to our students in exile, many of whom are down and out, is that there is a little something on the inside that God has given you. Those of us who love you are going to try to cultivate that special little something down on the inside of you. Behind those glazed eyeballs may be the cure for cancer—we do not know. We are going to struggle to give you a chance. We know that just because it rains you do not have to drown. On the one hand we need equal opportunity by law, but then we must match it with the superior effort.

We know we need superior effort. If you are behind in the race for whatever reason you cannot catch up by becoming a mass media addict watching four hours of television every night, being entertained rather than educated. We know that you cannot catch up by pickling your brains in liquor and using easy access to guns. We know you cannot catch up crying, drowning in your own tears, being cynical. We know you cannot catch up cursing the darkness and violating your neighbor. Tears and sweat are both salty and both are wet. But somehow sweat speaks to human progress in a way that tears never did. Let me tell you, God reigns on the just and the unjust alike. And even though the victim is not responsible for being down, he still has to be responsible for getting up.

In this relationship between slave and master, the master never gets tired of being master. Since there is no history of retired slave masters, the slave must assume the initiative to resist the drugs, the alcohol, and the diversions, and the decadence. The slave must rise up and push forward. His disadvantage is that he has weights on his ankles. But the advantage is that if he rises his legs will be stronger. He must look at his situation and say to himself: "I'm in the slum, but the slum is not in me. I'm going to rise above my circumstances." He must say: "That which I got was hard to get, but now that I've got it and it is mine, I know what I know, and nobody can take it from me." A fully developed personality can rise above the slum and slum living. If your personality is not fully developed you can be in a castle and you will turn it into a slum. If your personality is developed you can be in a slum and turn it into a castle, for mind is still stronger than matter. You can rise above your circumstances.

We meet people every day just telling our children how to pick up a welfare check or how to sign a check. Tell them there is a way out. Tell them that the laws of convenience lead to collapse, but the laws of sacrifice lead to greatness. Tell them there is a way out. Tell them that just because they are down, they do not have to be out. Tell them there is a way out. Tell them not to use pill power and cop out. Tell them to use will power and cope with. Tell them that way down on the inside there is a special something in everybody—you call it Logos, I call it God. But it is way down, a part of you.

Of course the scientists say you can't, but that little something says, "I can." When they say you won't, that little something says, "I will." When the society says you can never make it, that little something says, "Just watch me, because I'm made out of a special something." You see every now and then when our children are walking in the miry clay, walking in these tattered streets, with these torn lives, they must walk and meet ideas. Not necessarily another dollar or another dime.

I grew up with all these feelings of thinking about it twice and feeling a special sense of inferiority in spite of all the teachings of my mother and grandmother. I could not avoid a certain amount of self-doubt because I was a rejected child. When we walked by three white schools as we were going to school every day and I would ask Mama, "Why can't I go there?" her answer never was clear. There was a special sense of rejection. I got on that bus and paid that dime and had to go and sit in the back of the bus by law. No matter how positive I thought, there was a sense of rejection there. I went to that library and that lady told me I couldn't read those books, I would have to go to the colored library. I felt the sense of rejection there. We had to walk by white churches on Sunday morning with green grass and steeples speaking to God, and I couldn't go there or I would be arrested. There was a special sense of rejection there. Everywhere I went there was rejection—even in rejection, where preachers split their theology and lost their moral foundation because I was a black boy.

All of their gods spoke one day, and I went and met some people one day. I got introduced to a thought one day and I liked it; to a sentence, to a paragraph, how to read, how to write, how to count. Somebody told me one day about Aristotle and Plato, and I heard about Descartes, Tillich, and Niebuhr. And I found a great kinship with the great ideas of ages. I began to come out of my shell because an idea pulled me above my circumstance. Then I went beyond that and something hit me one day. I found that when it thundered and lightning struck out there was a part of all that vast universe that was bigger than segregation, bigger than slavery, bigger than that backyard bath, bigger than that clothesline on Monday morning, bigger than all of that. There was a God somewhere. I found that one day in my life. It meant an awful lot to me at that time because I was rejected by some, but I was accepted by One that was superior to all of that. I could say to myself: "I'm somebody. I'm somebody because I am God's child." I say to myself: "I'm somebody because I count. Because I'm a part of this universe. I'm in this slum, but this slum is not in me. Better watch me now because something is going to happen in my life."

At first blacks could not even use welfare. Welfare was for whites. Welfare was for the unemployed. Blacks were unemployed. We were called lazy. White folks were unemployed—they called it a depression. We could not even apply for any money, we had to use something else to come out of that mess. When I met God and understood Him, Jesus was a little clearer to me. I learned to read about Jesus, and God became a little clearer, and the Holy Scriptures knocked off the rough edges. I say that to you because every now and then you need something that is not available from the State Department. Every now and then you need something else. Every now and then you need something that the cynics of doom do not have to offer. You need another little special something. A special something. You all better say Amen now.

There is another little something: if you ever get it on the inside, then you will not stand too much rejection anymore because you know you count. You might be ignored and disregarded, but you know that you count. Tell these children that they count, tell them that they are somebody. Tell them "down with dope and up with hope." Tell them that they are God's children. Tell them that in their minds they have infinite potential. They can be whatever they want to be—tell them. Tell them that they count. Tell them that they can conceive it and believe that they can achieve it. Tell them it is not their aptitude but their attitude that determines their altitude with a little intestinal fortitude.

Affirmative Action—
Past, Present, Future

THE WHITNEY M. YOUNG, JR.,
MEMORIAL LECTURE

JAMES FARMER

IT ALMOST GOES without saying that I am honored on this occasion because it allows me to reminisce about my friendship with a great colleague, the late Whitney Young. The anecdotes abound just as Whitney's energy was boundless. I recall once seeing him dashing through the halls of the Senate office building. As usual he had gone without sleep and he looked a bit depressed. I asked, "What's the trouble, Whitney?" He said, "Jim, it's awfully tough trying to be a civil rights leader without going to jail these days," and that was true.

Whitney served a unique function, and he once described that function before a group of business executives. We were conducting a seminar, and the heads of the various civil rights organizations were there. The question was raised as to why the organizations did not get together and combine their forces. Whitney took the ball immediately and said: "Of course we do meet together and we do plan together, but we have a division of responsibilities." "The Urban League," he said "is the State Department; the NAACP, the War Department, and CORE is the Marines." Whitney indeed used that figure of speech quite frequently. Time after time when he was in negotiations with business executives about employing

JAMES FARMER is Executive Director, Coalition of American Public Employees, Washington, and Founder, Congress of Racial Equality.

more minorities and poor people and they were recalcitrant and did not want to yield, invariably Whitney would say, "Look, you had better deal with the Urban League and with me; if you don't you'll get Farmer and CORE," and that did it.

He was a man of utmost sincerity who really believed in what he was doing, and that stood out at all times. I am sure it was partly because he came out of the social work profession. I cannot imagine anyone becoming a social worker unless he cares about people and cares deeply. He would not do it for money—that is certain. He or she might become a doctor and hope to make a million dollars, but not in the field of social work. Whitney cared deeply, and when the real history of the civil rights movement of the 1960s is written— and it has not been written yet—Whitney's contributions will be better understood and much more appreciated than they are now. I think his greatest contribution was probably that of affirmative action. It was Whitney himself who devised the concept. We in CORE used to claim it—but we had no sense of public relations at all.

When we went in to talk to Lyndon Johnson, who was Vice President then and head of the President's Commission on Equal Employment Opportunity, we spoke of what we called it—compensatory preferential hiring. "I cannot imagine a worse term than that—more calculated to raise all hackles," he responded. "Well, it's a good idea, but don't call it—what do you call it, a compensatory what? That's horrible! Why don't you call it what Whitney just talked about, affirmative action? That's what we need to march forward and to take the lead to advance and to be affirmative and positive in what we're doing." So I will yield to Whitney: it was his idea and it was a concept that certainly needed enunciating.

We look back on those historic days of the early 1960s, dramatic days indeed, when some of you probably were involved, or your sons, your daughters, your mothers, your fathers, your cousins, your classmates—white and black poured out so much love and commitment, dedication, and blood

more times in their lives than we care to remember. We won
lots of victories, and there is no demeaning those victories in
pointing now to their limitations.

Those victories were clear, and all one has to do is to
travel, especially in the South, to be impressed by the
changes that have taken place in the social fabric—at least on
the surface. The system of iron-clad segregation of the races
in places of public accommodation and in public transportation has become a thing of the past. That was a contribution of those willing warriors of the early 1960s, of whom
Whitney was one of the leaders. Many persons whom one
would not expect to accept changes so quickly are now accepting them. If twenty, even fifteen years ago somebody
had told you that George Wallace in the early 1970s would
crown a black queen at the University of Alabama, you would
have sent him to the nearest mental institution. But George
Wallace not only crowned her, he kissed her. The changes
are there and one sees them, and I find it exhilarating to
travel through the Southern cities now. The South is almost
like a different country compared to what it was like prior to
the 1960s.

I recall a family reunion in Ocala, Florida, two or three
summers ago. My mind had to drift back to an earlier visit
more than a decade earlier. The first visit was touch and go.
Our meeting was in a church, and the Ku Klux Klan rented
the building across the street. Their members paraded in
and out with their guns, rifles, and shotguns in plain sight.
The sheriff and his deputies were driving around the block.
We did not know which side they were on—well, quite to the
contrary, we did know, and it was not our side. The focus of
the struggle then was public accommodations, which now
seems like a rather superficial objective, but it was something
of great symbolic importance. At the more recent visit there
for the reunion—and that sort of family reunion is a growing
tradition in minority communities now that we have discovered we have roots—we made an important discovery. All
members of the clan, not the KKK, but our clan, gathered in

Ocala, and the red carpet had been rolled out for us. Stores from which we had been thrown out a decade earlier had signs in the windows welcoming us. The sky did not fall. We filled up two motels, and Dick Gregory was down for a brief time. He stood in the courtyard with me looking around and he said, "Gee, Jim, they have this place decorated so nice—wall-to-wall us." And so it was. I walked through the streets and stopped in eating establishments that had been the focus of the earlier struggle. I was served every place, but what impressed me was that the people served me not begrudgingly, but apparently willingly. Many were the same ones who a scant decade earlier had been shouting, "Never!" Now they were accepting the new state of affairs as though that was the way things always had been or the way things should be. I was impressed with the capacity of the nation for change.

I have become even more impressed since then with the limited nature of the changes which came out of the 1960s. Within the past few years there has appeared to be an erosion of some of those victories, particularly in education and in employment. In 1970 the research department of the National Urban League informed us that the percentage of young blacks attending college was approximately the same as the percentage of young whites attending college. We all applauded those new statistics. Now, however that is not the case. The percentage dropped, and that gap has widened because there is much less emphasis on affirmative action or seeking ghetto and barrio youngsters for college. There are fewer funds available for scholarship aid from the federal government. There has been a step back in that regard. It is a little like the "Nixonian" waltz that Nixon did on domestic issues. The "Nixonian" waltz, you may recall, consists of a step forward, two steps backward, a hesitation, and a side step.

There has been erosion in education and there has been erosion in employment too. Partly because of the recession, the unemployment figures among blacks and other minorities, including Chicanos, Puerto Ricans, and Native Americans, are more than twice as high as the national average. In the cities we know that the unemployment among ethnic minority youth is ranging from 35 percent to 55 percent. We know, too, that the income gap between the majority and ethnic minorities has widened, not narrowed. For blacks, for instance, the average median income is only 62 percent of that of whites. We have been struggling with employment for a long time, and obviously the front seat of the bus becomes hard and rocky; the hot dog at the lunch counter, so hard fought for and so dearly wanted in the 1960s, turns to rubber in our mouths when we realize that our victories were largely victories for those of us who have a certain measure of affluence: those who like myself are in the middle class. I am not antimiddle class; if I were, it would be an act of supreme self-rejection, for I am of it and from it. But I face the fact that we did not succeed in significantly elevating the status of the poor. Whether they are the Chicano poor, Native American poor, the Puerto Rican poor, the black poor, the white poor, what does the youth in the ghetto or barrio care about the hot dog at Howard Johnson's or the 57 brands of ice cream? He could hardly care less, for he is as concerned as you who work with the problem every day are concerned about the rats that still bite the children, with the alienation, with the absence of the American dream. You have seen as often as I have the faces of the under class in American society. We did not move that under class into the mainstream of the nation's life. If other things were our successes, then that was our major failure. You work with them, you know their faces, and you know they come in all colors. They are white, they are brown, they are black, they are red. Just two weeks ago, walking through the poor sections of the inner city in Washington, D.C., I looked at the faces of people who have given up hope—if they had any. They are content merely to exist and they are not really so sure about that. They have gone back into a kind of invisibility.

Michael Harrington and his memorable and influential

book *The Other America* pointed out about 1963 or a year or two earlier that the poor were invisible and we did not see them. Social workers saw them frequently, but most of us did not see them. They were hidden, our main streets and roads by-passed the communities so that our eyes were not shocked by the sight. When our commuter trains came into the city, we looked up from the *Wall Street Journal* or the New York *Times* long enough to catch a glimpse of the pain and misery through which we were being transported. The poor, he said, wallowing in the culture of poverty are invisible, are hardly aware of their own existence.

That began to change in the later or middle 1960s, partly because of the war on poverty, which again was in part a Whitney Young invention in his consultations with Lyndon Johnson. And along with that war on poverty was "maximum feasible participation," with the poor becoming visible; no longer hidden, they were fairly bursting with existence. The voice with which they spoke, which had been so long silent, was a raucous voice, and most of us, except probably social workers, were not accustomed to what we saw or what we heard. In the early 1960s, the movement people sang one song, "I'm Going to Sit at the Welcome Table One of These Days." In the middle 1960s the formerly invisible CORE members sat at the welcome table, but many of us were shocked by the fact that they did not know what fork to use and that they did not know politeness and cultivation of language. They were blunt, and many were irritated. For that and for other reasons probably more important, the war on poverty has been largely dismantled. Maximum feasible participation has become a thing of the past. The poor have become rather silent again and have gone back behind the cloak of invisibility.

There have to be ways for these folks to move into the mainstream of American society: by sharing resources, by income redistribution, by seeing that they get education even though they have been handicapped by poverty—a poverty that is compounded by racism in the case of the ethnic minorities. "Ghettoized" and "barrioized," they have become in so many cases the suburban version of Edwin Markham's "The Man with the Hoe." Markham wrote that poem after viewing Millet's famous painting:

> Bowed by the weight of centuries he leans
> Upon his hoe and gazes on the ground,
> The emptiness of ages in his face,
> And on his back the burden of the world.
>
>   .   .   .   .
>
> Whose was the hand that slanted back this brow?
> Whose breath blew out the light within this brain?
>
>   .   .   .   .
>
> How will it be with kingdoms and with kings—
> With those who shaped him to the thing he is—
> When this dumb Terror shall rise to judge the world,
> After the silence of the centuries?

We have urban counterparts of "The Man with the Hoe." I think that as a nation unless we close the gap and find ways to integrate the hard core into the nation's life we are courting disaster. That is why affirmative action was born.

First, in the 1940s and 1950s, we fought for employment, for an end to employment discrimination. But that was when we sought "color blindness" as an objective. Race or color was not only not to be a criterion, but was not even to be considered. The Fair Employment Practices laws, the first equal employment laws, were "color-blind" laws. The first one was an executive order issued by President Franklin D. Roosevelt in 1941, and then there were state laws passed and federal laws, but what the laws said was that employers and their counterparts in education and in the admission offices of schools must be absolutely color blind—must not even be aware of, or show an awareness of, the color or race of an applicant. We said to the employer: "Just hire the best qualified person who happens to apply and you will have fulfilled your obligation to society. You are a good person then." Didn't work. We would go back to that employer two years hence and say, "Now that you have practiced fair employment how many Chicanos and blacks do you employ?" And his answer would be, "How in the hell should I know? I'm 'color blind'!" We took a visual check and found out he had none. He said, "So what! You told me to be 'color blind' and I am." Employers did not and do not look through "color-blind" eyes.

Those early laws were a step forward, an important but inadequate step, as events show. In New York in the CORE days, about 1962, we had a campaign against job discrimination in a chain of hamburger joints. The only blacks and Puerto Ricans they employed were janitors. We tried to talk with them, but they said there was nothing to talk about. We then used our usual techniques: we marched, picketed, sat in while we had garbage thrown at us, and there was even a cross burning—in New York, not Alabama. We persisted, of course, and finally management sat down to discuss it with us. The manager of the chain said to me: "Mr. Farmer, you're absolutely right. The only blacks and Puerto Ricans in our employ are in the janitorial service, and we agree that's wrong. We feel very bad about it and we would like to change it. In fact, our projection is that within the next three months we're going to need about sixty sales personnel." That was their euphemism for counter people. He said: "We would love to hire Puerto Ricans and blacks for those new jobs but we can't do it." "Why can't you?" I bristled. He said: "It would be against the law. We're supposed to be 'color blind.' We get our employees through the State Employment service, and if I go to the State Employment service and ask them to send me sixty blacks and Puerto Ricans they will immediately charge us with violating the State Fair Employment Practices law, which said you must be 'color blind' and may not consider race." I thought he smiled triumphantly, so I asked for a recess and called an old friend who worked for the State Employment service.

"Now, Joe," I said, "you realize that the law is our king." He said, "of course, it is one of those 'color-blind' laws that you and people like you fought so hard to get just a few years ago." I explained our problem to him and asked, "What do you suggest?" Joe said: "Jim, I'll tell you what. Go back into your negotiation session and ask this manager to call me. Tell him don't write—call, and tell me his needs and I will then call our office on 125th Street in Harlem and ask them to send him sixty qualified applicants regardless of race, color, creed, or national origin." Of course there was the recognition of the limitation of the early Fair Employment Practices Law.

Well, Whitney Young and others sat down to devise something that would get around this. How could we change it? And that was when affirmative action was born. We said to employers then that it was their job to go out and seek those who have been excluded and bring them into employment and into the schools. In the past, by the way, we had not even kept ethnic records. It was illegal under the Fair Employment Practices Commission to keep ethnic records. One did not know how many blacks were employed unless one took a look, and then one might miss a few. The same was true in schools.

I remember writing to the presidents of some colleges to inquire how many black students they had. And I got some very angry letters, saying, "How dare you ask such an insulting question? We're 'color blind' and we don't keep any such records as that." We did not know where we stood, but we were telling employers to go out and seek minorities. Advertise in the minority papers. If you recruit in high schools, recruit in the predominantly black high schools or in the predominantly Hispanic high schools in the barrio. This worked tentatively, and we began to make some advances. New jobs were opened up, especially in companies that did business with the government and wanted a contract. After all, if they were going to keep their contract they had to show some minorities—usually visible minorities, you know, the black who sat by the door.

A friend of mine got a job in those years, and he said,

"Jim, I don't have to do anything but sit close to the door and look very black." He finally was fired because he was not dark enough. They wanted more visibility, wanted to be sure that when the "feds" came by they didn't miss him, that they saw him—and counted him. Of course, now they could put a black woman there and could count her twice: as a woman and as a minority black. But we got new jobs. I don't knock those jobs, I just regret the fact that they were so limited. They affected a few thousand people, but we did not change the pattern. We did not move the under class into our society. The ideal concept was adopted by the government.

They tell the story of President Kennedy stepping off a plane one day and observing the Honor Guard that was there to greet him. He noticed that it was all white—no blacks or other minorities. He called an officer over and said, "I see there are no Negroes in the Honor Guard." The officer smiled and said, "That's correct, Mr. President. You see, none has applied." The President allegedly said, "Well, go and find some." That was not a case of "color blindness," for the "color blindness" era had ended then; it was "color consciousness" for the purpose of eliminating "color discrimination."

The nation is not now color blind and was not color blind, so it is fanciful for us to assume a color blindness in society and to build our programs around that assumption. They are bound to fail, so it is color consciousness that we were asking. Be aware when an Hispanic comes in, when a black comes in. Go out and seek them, and if further training is needed, provide that training. It is a responsibility to make the nation whole and to defuse a time bomb on which all of us sit. All too frequently we would go back to an employer, to a supervisor, a line manager, and say: "You have had two years practicing affirmative action, you have been seeking minorities. How many have you found?" The answer would be, "Well, now, Whitney, Lord knows I've tried. I've tried hard, but I couldn't find any that were qualified." How often have we heard it? How often have you? Now what wisdom would it take on our part to know whether he had tried adequately? We could ask: Where did you advertise? Where did you go to seek members of the minority groups? How hard did you seek them? But we could not prove that he had shown good faith or that he had not shown good faith. This was still parenthetically within the merit system.

I saw how the merit system works while I was with HEW for about eighteen months. The merit system sometimes becomes a "buddy" system. Some of the employees—heads of offices—who reported to me were the heads of these boxes that had straight lines or broken lines going to the Assistant Secretary on the organizational chart. Sometimes they would have an opening, say, for a GS13 or 14. What happened? Here is the way it worked. It often happened that this GS15 or 16 who was assigned the responsibility of locating someone would call an old Yale classmate or roommate in Denver and chat for a while about, "Mary and Elaine and their respective families, the children and how are they doing? Has your daughter straightened her teeth yet? Is she still wearing braces? How are things?" And then, "Oh, by the way, I have an opening here—a pretty good job, GS13. We need somebody and we need somebody good." "Hey!" says the friend, "I know a fellow who worked with me in Seattle in the regional office a few years ago and he was pretty good too. He's a 12 looking for a 13. Say, I tell you what, I'll send along his form and give you the information on him."

So he would send his form 121, or whatever, and the list of possible candidates would of course come over from the Civil Service Commission, and a panel would be sent up to go over all the eligibles, including this one from Seattle who was thrown in. It was very interesting that most of the time the friend of the friend from Seattle got the job, came out on top of the list. I would ask, "Now, did you look at minorities too?" "Well," he would say, "the Civil Service Commission doesn't tell us which are minorities." It was illegal to keep ethnic data—they didn't tell us which are minorities. "Couldn't you look at the schools they went to?" Yes, but they didn't know whether Talladega was a black school or a white school or Tougaloo—"we just couldn't tell." "Could you tell from the section of the city they lived in?" Well, they didn't know the names of those streets, so how could they tell?

No, the merit system is not always a merit system. It tends to be a "buddy" system, but we were not a part of the "buddy" system. Unless one takes affirmative action and conscious action I suggest to you, my colleagues and my friends, there will be no significant change in the employment picture. Unless race is considered, unless color and ethnicity are considered as factors in employment, then the minorities in our land will continue to be at the bottom of the totem pole economically. It is something none of us white or black or whatever class should want to see continue to happen.

When affirmative action was not working as well as it should we had to have some way of telling whether the employer was acting in good faith, and the numerical goals and time tables were devised. Now that is tricky. Of course it is, because it sounds like quotas. I do not like quotas and who does? I recall too well that in the 1940s and 1950s, especially the late years of those decades, we fought against quotas. We fought against quotas especially in educational institutions, professional schools, graduate schools, and so forth. Quotas were used to exclude or to limit the number of minorities. In New York we were battling against that policy in upstate universities. There were quotas on blacks, quotas on Puerto Ricans, quotas on Jews—in most cases they didn't say quotas on Jews; they said, "We have quotas on people from New York City." That was euphemism, but everybody knew what they were talking about. Everybody knew what they meant. We fought against it and we won that battle.

So far as I know we knocked out those quotas because they were used to exclude or limit the number of minorities who got in and to suggest that a kind of benign quota be used. The numerical goals and time tables I will not argue. We can make an excellent case for a distinction between numerical goals and time tables and quotas. Or one could argue that one is flexible and the other inflexible; one is a goal and objective and the other is something that must take place all at once and now. I would not argue that because I think it would in a way be begging the question and would not be confronting the major issue.

The point of the matter seems to be that times make "ancient good" uncouth and that things which we had to fight against in an earlier decade (for they were used to exclude) now may be necessary if color consciousness is to wipe out color discrimination in order to include those who have been excluded. I would consider that to be a basic distinction and a real difference. I am not happy about it because I can understand how people would resent it, especially a Bakke or a Defunis or many other individuals. I do not know whether those two were highly qualified. They scored fairly high in their examinations and their tests—higher than many who were accepted; lower than some who were accepted; lower than some who were not accepted. Let us assume that Bakke or Defunis is a paragon of academic excellence and has worked hard burning the midnight oil, coming up through grade school and secondary school, studying when he or she might have been playing stick ball or shooting marbles. Now if he or she feels that the application should have been accepted and it was not, I can understand the hurt and the frustration and it pains me too, believe me. But as I look upon history and the history of social change, very honestly I do not know of a single instance where significant social change can take place, especially when you are dealing with deep-rooted societal ills, without some people being individually or personally injured. I wish that were not the case but I think it is.

The goal is important to make a nation whole. I would view affirmative action as a temporary expedient. The objective was Martin Luther King's dream: a society where race is unimportant and irrelevant, where it is the content of the character and not the color of the skin that is important, where we are indeed color blind. That is the ideal; the tactical and strategical problem is how to arrive at that point. How do we get there? I suggest that it will take affirmative action on a much more massive scale than we have had. Enforcement and implementation will take much more effort too. Affirmative action alone will not do it. I wish that Bakke had pointed his guns at the American Medical Association rather than at his black would-be fellow students. The American Medical Association has fought hard against having enough medical schools, against the proliferation of medical schools. Why? Supply and demand. Keep the supply of doctors down low while the demand is high, then we can make a million dollars. It is quite simple, and that is the reason we do not have the educational facilities for all.

We are in complex times today, and I sometimes long for the simple era of the 1960s when everything was clear and simple and fitted neatly. When the issue was the hot dog at the lunch counter. When those college kids, black freshmen, sat at a lunch counter at Woolworth's in Greensboro, North Carolina, on February 1, 1960, and said, "A cup of coffee please." Here they were—polite, courteous, well-dressed— this was a different era—asking for a cup of coffee. Who in his right mind with any semblance of decency could say they should not be served that coffee? Here were the goons, their opponents—the duck-tail haircut, leather jacket crew coming in grinning and crushing cigarette butts out against the back of their necks, clubbing them. This scene led the conservative writer James J. Kilpatrick to observe, when he was editing the Richmond *News Leader,* "It's a reversal of roles—gad, it gives one pause to think—who are the good guys and who are the bad guys?" Who in decency could say those kids should not be served, if they had the money for the coffee? Who could argue that a person should not have a seat at the front of the bus if he had the money to pay for the seat? This was when good was in conflict with bad. Right versus wrong.

Furthermore, you could tell when you had won. If you got that hot dog and you didn't get clobbered in the process and if you sat on the front seat of a bus and were not beaten,

jailed, or thrown off, you were victorious. Now we are in
shady areas where it is not good against bad, it is right versus
right. Rights invariably come into conflict, in time, as in seniority layoffs when minorities say, "Hey, wait a minute. You
can't lay me off first because I don't have seniority, because if
you hadn't been excluding me all these years I'd have seniority now." But many of the unions say, "Oh no, sorry, seniority is a rule, it is a principle." But the minority say, "Well, it's
as if you're going to penalize me for not having seniority that
you kept me from getting. That is compounding a felony, as
it were." These are complex issues, and issues, I regret to say,
have divided friends.

In dealing with these issues being on the other side does
not make one an evil person. I resent hearing people say that
anyone who sides with Bakke must be a racist. That is nonsense, complete nonsense. When two people of ultimate and
infinite good will may disagree on issues I happen to think
that not enough light has been shed on one side of some of
these issues; there is not enough perspective of the broad
picture, but those who disagree are not necessarily racists.
This is not to say that no one who supports Bakke is a racist;
some are, but one is not automatically a racist because he
supports Bakke. These are the kinds of issues we have now,
where people of good will may be on different sides. That is
why the issue requires more thought than ever before. What
is required today is not so much demonstration as cerebra-
tion, as thought, as thinking, as dialogue, to find, indeed,
compromises. I do not know what the Supreme Court will
rule in the Bakke case. I suspect, of course, that the court will
side-step the basic issue. It will probably find that there was a
loophole in the case and therefore it should not have been
accepted. And it will try not to accept it. Without dealing
with the fundamental issue, the issue will plague us. There
are other cases coming through the courts, and if Bakke does
get a definitive answer there will be other cases.

Furthermore, affirmative action has pit minorities against
each other. I do not say that the *issue* had done that, I think

that people who are opposed to affirmative action have done that by pitting minorities against each other—Chicanos against blacks and blacks against Chicanos, Puerto Ricans against blacks, and so forth. That game is being played with women, too, against minorities. The thing of it is that only so many jobs have responded to affirmative action or have employed women. It is called reverse discrimination. I think it is a misnomer and I think it is a kind of cheap-shot labeling which has been used largely by the press. Actually, rather than reverse discrimination it is an attempt to reverse discrimination. Maybe it is a bungling attempt, and perhaps there are better compromises. For example, several years ago, when I was speaking before a group of college students, management interns in the Defense Department, one young white student said: "Mr. Farmer, let's use a little imagination in the Defunis case [that was the University of Washington Law School case]. Suppose they had done it this way. The University of Washington had 100 slots for students. Suppose they selected 100 of the best qualified or the 100 best qualified—it might be hard to say whether number 101 was as qualified as 99, but say 100 highly qualified students—then no one could say student A is more qualified than student B because he scored three points higher in a test which might have been culturally biased and not his specialty. Anyway, one could say that if both A and B scored well, both were qualified in at least that aspect of qualifications. Maybe another student who scored less well or could speak better could influence a jury, could talk with the judge. They could pick 100 then. Suppose the University of Washington Law School then selected the 25 that they needed, if they had places for 25, by random selection, by a lottery. If a Defunis had not been in the 25, or had been in the 100 but was not in the 25, could he then charge reverse discrimination?" Now there are flaws in this suggestion, of course, but the big question is: how do you select the 100? What is the selection process? I think that we put too much emphasis on testing because the tests do have cultural biases, partly in language.

The government people who tested Harlem students to find out what kind of manpower jobs or training would be most effective were astonished, "absolutely flabbergasted," at some of the replies. One question was: "If you were an employer would you hire a person with real convictions or not?" One answer was: "No, not with any convictions and certainly not with real convictions, because those must be felonies."

Really, the tests are *not* adequate. Even the people who devise the tests and are trying to prepare new ones regret that the educational testing service has not accepted many of the new tests, such as the so-called "cultural pluralistic" or "cultural specific" test. We will get them, but there has to be counseling, and that is where social workers can come in. I think too that your profession is going to have to work with other disciplines on this problem if we are going to deal with it and deal with it adequately. It is not a one-discipline problem. The teachers, the social workers, the psychologists, the nurses, and the doctors will be necessary if we are to rebuild or help people who have been underclassed to rebuild themselves and move into the nation's life. We are for ourselves, we are for the nation. In the words of Hillel: "If I am not for myself, who will be for me? If I am for myself alone, what am I? And if not now—when?"

Report from the President's Commission on Mental Health

BEVERLY BENSON LONG

THE PRESIDENT'S COMMISSION on Mental Health was established by Executive Order signed by President Carter on February 17, 1977, to review the mental health needs of the nation and to make recommendations to the President as to how the nation might best meet these needs.

A six-person group chaired by John Gardner did the initial screening of potential members of the Commission, and Mrs. Carter made the final selections. Mrs. Carter was named honorary chairperson and presided at the public hearings.

Although the twenty commissioners represent a wide range of interests related to mental health and mental retardation, I believe we have produced a landmark report—a summary of where we are and how we need to proceed to attain a higher level of mental and emotional health in this country.

Dr. Thomas Bryant, an M.D. and a lawyer, was named chairperson and Executive Director.

In addition to the Commission, 32 separate task panels were appointed. These were made up of about 450 of the nation's outstanding mental health advocates who volunteered innumerable hours to the Commission. The reports of the panels have been published in three separate volumes.

It is generally conceded that mental health is an integral and basic aspect of what we call health or well-being. In

BEVERLY BENSON LONG is Vice-president for Program, National Association for Mental Health; Chairperson, Governor's Advisory Council for Mental Health-Mental Retardation; member, President's Commission on Mental Health.

twenty-six states the services are grouped under human resources, and physical health and mental health budgets and programs are separate. In others, mental health is a component of health. We found many different structural and administrative arrangements. At the federal level, mental health is a part of HEW and is subsumed under over-all health.

It probably makes little difference how structures are composed for delivering services, but how we identify, weigh, and coordinate the components makes *all* the difference. This is where mental health is still unrecognized. To most people, "health" means *physical* health. There is painfully clear evidence of this fact in the composition of the health systems agencies (HSAs) and boards. The Health Planning and Resource Development Act, P.L. 94–641, provides for *all* health planning and coordination, but at the national and local levels mental health representation is almost nonexistent.

The federal health expenditures are about $63 billion, of which something less than 6 percent goes to mental health. The states, on the other hand, spend enormous amounts of money for the mentally ill, about 80 percent of which still is for institutional care.

In 1963, John Kennedy said in a speech to Congress:

Mental illness and mental retardation are among our most critical health problems. . . . waste more of our human resources, and constitute more financial drain upon both the Public Treasury and the . . . individual families than any other single condition.

Nearly a decade later, the Governor of Georgia, now President Carter, said: "Mental illness is the most costly health problem in America today, both in dollars and in wasted human lives."

One third of all the hospital beds in this country are occupied by the mentally disabled. More than half of the prescription drugs are given for emotional symptoms. From 50 percent to 60 percent of the people who have "physical" problems are really suffering from psychological stresses.

Because so many people think that the absence of mental health is a disease entity—such as diabetes or measles—or a condition—such as a broken foot or nearsightedness—we are still not allocating funds commensurate with the need.

The federal government accounts for one third of all health expenditures in the United States (about $63 billion), yet it spends 94 percent for *other* than mental health-related problems.

At lease six times as much Medicaid money is spent on physical health care as is spent on mental health care. Medicare expenditures for physical health care are seventy-five times those for mental health care.

The Commission report says: "We will have to devote greater human and fiscal resources to mental health. There must be a more realistic balance in the allocation of resources between physical health and mental health." [1]

The President, who received the report at a White House ceremony on April 27, 1978, called it "a superb analysis of the problems we face in giving mental health services." He said it would not be costly to implement because it does not stress new programs, "but," he added, "it will save enormous amounts of public funds."

As a public commission, we concentrated primarily on what publicly funded mental health groups can do to improve mental health in the United States and, more specifically, on what the federal government might do to encourage and catalyze, to exert leverage, to provide leadership.

We recognize the need and strongly urge the federal government to encourage partnership among the federal, state, and local agencies, between the public and private sectors, and among those working in general health and in other human services. Not unexpectedly, we call for more clearly defined areas of responsibility and accountability, for coordination and unification.

The report is a clear reinforcement of the efforts of the 1961 Joint Commission to stop the neglect of the mentally ill,

[1] *Report to the President from the President's Commission on Mental Health* (Washington, D.C.: Superintendent of Documents, U.S. Government Printing Office, 1978).

to provide mental health services in the community and to see that human dignity is nurtured and enhanced.

FINDINGS OF THE COMMISSION

We have more outpatient and community services than in the 1960s, we have more providers of care, we have more knowledge and better treatment methods, and there is even less stigma attached to mental illness patients. Despite this progress, however, many problems remain in 1978:

1. The magnitude of mental health in relation to "health" problems is not acknowledged.

2. The interface between mental health and physical health is all but ignored.

3. The capacity to coordinate and integrate social, physical, and mental health services is practically nil. There are 135 federal programs in 11 major departments and agencies which have a direct or indirect impact on the mentally impaired, yet little, if any, coordination exists among them.

4. Personnel is badly distributed.

5. Financial arrangements keep people in hospitals and institutions.

6. Literally millions of people in the United States who have mental health problems are unserved, underserved, or inappropriately served.

Every one of our 117 recommendations is keyed to move us toward having appropriate services available close to where people live.

Our recommendations are divided into eight groups: community supports, service systems, finance, personnel, protection of rights, research, prevention, improving public understanding. We make specific recommendations with regard to adjustments in service delivery, financing, and personnel deployment and training. We speak strongly about research. But two areas are emphasized for the first time by the Commission, namely, community supports and primary prevention.

Community supports. Community supports—the personal and social networks of families, neighbors, and community organizations—need to be a much more recognized part of a responsive human service system.

Prevention. We note that "at present, our efforts to prevent mental illness or to promote mental health are unstructured, unfocused, and uncoordinated. They command few dollars, limited personnel, and little interest at levels where resources are sufficient to achieve results."

We recommend that

HEW immediately establish within NIMH a Center for Prevention. The Center would undertake and support research in primary prevention; would take the lead in initiating, stimulating, and coordinating all federal prevention activities; and would provide the link between similar work at state and local levels. The Commission recommends an initial budget of $10 million, to be increased over a 10-year period until it is not less than 10 percent of the total NIMH budget. The Commission concludes that: Although effective programs to reduce distress and emotional disorder can and should be developed for the entire life span, we believe that helping children must be the Nation's first priority in preventing mental disability.

Service systems. The Commission cites the accomplishments and progress since 1963 when the community mental health centers (CMHC) legislation was passed. The centers receive less than 5 percent of the total monies spent on mental health, yet provide 30 percent of the total episodes of care. They now cover about half the population. Each federal dollar has attracted three more dollars for community care. Where a center has been in operation for three or more years, hospital admissions for mental health problems have been reduced by one third.

The CMHC Act provides practically all of the federal dollars which now go into community mental health services. Whereas states spend some ten to twenty times as much as the federal government spends on mental health services, about 80 percent still goes into hospitals and institutions. In addition, Medicaid and Medicare payments promote the current unconscionable level of state hospital and nursing home budgets.

In assessing the role of the centers, we found that it is time for some mid-course corrections. There is need for more flexibility in the required services, for some geographical adjustments, and for across-boundary sharing of resources in some cases. There is an urgent need to help the severely underserved areas secure services. The report makes recommendations to accomplish these goals under the existing or amended CMHC Act. There is an urgent need for the states to move the monies as well as the patients back into the communities.

On another front, while mental health advocates struggled for better services, general or physical health was in an era of unprecedented turmoil. Costs have escalated at a phenomenal rate. The Congress in 1974, in an attempt to rectify this almost out-of-control situation, passed the National Health Planning and Resources Development Act, aimed at cost containment and equity of services.

These over-all health developments and the lessons learned from experience with a federally catalyzed system of CMHC services have provided a new stage for moving toward the goal of adequate and available health, including mental health.

We saw the developing network of HSAs under P.L. 93–641 as a key to more flexible mental health services and to a better coordinated system of state and community care. We recommend a new federal grant program whereby community mental health services can be established on a more limited basis than under current mental health legislation and would bring services to populations with special needs.

A word of caution, however. The report recommends very strong and very clear requirements for these planning bodies. We suggest a 25 percent mental health representation on the boards, and expertise on the staff. In order to develop the needed programs, we recommend new monies amounting to $75 million the first year and $100 million in each of the next two years. The new monies would be allocated for mental health services only on approval of the local HSAs.

We are not saying that CMHC development should be

stopped and that when we get new legislation we should start something else. We are saying that the momentum should be kept up and that special efforts should be made in regard to the 110 unserved areas and in places where services and needs are out of balance. Eventually, there should be a transition which will better unify and coordinate health programs with mental health programs, state with local, and public with private.

We include some fifty complete recommendations which, if implemented, will move us in the proper direction. Special priority should be given to the chronically mentally ill. Again, we strive for states and the federal government to work together. We recommend that $50 million annually be allocated for incentives to establish a federal-state partnership to phase down large hospitals and provide community services.

Medicaid and Medicare must be made more responsive to the mentally impaired. Mental health benefits must be on a parity with physical health benefits and services *must* be coordinated. We speak of the need for a national health insurance program which adequately deals with the needs of the mentally ill.

Research. We strongly recommend correcting the discrimination which has caused mental health research to drop 50 percent in the past decade. Despite the fact that one third of all hospital beds are occupied by the mentally disabled, only 3.5 percent of the U.S. government's health research funds go to mental health.

The President has directed the Domestic Policy Council and the Secretary of HEW to set in motion specific implementation processes. This is being done on a priority basis.

Discharged Mental Patients

STEPHEN M. ROSE and
DONNA L. CHAGLASIAN

In PRESENTING AN alternative approach to any sanctioned or traditional practice, it is first necessary to discuss the forms from which we want to depart. We shall do this briefly, since the material is thoroughly described elsewhere.[1] Based on data presented in numerous studies and from our own work, we assert that all of the humane changes and intended benefits of transferring from institutional or custodial psychiatry to community mental health have failed to materialize in the experience of former patients. We also believe that the truth of this statement has varying impact, with the seriousness of the deception increasing in proportion to the time spent in the hospital. In other words, the longer time a patient has spent in the institution, the greater the likelihood that present living conditions reflect past custodial arrangements.

The situation in New York State, which we think is qualitatively similar to other places, is that large numbers of people were dumped out of public mental hospitals into communities unwilling to accept them and ill-prepared to provide for

STEPHEN M. ROSE is Professor, School of Social Welfare, State University of New York at Stony Brook.

DONNA L. CHAGLASIAN is Field Work Instructor, School of Social Welfare, State University of New York at Stony Brook.

The preparation of the paper has been supported in part by a training grant from the Social Work Training Division of the National Institute of Mental Health.

[1] Stephen M. Rose, "Deciphering Deinstitutionalization: Complexities in Policy and Program Analysis" (unpublished, 1978); Stephen M. Rose, "Deinstitutionalization—a Challenge to the Profession (paper given at the National Conference on Social Welfare, 1978); Comptroller General of the United States, *Returning the Mentally Disabled to the Community: Government Needs to Do More* (Washington, D.C.: Government Printing Office, 1977).

them. We further believe that the dumping grounds more often than not continue to be private, profit-run nursing homes, intermediate care facilities, and single-room occupancy hotels, most of which have at least two people per room. We know that most nursing homes, intermediate care facilities, and adult homes are larger in size than many discharging wards, and that the inadequate services which characterize state hospitals are seldom replicated once patients are discharged into these facilities. Public interest research[2] has presented a devastating critique of the failure of the community mental health centers (CMHCs) to deal adequately with the problems of aftercare (particularly for the institutionalized former patients) or with prevention of rehospitalization. This research has received substantial legitimacy from the study conducted by an unquestionably impartial group—the Office of the Comptroller General of the United States.[3] In New York, equally severe criticism has been made by the Assembly Joint Committee (Mental Hygiene/Ways and Means, 1976), the Legislative Commission on Expenditure Review,[4] and the Office of the Special Prosecutor (1977). Charles Hynes, in his interim report to the State Attorney General, reflects his appraisal: "The discharge of mental patients from psychiatric hospitals without insuring the delivery of aftercare services makes deinstitutionalization a procedure of patient abandonment, rather than a progressive program of patient care."[5]

Complicating the problem of patient abandonment, in addition to the wholesale lack of adequate support services and grossly improper housing, is an inability to understand conceptually the "community" into which people were thrown.

---

[2] Franklin D. Chu and Sharland Trotter, *The Madness Establishment: Ralph Nader's Group Report on the National Institute of Mental Health* (New York: Grossman Publishers, 1974).

[3] Comptroller General, *op. cit.*

[4] State of New York, Legislative Commission on Expenditure Review, "Patients Released from State Psychiatric Centers" (1975).

[5] Charles J. Hynes, *Private Proprietary Homes for Adults—an Interim Report* (Albany, N.Y.: New York State Deputy Attorney General, 1977), p. 41.

In practice, and despite countless and fruitless hours worrying about catchment areas,[6] communities as economic and
social entities could not be understood from within the psychiatric world. Operating from the individual defect or medical model,[7] social reality could not be understood as a complex of objective historical and economic conditions and so
was neglected even in the CMHC programs. For the tens of
thousands of long-term patients, who were never seen in
CMHCs and were simply deposited outside the hospital as
part of deinstitutionalization, the issue of the social environment was never approached. It simply amounted to whatever
entrepreneur could build a facility or appropriate space to
receive patients from state facilities.

Just as most local communities have little or no power to
contend with economic realities of a more overt and larger
scope (unemployment and inflation, for example) than deinstitutionalization, they had no political capacity to enter into
the community mental health arena. The net result, in areas
such as Long Beach, Bay Shore, and Sayville on Long Island,
was a combination of inadequate service provision, inadequate resource bases for constructing services, and tremen-
dous antagonism on the part of those many community residents who were not profiting from a large influx of formerly
institutionalized patients. In turn, the vast majority of the
dischargees had never heard of these towns, let alone lived in
them.

Former patients, workers, and residents had one thing in
common: all were exploited by, and manipulated through, a
policy outside their control. Former patients, who for years
had heard that it was necessary for them to remain in the
hospital, were now told it was necessary for them to leave;
social workers who were to provide impatient services now
were told to place their patients elsewhere, and given quotas

[6] Anthony F. Panzetta, "The Concept of Community: the Short Circuit of the
Mental Health Movement," *Archives of General Psychiatry*, XXV (1971), 291–98.

[7] Stephen M. Rose, *Betrayal of the Poor* (Cambridge, Mass.: Schenkman Publishing
Co., 1972); Roland L. Warren, Stephen M. Rose, and Ann F. Bergunder, *The Structure of Urban Reform* (Lexington, Ky.: D. C. Heath & Co., 1974).

for discharge; and community residents, who had been told to fear mental patients, were now told to welcome them into their neighborhoods. Whatever the reactions of these three groups, the process of dumping continued. In most states, hospital populations were reduced by about two-thirds in less than fifteen years, while first admissions and recidivism rates skyrocketed. At the same time, evidence of fraud and other abuses of the former patients accumulated, community hostilities were inflamed, and the number of workers in the state systems decreased. Treatment, however, remained much the same even while being shifted from distant hospitals to somewhat closer clinics. And the basic mode of interaction, refilling prescriptions for potentially dangerous and unscientifically grounded medications,[8] was maintained, along with other therapeutic pursuits which neglected to take into account both former patients' needs and the needs of the communities into which they were placed.

Our project did make this effort. We had to determine first how we would define the needs of the former patients with whom we worked. This population is comprised of a variety of people aged thirty-four to seventy-seven who have in common the fact that they lived for many years in large, custodial state hospitals, were discharged without consideration of what they wanted for themselves or what they knew about life "on the outside," and were placed in private congregate-care facilities—either adult homes or hotels. They have in common the fact of their manipulation by mental health policy-makers carrying out a fiscal policy masked in humane mental health rhetoric; their domination by a landlord system at best as controlling as the discharging hospitals; and their exploitation via the profits being reaped by the private sector from their placements. We began our analysis with an acceptance of these characteristics—domination, exploitation, and manipulation—as unintended, concrete facts of daily life for former patients, and we accepted their behavior, worker

[8] George E. Crane, "Clinical Psychopharmacology in Its 20th Year," *Science*, July 13, 1973, pp. 124–28.

cynicism, and community hostility as misdirected but appropriate subjective reflections or echoes of these facts.

In our target population, we found that the objective situation also had its expected subjective repercussions: people still saw themselves as mental patients, even though some had been discharged a year or more. Almost everything in their daily lives replicated the hospital wards, and daily this functioned to reproduce a mental patient self-image, one which aided the landlords in maintaining a docile, acquiescing residence with even less freedom than was available in many hospitals. The objective economic and social conditions were refracted through the subjective experience of former patients which then reproduced the objective situations monotonously.

It took some time for us to recognize the extent of this interpenetration between continuity in oppressive social environments and former patients' behavior and modes of interacting with us. When we did see the extent and scope of the oppression, it made our program strategy clearer. We had to develop a system of integrated dimensions in our program which recognized both the subjective or psychological needs of the former patients and, even more important, the objective or social bases which forged and defined those needs. Our program therefore took on a complex nature: we had to work for change in the objective context as a vehicle for producing subjective change in our program participants, and we had to comprehend the objective situation *as they understood and related to it themselves* in order for us to develop a supportive, direct-service approach which recognized their life experience as a valid, legitimate reflection of the lives they were forced to lead.

The outlines of a strategy formed: we had to engage ourselves in the political, economic, and legal aspects of postdischarge contexts, yet we had to engender some direct-service basis through which we could identify and act on structural problems. We also had to engage the former patients in a process of support and validation so that they could tell us about their experiences. Once we could establish a process for receiving this information, we could move to identify an objective basis for their thoughts about themselves, their feelings, and their generalized acquiescence. This led us to our program design which, of necessity, included a direct-service strategy and an advocacy or organizing strategy which were mutually supportive.

DIRECT-SERVICE COMPONENTS

Our first task was to develop a process for involving the people in forms of interaction which provided support for them and a basis from which to talk about their life situations. It would not be any typical form of therapy, nor would it be based on any theories of psychopathology, both of which act to sever the continuity or dialectical relationship of objective (social and economic forces) with subjective or psychological response, or of producing and reproducing destructive behaviors and perceptions. We had to maintain our belief in this social world where people who had been acted upon in systematic and coercive ways reproduced the situations that dominated them. They were, as Freire says, submerged in a reality of oppression which kept them behaviorally and ideologically domesticated.[9] They were compliant with both house rules and the self-image those rules perpetuated. The scope and extent of this immersion in oppression, in dehumanizing modes of daily life, could only be learned from them.

We began by trying to involve them in planning activities, in refusing to acknowledge our more powerful role, and in moving quickly to identify sources of domination, exploitation, and manipulation. And in doing this, we replicated the very characteristics that were our targets. Involving people who perceive themselves as mental patients in program planning meant that they asked for programs appropriate to mental patients—the recreational and busybody things which

[9] Paolo Freire, *Pedagogy of the Oppressed* (New York: Herder & Herder, 1971).

they had been offered in the hospital to maintain a mildly entertained and domesticated group whose ability to perceive their own real needs and interests had been damaged by hospital treatment. To go along with them meant sustaining the oppression, while doing anything else meant continuing the manipulation and domination by obscuring it. In refusing to accept our leadership role, we did not differentiate ourselves from hospital staff in allowing patientlike behavior to be validated. And in moving quickly to identify and act against sources of exploitation, we exploited by superimposing our need to feel valid in our work over their need to trust the situation, learn about it, and act.

Our familiarity with the work of Freire fortunately helped us clear our minds about our own work, a process which we still engage in, since the need for criticism and support among the workers is always great. We were able to see that we were not entering into and understanding the reality as the former patients experienced it and related to it. We were substituting our reality for theirs, and forcing them to respond to us rather than the other way around. Once we identified this obstacle to our intentions, we could move to redress it. We backed off from false participation in planning (or, as Freire calls it, "false charity"); we assumed the leadership position that we actually held in introducing programs and leading groups; and we struggled to develop formats in which we could elicit descriptions of daily life and experiences rather than tell them what we saw and felt.

The community meeting was the first organized group which we introduced. It had three overt purposes: to discuss plans for the day and the week; to discuss resources that people might use and how to get them; and to discuss any difficulties people were having or feeling in their lives. We made clear that we felt the community meeting was a proper place to do all of this, since all of the participants had in common their hospital experience and their living situations and could be helpful in sorting out how they have handled problems. Our message was twofold: the former patients could be seen as resources for one another and group support is a basis of strength.

The resources issue led us to introduce to the group the tasks and functions of the state aftercare clinic and the Adult Protective Services (APS) workers. Representatives from both programs were brought to the community meeting to discuss their responsibilities. We were able to use these experiences, particularly those of the APS worker, to identify real problems that had an objective existence.

Once we could identify these problems, a format was set up to elicit reaction to those problems. People were able to discuss whether or not they ever saw the face of their Supplementary Security Income checks, whether or not they had a proper Medicaid card, whether or not they received medical attention, and so on. As a member talked about what happened in his/her home, others could be involved in comparing their experiences. People began to see their common situation, and slowly learned that how they felt about themselves and their situation had an objective base, that it came from real forces in the external world.

Our experience with the community meeting, and with the struggle to introduce external world variables into the thought process of our members, led us to organize several other groups which had the same purpose. A health group was started, to which were added a discussion group (to address daily life issues), a women's group, a men's group, an exercise group, a sewing group. In each case the group focused on an aspect of daily life which could be examined and generalized. The health group, run by a nurse, could do hypertension screening and talk about other health-related issues while discussing the quantity and quality of health care available to them. The discussion group could talk about rent, landlord behavior, and former patients' experiences in the facility while raising questions about the law and its acceptance or rejection by the landlord. The women's group could talk about individual histories while looking at common bases in social roles and at what happened in the project itself. The men's groups could explore issues related to being part of the labor market and its impact on self-perception while raising questions about the idealized role expectations people had in the light of high unemployment. In each case, to the best of our ability, we tried to identify the reality of oppression as objective, to identify common bonds, to build community or solidarity, and to restore the objective/subjective dialectic which is human life. We tried to shift the focus from internal invalidation to external and understandable aspects of social reality.

Ironically, to a casual observer, much of what we may do resembles in form what happens in hospitals and day treatment programs. As mentioned, however, our theoretical orientation and practice principles differ substantially: we see ourselves as restoring what psychopathological theory and practice have taken away—a sense of autonomy, dignity, communality, and connection with the objective world. We think that a vehicle for advancing these processes (which we see as movement and development rather than as objectives or goals) will provide a basis for, and subsequent feeling of, community among the members of our program, decrease competition and contempt, and create critical understanding of the context in which they live. As such, our activities and group meetings do not exist as isolated events—they all work toward establishing support, validation, and connection as a basis for generating a critical appraisal of life situations and action. Working in this way often produces a new awareness of previously unknown needs: working on a newsletter discovers major problems of illiteracy and difficulty with eyesight which lead to a reading group and an examination of medical care. Discussions about eyesight in the health group reappear in the community meeting as discussions about Medicaid cards and health service delivery, which in turn leads to discussion of the extremely poor public transportation system. Each theme or need identified in one of the smaller groups is reported to the community meeting, both spreading the knowledge we have gained and reaffirming the objective world obstacles to a more enhanced life. The themes are then repeated as each group records its progress in our newsletter. Over time, people begin to respond, making suggestions for action, or taking action themselves.

Several months after we introduced a legal services attorney to the project, and after he had explained various aspects of the law and negotiated with a landlord for one of our members, another member sought his counsel to register a grievance about withheld money. This contest was won, encouraging others to seek legal assistance. The money problems led to identification of a medical problem which led to another legal action to ensure that the plaintiff received a proper Medicaid card. Each step was discussed at the community meeting, with the member and the attorney participating. The objective victories are shared, with equal validation given to the subjective experience of acting and fighting for one's rights. At the same community meeting, another member may report on the death of a goldfish, on the visit to a relative, or on a coming birthday. Personal experiences and political experiences commingle, creating a blend that emphasizes both aspects of our work together.

Other activities occur with regularity: writing a monthly newsletter, cooking and cleaning up, planting and caring for a garden, learning to use the bus, walking through the town, playing various games. All are done to encourage activity, participation, cooperation, and enjoyment of being together, of having fun. Food preparation has been a major focus since it has meaning well beyond the fulfillment of a basic human need. Among the institutionalized, eating was a time for maximum competition—eat as much as you can as fast as you can, or else there will be nothing for you. The way people ate at the beginning told us much about the way they had been forced to live, and what we had to contend against to bring about communality. As we struggled to open up this new avenue of relationships, we used eating as a measure of our development. We also used it as a point of criticism, often turning a meal into a community meeting for that purpose.

Cooking brought into perspective another need. People who had spent ten to fifteen years in a state hospital had either lost whatever skills they had, or succumbed to the idea that they were incompetent in the real world. We had to turn cooking into a forum for active participation rather than an arena for individual excellence. Cooking became a task of breaking down the process to include as many people as possible, and to communicate skills from one person to another: today's can opener becomes tomorrow's teacher of can opening, thus building confidence, communication, and mutuality. Gradually, as more and more people had the experience of helping to prepare coffee or meals, a sense of sharing, enjoyment, and satisfaction emerged. Since we never used participation as a test of daily living skills, people could approach more complex tasks comfortably and even volunteer to help. The sharing that took place in the kitchen eventually showed up at the dinner table. After each meal the cooks are applauded, and applaud themselves—and the food is good!

Meeting real needs based on entering the reality of the former patients has produced an ever-expanding set of new needs. Increasingly, the new needs are the real or concrete needs of people (social, economic, political) as contrasted to the artificial needs of mental patients. As suggested, the basis for the existence of these needs and for responding to them lies in the objective world and in the necessity for acting to change it as well.

INDIRECT SERVICE COMPONENTS

Of primary importance in the beginning was our recognition of our position as "outsiders" in the Sayville community. Even though we had been invited to develop some type of program by a local State Assembly member and an agency director, we nevertheless came from the university, some miles away. We also knew about community hostility toward former patients, and about the effort of one small church group to provide some type of outreach to residents of one adult home. We thought that positive contact must be established as a base for our own program initiatives, and made an early contact with the church group. As a vehicle for publicly acknowledging the existence of former patients and their needs—there were no programs for them within a fifteen-mile radius and no public transportation—we worked with the church group to hold an open meeting for community members to discuss needs, problems, and possible responses.

The meeting had the function of identifying all the various interests and forces in the town: those people who were willing to work together to develop a recreational program; those who wanted all former patients thrown out of the town; the service providers who offered empty promises and shifted blame or made false apologies for the present situation. Most significantly, however, the meeting led to organization of the Sayville Community Steering Committee, which brought a number of people together for continuing discussions.

Sayville Community Steering Committee. Work with the Steering Committee has been a useful but often frustrating experience. The committee began with a strong tendency to give two or three dances or picnics per year "for them," and to provide opportunities for some people in the community to exercise their religious energy by directing it toward "other-worldly" goals. But it also contained a different source of support: some of the members were quite willing to listen to issues, visit proprietary homes, and struggle to understand the objective context of former patients' lives. Our task was one of supporting the leadership, keeping the meetings going, providing information and educational materials, and reflecting back to the committee members what the people who came to our program told us about their daily lives and needs.

Over the past two years these two tendencies have remained. The Steering Committee has initiated and provided for residents of the homes several activities which had some broader base of community support, and it has decreased fear of the former patients among those community residents who have attended. It has also engaged in some examination of conditions in the homes, occasionally questioned political representatives about those conditions, and served at times as a mild advocate for former patients' needs. As a vehicle for wider participation and education, the Steering Committee and the Sayville Project coproduced a slide-tape presentation about the situation in the community, a process which required many hours of discussion about what the narrative should contain, about what each slide represented and what it was to demonstrate. Eventually, a completed presentation discussed why former patients lived in the community, what resources were and were not available to them, what some of their needs were, and how the community could respond in a positive manner. The presentation was then made available to church, civic, and other community groups, with Steering Committee and Sayville Project members participating. The process of producing the final product, of course, turned out to be as valuable as the product itself.

CASA. We invited agency representatives to the Steering Committee meetings, and found that often the meetings were the first source of contact with workers from agencies whose functions and responsibilities should have brought them together frequently since they dealt with the same general client population, and often with the same individuals. We also learned that none of the agencies with responsibility for some aspects of former patients' lives had ever made community contacts. As this process unfolded, agency representatives were invited to attend the Steering Committee meetings regularly. Soon the committee began to function as a clearinghouse for information and a source of coordination. These useful tasks, however, were often deflected by

Steering Committee members with more "otherworldly" or recreational/charitable interests. As a result, we organized a separate group made up of several members of the Steering Committee who lived in the community, representatives from the discharging state facility and its aftercare clinics and from the APS.

Our new organization was dubbed CASA, for Community After-Care Services Association. It had the purposes of coordinating interagency and agency-community concerns and identifying obstacles to improved service delivery. Its membership was made up of Sayville residents, some line workers from involved agencies, and Sayville Project staff. We assumed leadership in converting anecdotes and "war stories" into recognizable general issues, and used the group to educate the members further about the objective basis for former patients' behavior and modes of living. Once issues could be generalized, we moved to identify the scope and proper definition of the problem: was it a gap in service delivery, a deficiency in service design, or a problem of implementation, policy, and/or legislation?

CASA meetings always began with specific situations that were brought either by Sayville Project participants on the basis of our direct-service experience or by other CASA members. Our major task was to elevate the level of concern from anecdote to issue, and to shift the focus from defensiveness on the part of agency members to a more comprehensive overview of the situation. As we compiled "war story" after "war story," we were able to infer and identify the existence of larger problems than the behavior of individuals, whether former patients or workers. The problems began to emerge as systemic, a view that we encouraged and developed. It was only when this level of preliminary understanding was reached that the CASA group began to see other sources for criticism than one another. The sources that required examination included three state/county bureaucracies which had vaguely defined responsibilities for af-

tercare. The conclusion reached, converting hostile an-
tiagency rhetoric into a more thorough outlook, was that
CASA should engage in policy analysis and research.

With our leadership, CASA systematically went over repeated cases of abuse and neglect of former patients, and
struggled to generate issues that went beyond case circumstances to the context in which those cases existed, the private housing market. A brief questionnaire was mailed to the
appropriate agencies under the CASA letterhead. This process itself was a solidifying experience for the CASA membership since we had moved beyond talking to some form of
action. When agency responses trickled in, they were analyzed in the context of larger scale research about deinstitutionalization. This led to a position paper on the issues of accountability, and an analysis of where gaps in the system
existed as a result of inadequate legislation, policy, and/or
implementation. The CASA policy position paper, which we
took the responsibility for preparing, was a basis for discussion and soon led to our adopting a series of recommendations for legislation which we then presented to the State
Assembly Subcommittee on Aftercare.

Maintaining contact, or instituting it where necessary, with
state legislators is an important aspect of our advocacy work.
We have the convenience of working with Assembly
members from Sayville and neighboring areas which are considered "impacted" or "saturated" communities in terms of
numbers of former patients. These people can be an important asset in progressive reform through legislation and evaluation of state programs, but they must be worked with carefully since large numbers of their constituents often form
hostile citizens' groups and berate former patients for wan-
dering the streets, and so forth. Contact with the legislature
or with state officials can be maintained by inviting them to
visit the program, by conducting an active correspondence
about mental health issues which appear in the media, and
by appearing at every opportunity to present testimony at
hearings which articulate our perspective on the issues.

Again, the tasks involved are to generalize from individual cases, attach accountability to state or local agencies, and present an analysis of problems that shifts the focus from treatment to meeting specific or objectively based needs.

Effective impact on legislators must be seen in relation to their constituents. This means that an effort must be made to establish linkages to citizens' groups, however antagonistic and outrageous they may appear to be at first. We made these contacts through other community members with whom we worked—the CASA members. Representatives of the hostile Civic Association were invited to CASA meetings, and then invited to become part of CASA. CASA then was asked to address the Civic Association, following two meetings the Association had held with mental health service providers and politicians. Our focus was clear. We supported their anger, but suggested that it was misdirected at former patients and that we would present data to identify the correct sources of their feelings: the state fiscal structure and the entrepreneurial home owners. An analysis of who benefits from deinstitutionalization—the state and the private sector—provided community members with the first realistic or correct assessment of what had happened, and how they, along with former patients and line workers, had been subjected to policy and promises that were false and outside their control.

Our efforts were directed toward constructing a stronger base of community support for our work, involving community members in CASA, and increasing the advocacy role of that group. We struggled to turn our interactions with the members of our daily program into policy—legislative and service-delivery issues which required action to change the context in which former patients lived. Undertaking study of the issues, analysis of the structural impediments to better services, and presentation of legislative recommendations further clarified the structure of interaction and decision-making, allowing us additional identification of political points of entry. As this information unfolded, it was fed back into our direct-service program. The more we learned about the law and its potential, the more we could communicate to Sayville Project participants, and the greater would be the likelihood of legal challenges to landlord domination, exploitation, and abuse. The stronger the participants felt about their rights, the more likely they would be to initiate legal redress.

The process is a continuing one. To the extent that we can provide supportive legitimation to the former patients, through acknowledgment of, and communication about, the objective world, the stronger they become subjectively. The degree to which they reestablish connection with the objective world will determine the extent to which they feel more human, less like patients, more able to act in their own interests. And as they act, slowly and painfully, with fear and uncertainty about themselves, the more in doubt the mental patient status becomes. The process is continuous, with each step emerging gradually in the context of support given through our direct-service program leading to identification of new needs, and new needs producing the necessity of learning more about the objective context and how it must be confronted to produce change. Each change must then be followed up—to ensure, for example, that landlords in fact transfer SSI personal allowance money to the residents, or that legal recourse is initiated when required.

Slowly, the process of conversion from mental patient to person or citizen takes place. The persons coming to our program slowly recognize each other as persons, and support each other as people rather than accept each other as patients. And, slowly, they begin to act to reduce domination, to reduce exploitation, and to reduce manipulation. Put another way, as they begin to understand parts of the objective world critically, through a process of group support and validation, they slowly begin to act to change it. Our responsibility is to stimulate this process, to encourage it, to allow it, to reflect the pace and needs of the participants, and to carry its message into political and economic arenas for structural transformation. To do this requires our constant attention at

the direct-service level where we struggle to build "community" among the participants, and at the indirect-service level
where we struggle to establish concrete or objective bases for
that community.

Into the Lifeboats, Wealthy and Powerful First

PAUL ABELS and *SONIA LEIB ABELS*

THE PURPOSE OF this paper is to provide an account of the persistent and pervasive forces that are shaping our understanding of the value of human life. We hope to initiate this dialogue within our profession for we believe that issues such as population control, abortion, euthanasia, and death have been viewed primarily within the context of the individual, rather than what in regard to the effects are on the social collective.

Throughout the generations prophets have forecast the end of the world—"repent," they urged, and perhaps you might be saved—but never before has the rallying call been "save yourself by murder." Visualize the earth as a lifeboat, suggests Garrett Hardin, and imagine that "the 50 of us in the lifeboat see 100 others swimming in the water outside, asking for admission to the boat, or for handouts. How shall we respond to their calls?" His answer is simple, admittedly abhorrent, but deemed necessary: "Future survival demands that we govern our actions by the ethics of a lifeboat."[1]

Hardin uses the traditional laws of survival at sea as a metaphor for nations. The wealthy countries are in the lifeboat, and the poor developing countries are struggling in the storm-tossed waters. Only those considered worthy (decided how?) should be permitted access to those resources, or all

PAUL ABELS is Professor, School of Applied Social Sciences, Case Western Reserve University, Cleveland.
SONIA LEIB ABELS is Associate Professor, Department of Social Sciences, Cleveland State University, Cleveland.

[1] Garrett Hardin, "Living in a Lifeboat," *Bio Science*, XXIV (1947), 562.

will go under. The rules are that food is not to be given away, and population expansion shall be controlled. In his latest book[2] we see that his commitment is not only a metaphor for nations, but an attack on all altruistic institutions, similar in some measure to that of his predecessor, Herbert Spencer.

The "worthy poor" refrain has sounded before, but rarely so universally, and never at a time when the fear of scarcity and destruction was international. Hardin's tune has been sung before. In his famous "Tragedy of the Commons" he examines the need for population control but is not yet ready to let the offenders drown.[3]

THE NEW ETHIC: SOCIAL DARWINISM IN NEW BOTTLES

The idea of being safe and snug in the lifeboat, and feeling appropriately chosen, is very compelling. Certainly the reasons for one's selection are rational. To follow Hardin's approach, those that have, do not share, they make the rules and enforce them.

But was there not an unwritten law of "women and children first"? Whatever happened to the noble concern that reflected consideration for the weaker or more helpless? This was seen as a more "civilized" view than concern for one's own survival at all costs.

There was a time in the course of civilization when rather than keeping them out of the boats, people who lacked certain characteristics were forced into boats. These boats plied the Rhine, taking people who were thought to be insane from communities that did not want them, and dumping them miles up or down river on the shores or at the ports of other cities. It was an attempt to solve the local mental health problems. Such a boat was called a "ship of fools."

Throughout history there have always been victims, and a

[2] Garrett Hardin, *The Limits of Altruism: an Ecologist's View of Survival* (Bloomington, Ind.: Indiana University Press, 1977).

[3] Garrett Hardin, "The Tragedy of the Commons," *Science,* CLXII, No. 13 (1968), 1243–48.

common mechanism was to blame the victims for their own misfortunes and then suggest drastic population control programs:

In the late nineteenth and early twentieth century, American pauperism was believed to be an inherited condition, and many eugenicists recommended sterilizing people on the public dole. During the same period many programmers, including Margaret Sanger, believed that immigrants to this country were inferior in mental capacities to native Americans, and that sterilization ought to be used to prevent contamination of the gene pool.[4]

Even though these ideas have faded, their faint pentimento can be ascertained underlying some of the current proposed solutions to the social problems facing our society. They are manifested in our changing values in relation to: population control, abortions, suicides, death and dying, and euthanasia.

Discussions of these issues in communication with abortion, for example, usually focus on the individual's right to decide his own life, or on the right of the unborn child, rather than on helping to raise our moral understanding. The social consequences of an individual's actions for our society are generally not considered. The common denominator that spans all these issues is life and its alternative, death.

Our more open acceptance of death may not be an enlightened moral view, but rather subtle socialization of the view that we have too many people, that we no longer "need" people, accompanied by a devaluing of life. With the shrinking need for people to carry out traditional work roles; with vanishing frontiers and machine-made, mass-produced goods; with increased life spans, a static or shrinking population level is acceptable. We have seen communities close off entrance to newcomers and, as in the case of St. Petersburg, try to limit population size by law. These communities are faced with serious land-use problems, and resolutions are made on the basis of the "ins" against the "outs."

[4] Drew Christiansen, "Ethics and Compulsory Population Control," *Hastings Center Report,* February, 1977, p. 31.

At least since the days of Malthus, we have created the specter of being overrun by too many people, particularly by people believed to be less fit, yet mysteriously more prolific and less socially concerned breeders. Hardin's philosophy has obvious roots in social Darwinism, but its theoretical relation to I.Q. controversies, immigration laws, birth control, sterilization, and abortion is a tangled web. It is evident that some people active in the fields of eugenics, immigration quotas, and population control were and often are interchangeable in their affiliations. Some are motivated by important principles, such as preventing deaths by illegal abortion mills, or insuring a good home for each child. Some motivations are less clear, such as, for example, promoting "survival of the race," or not permitting deformed babies to live. The social work profession has struggled with these issues, and our historic roots show the split in our own moral heritage. This may best be illustrated by the Bollenger baby case.

CONFLICTING VALUES: THE BOLLENGER BABY CASE[5]

In November of 1915 a Chicago surgeon, J. H. Haiselden, contrary to accepted medical ethics, refused to operate on the defective Bollenger baby, four days old. This he did, he affirmed, "in the interest of the human race and more particularly of American manhood." He explained that the boy was extremely defective and would probably remain so throughout his life. He believed that the infant was dying, but there was no doubt that his life would be prolonged if an operation were performed. Dr. Haiselden's position was that, with the consent of the parents, which was willingly given, "nature should be allowed to take her course." The child was allowed to die.

There were, as might be expected, serious differences of opinion. Widespread discussion ensued, and there were many medical and lay people on both sides of the question.

[5] Summarized from Wilbur Marshall Urban, *Fundamentals of Ethics* (New York; Henry Holt, 1930), pp. 41–44.

"It has always been my opinion," wrote one physician, "that all children born with a congenital abnormality are a detriment to society. I distinctly believe that it is humane to cut off their future sufferings and those of society."

The moral reaction was immediate and extensive. Meetings of the Chicago Anti-Cruelty League and of the Illinois Humane Society were held. There were threats of court action, but to the surprise of many, the two societies announced support for Dr. Haiselden. Jane Addams, of Hull House, condemned the act absolutely:

"Life," she insisted, "can be taken away only by the one that gave it, and should be prolonged at any cost. What right has this doctor to take a human life? Everything is born into this world with an inherent right to have a chance to live. The letting of that baby die when its life could have been saved, is a crime against the race instead of the benefaction claimed.[6]

It is important to note that social workers became involved in a nationally publicized way. None, to my knowledge, has been similarly quoted on the Karen Quinlan case, or other euthanasia cases, although differences have been expressed on the abortion issue.

Here we see highlighted two different views. Both the Chicago Anti-Cruelty League and the Illinois Humane Society, clinically oriented agencies, and related to the Charity Organization Society (C.O.S.) philosophy, supported the physician. Jane Addams, of the settlements, opposed. Historically, it could be pointed out the C.O.S. was more Social Darwinian (survival of the fittest), the settlements more community- or people-oriented.

Friedlander notes of the C.O.S. that "the founders of these societies represented the 'bourgeois benevolence' of wealthy citizens who felt morally obliged to alleviate the suffering of the poor and hoped thus to minimize political unrest and industrial strike."[7] Whether or not this statement truly repre-

---

[6] Jane Addams, quoted in *ibid.*, p. 42.
[7] Walter Friedlander, *Introduction to Social Welfare* (New York: Prentice-Hall, 1955), p. 106.

sents what was in the hearts and minds of the C.O.S. workers is open to serious question, but it is clear that there was a strong element of social control philosophy in their approach, a "better-than-thou" view, as well as a belief in the worthy and unworthy poor. For example, in order to obtain aid from the C.O.S., women whose husbands drank were required to obtain a divorce. Women who were abandoned by their husbands could not qualify, either, because this might promote continued and increased abandonments.

The settlement's major emphasis, on the other hand, was to help individuals by working with them in the community, and helping the community change itself and society. There was an attempt to share experiences and live with the people, to form collectives, and to instigate appropriate social action. Many of the settlements were in fact communes, particularly for women, and training grounds for liberal reform. The two differences in philosophy were often evident in other ways than in the Bollenger baby case. There were many conflicts between the settlements and the C.O.S.

"Jane Addams of Hull House referred to the honest outrage experienced by many people who come into contact with them [charity organization societies]." When they see the delay and caution with which relief is given, these do not appear to them conscientious scruples, but the cold and calculating action of the selfish man. On the other hand, "Mary Richmond warned her co-workers not to be swept away by enthusiastic advocates of social reform from that safe middle ground which recognizes that character is at the very center of social problems." [8]

The C.O.S. made an ideological virtue out of the need to police the poor, to preach self-restraint, and to attach cost accounting to moral uplifting, and was accused of "establishing standards of truthfulness and hard work for the poor which apparently did not apply to the rich." [9] Mary Richmond's colleagues focused on the "moral roots of dependency." [10] The

[8] Roy Lubove, *The Professional Altruist* (New York: Atheneum, 1972), p. 11.
[9] *Ibid.*, p. 10.   [10] *Ibid.*, p. 11.

dichotomy has lost some of its power, but periodically appears in the issues of clinical vs. social change, or the growth
of private practice. We have not yet provided the dialogue
around a contrast of views, which Piaget suggests helps people evolve to a high moral level.

Could social work function in a world of lifeboat ethics,
where any contribution to help the poor or finance a program to combat illness is seen to threaten humanity eugeni-
cally?[11] Imagine, if you will, a future world in which we can
survive only if we can limit the number of people. We would
do this in the kindest fashion, of course, but eventually
science and technology would be employed to enrich those
who were selected to survive and to prevent the development
of those considered surplus.[12] Certainly some would remain
for menial tasks, but not many would be needed in an advanced technological-computerized society.

Hardin would hold, we suppose, that these nightmarish futures or worse could be prevented by some drastic action
now. But would taking those steps permit us, once committed to action which is based on status as a prerequisite for
survival, to return to the idea of a world in which social justice has any significance? Have we become more human because we dropped the Horoshima bomb or because of our involvement in My Lai? Never mind that other countries
mistrust our motives because of these actions. What is our
own assessment of ourselves?

Would not the same logic apply to the handicapped, the
aged, the retarded, if a crunch were to develop in our own
country? Once we develop a triage mentality where would it
end? With which minorities? The poor?

Can there be a new ethics which revolves around supporting the powerful and maintaining a society of those who have
and those who have nothing? Ethics is related to the process
of moral decision-making, the selection of "good" choices. By
suggesting a "new ethics," Hardin admits that indeed this

[11] Allan Chase, *The Legacy of Malthus* (New York: Alfred A. Knopf, 1977), p. 375.
[12] The idea of "surplus people" is not new—it was the title of a film put out about
ten years ago dealing with unemployment, the aged, and minorities.

would be something "new" for our society—a turning from important historic values, not on the basis that they were not good values but as a matter of immediate self-interest.

Civilization as we know it would be altered as we decide what groups should live or die. It is a power play, pure and simple, and may fall apart on that basis, for unlike people struggling in the water some of the developing countries have the power to sink our lifeboat through their own manipulation of scarce commodities, such as oil and tin, or through wars which might soon suck us into world conflict. Should we expect less than war or blackmail if we ourselves, an "enlightened cradle of liberty," should suggest turning away from those in need?

We once were asked whether a nation could long survive half slave and half free. A moral stand at that time led to a greater unity. Can we long survive as a universe half rich and half poor? Could the answer lie in world unity, at least in the recognition that we must work on our unity with others? Jung noted that without the conscious acknowledgment and acceptances of our kinship with those around us there can be no synthesis of personality. Recent archeological studies suggest that one of the early steps in civilization which helped differentiate humans from apes was humans' ability to share food. This step led to genetic, environmental stages, which move us up the ladder. Mutual aid is built into every society in some form and is basic for that society's survival.

The metaphor of the ship can still serve us well, because the ship suggests an alternative metaphor. As Chesterton wrote:

> We are all in the same boat in a stormy sea
> and we owe each other a terrible loyalty.

THE FUTURE AS MORAL COMMUNITY

The profession of social work will increasingly be faced with moral decisions and value conflicts. Any decision which affects another person's life is a moral decision. Concern such as population control and genetic manipulation not only have an impact on a mother whose child may have a birth defect, but also have implications for social control and/or modifications of future generations. These are values—sociopolitical decisions as well as technical decisions—and the social work role and perspective have always been vital in this area. They will become even more crucial in the future, and we must develop the human capacity to deal with the problem.

Part of that capacity is related to the decision-making and inquiry process we use in our profession. One such process for aiding decision-making at a high level is Kohlberg's theory of moral reasoning discussed in an earlier paper by the authors.[13] In Kohlberg's view the essential ingredient of moral development is not social pressure, the super-ego, or habit, but rather a certain mode of reasoning and judgment. All forms of reasoning are products of particular cognitive structures. In his studies, six stages in the development of moral reasoning are identified within three levels—preconventional, conventional, and postconventional.[14]

At Stage 1, right is seen as obedience to power and the avoidance of punishment. At Stage 2, right is taking responsibility for oneself. At Stage 3, it is putting oneself in the other person's shoes. Kohlberg sees Stage 4 as the most common; it is the law-and-order orientation involving fixed rules and maintenance of the social order.[15] At Stage 5, it recognizes individual rights within society with agreed-upon rules, and holds to a social contract orientation. Perhaps many social workers operate at this level. At Stage 6, the final, postconventional stage, the value of human life is differentiated from the general will, persons reason ethically, use more universal principles, achieve a greater scope of consistency

[13] Sonia Abels and Paul Abels, "Inquiry through Comparative Reasoning: a Measure of Competence" (paper given at Big Sky, Mont., 1977, mimeo; Case Western Reserve University, Cleveland).

[14] Lawrence Kohlberg, "Stage and Sequence," in David A. Goslin, ed., *Handbook of Socialization Theory and Research* (New York: Rand McNally & Co. 1969), p. 379.

[15] William J. Bennett and Edwin J. Delahre, "Moral Education in the Schools," *Public Interest*, Winter, 1978, p. 88.

across their actions, and are motivated in ways that are more likely to be valid over a greater range of situations.

Note the high levels of moral reasoning suggested by the Carnegie Foundation for Children: "The devotion that individual parents now feel to their own children would be broadened to include everyone's children. The next generation's strength and well-being would become everyone's responsibility."[16] We view the characteristics of sixth-stage reasoning as a goal that is desirable for all persons. In social agencies it can lead to a "just community," and one might have greater confidence in practitioners and policy-makers who reason at this stage.

At the base of our profession are values and processes which indicate our concern for the dignity and freedom of the individual. These include the beliefs that:

1. All people are entitled to dignity, a respect for the person. All people are to be treated with dignity and respect, and all people are entitled to equal treatment. Respect for persons as ends in themselves is basic to equality.

2. All people are entitled to freedom which, according to Lukes, consists of three major elements:

a) *Autonomy.* People are free so far as their actions are their own, when they can make choices as a free agent. Autonomy is self-determined behavior.

b) *Privacy.* People are free when they are free from interference and obstacles, to express their own thoughts, with freedom from public interference in the inner domain as well.

c) *Human development.* People are free when they can chart their own life course, which means that they have the power to make the best of themselves, to develop to their potential.[17]

What Hardin suggests is that people are not equally worthy; some are more worthy than others, and in his view

---

[16] Kenneth Keniston, *All Our Children* (New York: Harcourt Brace Jovanovich, 1977), p. 219.
[17] Steven Lukes, *Individuality* (New York: Harper and Row, 1973).

this worth is not related to any achievement or self-develop-
ment, but to geography or birth. This is a view that many
others have had and which at various times in our own
country has led to immigration quotas, sterilization, I.Q.
tracking, and various forms of discrimination. He notes that
"there seems to be little danger of society's being deprived of
something valuable by the sterilization of all feeble-minded
individuals" and that "as long as our present social organization [democracy] continues, there will be a slow but continued downward trend in the average intelligence."[18]

Our profession's focus on building a moral community
would make the social worker a full participant in the pursuit
of a just society. Treating people with dignity requires that
people be treated as equals, that each person has equal access
to, and can expect the same consequences from, society. We
know that neglect of this concept is fast leading to friction
among all class levels, an alienated society, and the subsequent results of poor physical and mental health. Recent
studies have shown the linkages between the rise in the
jobless and suicide, death, and murder.[19]

There is only one profession that has historically been
trained and committed to a holistic approach to human services. Social work recognizes the interdependence of people
and the need for community supports. The consequences of
a lifeboat ethics mentality in our society would be increased
suffering and deprivation for the poor, ill, educationally deprived, and violated minorities. The outcome must be re-
sisted with dedication and its unproven but maligning rhetoric exposed to reflective analysis.

We have not seen many articles or heard many conference
discussions that seemed to reflect how our profession has
been influenced by society's changing morality. It is clear,
however, that any changes in that stance which further blame
the victims in our society will soon erode our profession's
ability to muster the necessary resources on their behalf. In-

---

[18] Chase, *op. cit.*, p. 374.   [19] New York *Times*, October 31, 1976.

dividual development cannot occur, however, without a society which provides support for human development. Today's issues are so complex that our profession may lose sight of the fact that we ourselves are shaped by society into accepting values which erode the worth and dignity of people. There is a strong movement in the social work profession to turn inward toward the meditative-psychological dimensions of existence, but we must maintain the balance needed for the social, harmonious living with all humanity. Our profession is the most appropriate to undertake this task, for we are the social profession.

Welfare Reform

IRWIN GARFINKEL

WELFARE REFORM IS not new. The 300-year history of welfare in the United States consists of one reform after another. Indoor relief was replaced by outdoor relief and vice versa, nonwork relief by work relief and vice versa, cash relief by in-kind relief and vice versa.

Why does welfare need to be reformed so often? Why does it need to be reformed now?

The overarching problem with welfare is that we have too much of it. That is to say, too much of our income-support system is income-tested. The cure, therefore, is to replace income-tested programs with universal programs.

By "universal," I mean a program in which benefits are not related to income. The net (after tax) benefit, of course, depends on the amount of taxes paid and will vary with income to the extent that the tax system does.[1] In this sense free public education, Social Security, and Medicare are universal; Aid to Families with Dependent Children (AFDC), food stamps, and Medicaid are income-tested.

"Universal" is not the opposite of "categorical." A categorical program is one in which eligibility is limited to certain groups, such as the aged, children, and so on. Categorical programs may be either means-tested or universal.

Universal is the opposite of means-testing, or income-testing, or welfare—which are interchangeable. Old Age In-

IRWIN GARFINKEL is Director, Institute for Research on Poverty, and Professor, School of Social Work, University of Wisconsin, Madison.

[1] It should be remembered that, to the extent that the beneficiaries also pay positive taxes, the gross benefits of income-tested programs are not equal to the net benefits.

surance and children's allowances are categorical universal programs; the Supplemental Security Income (SSI) is a categorical income-tested program. A program for which eligibility depends *only* on income (such as the negative income tax) is a noncategorical income-tested program. A program in which gross benefits are paid to everyone in society (such as a demogrant or credit income tax) is a noncategorical universal program. In one sense, a program in which only the poor participate may be said to be categorical. For the sake of clarity, however, I shall retain the distinctions between categorical and noncategorical and between universal and income-tested.

THE LONG-RUN CASE FOR UNIVERSAL PROGRAMS

Why am I convinced that the social work profession should favor universal programs?

To understand the most important of many reasons one must understand the basic economics of universal and income-tested programs. Programs that provide benefits to everyone, in combination with any politically feasible range of tax rates in the positive tax system, will provide greater net benefits to the poor, the near-poor, and lower-middle-income groups, and cost more to upper-income groups than programs that restrict benefits to the poorest. This is true of public education in America, for example, which provides net benefits (that is, greater benefits received than the taxes paid to support it) for the very poorest, the near-poor, and a sizable chunk of the middle-income group. The net cost, consequently, is borne by the upper-middle and upper-income groups. If we subsidized the education of only the very poor, only the very poor would receive more benefits than they paid in taxes, and the cost of the program would be shared among poor and lower-middle-income people as well as those with the highest incomes.

Only if a universal program were financed by a tax even more regressive than the Social Security payroll tax would this not be true. For example, start with an income-tested program with, say, a 50 percent benefit reduction (tax) rate and a $4,000 guarantee or basic benefit. Assume that the program is financed by a 5 percent proportional tax on all income in excess of the break-even level of $8,000. For a universal program with the same basic benefit to have a less progressive net impact, it would have to be financed by a regressive tax rate structure which taxed all income from the first dollar up to $8,000 at a 50 percent rate, and all dollars in excess of $8,000 at only 5 percent. I assert that such a regressive tax, if explicit, could never become law in this country—though implicitly that is what we accept each time we opt for a means-tested rather than a universal program.

This basic economics of income testing makes it clear that the choice between income-tested and universal programs rests on a decision as to what is a preferable income distribution.

A second critical economic difference between universal and income-tested programs is that compared to universal programs, welfare programs reduce the opportunity of the poor to better themselves through hard work and sacrifice because they impose very high tax (benefit reduction) rates on the poor. In the extreme case of 100 percent rates, this opportunity is completely removed. If the welfare poor earn an additional dollar, their benefits are reduced by that dollar. If they have savings, their benefits are reduced for each dollar those savings earn. High tax rates reduce incentives to work and save; 100 percent tax rates eliminate them.

The poor start out at birth with less chance of success than the nonpoor; they get less education and thus earn much less than the rest of us. A 50 percent benefit reduction rate reduces the payoff for a $2.50 per hour job to $1.25. What is the justification for reducing by even as much as 50 percent the already small degree to which a poor person can improve himself when we do not equally reduce the percentage by which much wealthier Americans can improve themselves? Is there any justification for preferring to aid the poor through income-tested rather than universal programs when the former exacerbate already existing inequalities of opportunity?

Another adverse factor inherent in high tax rates is the incentive to cheat. The higher the tax rate, the greater the incentive to underreport income. If the poor are neither better nor worse than the rest of us, a consequence of imposing higher tax rates on them is that more will cheat. Is this desirable social policy?

Other noneconomic considerations reinforce my case. First, many people who participate in a welfare program feel a loss of pride. To receive benefits, they must declare themselves poor. In this country, where so much stress is put on material success and where the dominant ideology is that "with hard work anyone can make it," to declare oneself poor is almost synonymous with declaring oneself to be a failure.

Second, subjecting rich and poor alike to the same set of rules reduces the likelihood of differential treatment by income class. Some differential treatment is, of course, still possible within universal programs. For example, it is possible to administer the work test in the unemployment insurance program more harshly against the poor than the rest of us. But middle-income and rich people will insist that they be treated with dignity. Given the pressures for uniform treatment in bureaucracies, therefore, the poor will get at least some of the same respect.

Third, universal programs are likely to have more political stability than income-tested programs because they provide net benefits to so many more people. Increasing the incomes of the poorest members of society to permit a decent standard of living will continue to be a government objective. Hence the political stability of institutions designed to achieve this objective is an important consideration.

Fourth, income-tested programs create a sharp distinction between beneficiaries and nonbeneficiaries. This accentuates class divisions, while universal programs mute such divisions.

Note, however, that there is little empirical research on the severity of stigma, or the differential effects of income-tested and universal programs on the dignity and self-image of the poor, or on political stability and social cohesion in society. Thus, while the social work profession has stressed these arguments, economists and other public policy analysts have remained skeptical. Nevertheless, the a priori arguments are strong enough to convince me that the stigma, social cohesion, and political stability costs of income-tested programs are greater than zero.

All these differences between programs are related to the values of equality and integration. Income-tested programs segregate the poor in separate, politically vulnerable programs, which exacerbates class distinctions and encourages the poor to work less, save less, and cheat more than the rest of us.

Universal programs integrate the poor into society by treating them more equally, subjecting them to the same set of rules and same incentives that apply to the rest of us. By increasing over-all economic equality universal programs also integrate the poor into society more than income-tested programs do with the same basic benefits.[2]

Possible arguments against universal programs do exist. Because universal programs cost more to the wealthy than income-tested programs, it might be argued that they reduce the incentives to become wealthy. Related to this is the argument that the total gross national product (GNP) might be smaller under universal programs.[3] What little evidence we

[2] Not every expansion of universal programs or every proposal for a new universal program is desirable. For example, across-the-board increases in the Old Age Insurance program are not a desirable way to expand that program. Rather, the minimum benefit should be converted into a flat pension or demogrant much like that in several Western European countries. Benefits should be high enough to replace SSI. Similarly, the income tax credit for elementary, secondary, and higher education should be defeated because the elementary and secondary provisions would weaken our public education system. The part pertaining to higher education, however, is preferable in principle to the income-tested approach of such programs as the basic educational opportunity grants program that the Carter Administration wants to expand. All specific proposals must be scrutinized carefully.

[3] The Institute for Research on Poverty commissioned a paper on these subjects for an Institute conference on income testing in transfer programs held in the fall of 1978. For a description of the conference see the Institute newsletter *Focus,* Vol. II, No. 3 (1978).

have, however, suggests that the disincentive effects of high tax rates on the wealthy range from trivial to nonexistent.[4]

A third possible argument is that either running the extra tax dollars needed to finance universal programs through the public treasury or enlarging the share of goods provided publicly will have deleterious effects on social cohesion and perhaps even on freedom. There is no evidence of this as yet, but my own hypothesis is that: (1) the extra human capital we tap by integrating the poor into society will more than offset any extra disincentive effects of higher taxes on the upper-income groups; (2) in the long run, freedom is more likely to flourish in an integrated egalitarian society; (3) the upper-income groups will also benefit from a more integrated egalitarian society because it will be more peaceful, less crime-ridden, and more confident and outward looking; and (4) a majority of upper-income people will be willing to pay more taxes to live in such a society if they are cognizant of the benefits to themselves as well as to others. None of these issues was raised in the debates on income testing in the 1960s.

SHORT-RUN TACTICAL CONSIDERATIONS

To understand why economists and public policy analysts have become so focused on income testing, we must recall the political environment. All the Great Society programs, with the exception of Medicare, were financed out of the fiscal dividend which came from restoring full employment. By 1966, President Lyndon Johnson was committed to financing a major war without anybody noticing it. So he had to ignore the advice of his economists that taxes should be raised to prevent inflation. Consequently, despite the fact that Lyndon Johnson was the biggest "social spender" since Franklin Delano Roosevelt, it was clear that tax increases were not politically feasible under him. (Payroll taxes, of course, were and

---

[4] See Robin Barlow, Harvey E. Brazer, and James N. Morgan, *Economic Behavior of the Affluent* (Washington, D.C.: Brookings Institution, 1966).

continue to be an interesting exception in that they are explicitly tied to financing a universal program.)

Then we had two Republican Presidents who would not
have considered any welfare reform proposal that required
tax increases. We now have a Democratic President who says
he will not consider proposals which would increase the
share of total income being taxed. Indeed, his initial directive
to his staff was to produce a reform proposal with a zero
incremental budget cost. Thus, the welfare reform debate
has taken place for over a decade in an environment in
which everyone close to government believed that the budget
for welfare reform was more or less fixed at current low
levels. Since economists are closer to government than other
social scientists it is not surprising that practical economists
accepted the implicit assumption that the budget was both
fixed and small.

In the case of fixed budget constraints (that is, in some
short-run situations) income-tested programs are clearly better than universal programs, in the narrowest economic
sense, for the beneficiaries. For example, if $5 billion can be
spent on either a children's allowance or a negative income
tax, the poor would get more dollars out of the latter since
the benefits in the former would have to be spread over all
children. If the total budget available for universal and income-tested programs is the same, there is a case for
income-tested programs on distributional grounds. Many
economists who advocated income-tested programs did so
with the intent of championing the poor and believed
that the total budget would be the same whichever program was chosen. If the basic benefits are to be the same
for both programs, however, universal programs are better
for the poorest beneficiaries because their net tax rate
is lower.

Which type of program is better for the poor, therefore,
depends on whether the total budget or the basic benefit is to
be the same for both—which sounds more like a political

science question than an economics one. During some short periods of time, such as the last fifteen years, the budget available for transfers may appear to be, or actually be, small and fixed, whether the program is to be universal or income-tested. But surely this is not the case in the long run. How else can we explain that, despite the recent growth of income-tested programs, total expenditures for universal programs in the United States are four times as large as expenditures for income-tested programs? Unequal budgets, of course, do not guarantee equal basic benefits. My hunch is, however, that in the long run basic benefits in income-tested programs will be no higher, and perhaps even lower, than those in universal programs—so long as there are people who fight for universal programs. That qualification is terribly important. In indicates that whether budgets or basic benefits are the same for both programs is not only a political science question, it is a political question. Unless political outcomes are inevitable, what advocates of the poor do will help determine whether the budgets or benefits will be the same for universal and means-tested programs.

Economists and other policy analysts, however, did not perceive this. As employees of, and advisers to, government they sought to serve government rather than to change it. Objective analysts would note that universal programs are better for the poor if basic benefits are equal and worse if budgets are equal. In any case, they took their *perception* of short-run political reality to be the only reality. They thus translated the apparent fact of life that taxes could not be raised into the implicit assumption that taxes and expenditures should be considered fixed in any universal/income-tested program comparison. This assumption found its way into the denominator of target efficiency, a criterion invented by academic economists and adopted by the federal government to evaluate alternative transfer programs.

Target efficiency is simply the proportion of the total (gross) benefits of a program that goes to the poor. Such a

measure has nothing to do with economic efficiency.[5] From
the point of view of upper-middle and upper-income people
who care only about raising the incomes of those with no income of their own—generally the poorest of the poor—an income-tested program is obviously more efficient than a universal program. But that is just another way of saying again
that income-tested programs are less costly than universal
programs to upper-middle and upper-income families.

It is only a half truth to say that universal programs are
more costly or inefficient than income-tested programs. The
full truth is more complicated: compared to income-tested
programs with the same basic *benefit* levels, universal programs are more costly to, and less efficient for, upper-middle
and upper-income people because they are of greater benefit
to the poor, near-poor, and lower-middle-income groups. If
one assumes that the total *budget* is fixed, of course, then
target efficiency does measure the extent to which alternative
programs are pro-poor. In my judgment, it is this implicit
political assumption rather than concern for the narrow economic interests of upper-income people that gives target efficiency its normative content and appeal.

But what if it appears that budgets are fixed in the short
run? Then advocates of the poor should urge political
leaders and all citizens to compare the merits of universal
and income-tested programs with equal benefits. If we do
not, who will? And if no one does, there will never be a
chance for universal programs. If political leaders refuse to
consider universal programs on the grounds that they are
"too expensive," they should be reminded that universal programs are more expensive only to some and that is because
they are more beneficial to others. If they still refuse to
spend anything but a small, absolute, budgeted amount on

---

[5] Kesselman and Garfinkel tested economic efficiency effects and found they were
trivial. See Irwin Garfinkel and Jon Kesselman, "On the Efficiency of Income Testing in Transfer Programs," Institute for Research on Poverty Discussion Paper No.
339–76.

any transfer program, we might have to accept income-tested programs.

I say "might" because even if we can get more dollars to poor people through income-tested programs, the short-run case for income-tested programs, while persuasive, is still not overwhelming. Short-run political or tactical judgments are always difficult. Men and women with the same objectives frequently disagree passionately about tactics. Do universal programs grow more quickly than income-tested programs? Do they grow quickly enough to offset the latter's short-run advantages to the poor? If there are short-run monetary advantages in income-tested programs, do they offset the non-monetary advantages of universal programs? These complex questions cannot be answered in the abstract.

Consider, for example, the explosion of income testing during the 1960s and early 1970s. Expenditures on income-tested transfers (including AFDC, SSI, food stamps, basic educational opportunity grants, housing assistance, and Medicaid) grew from a little over $5 billion in 1965 to $43 billion in 1977. The achievements of this explosion are notable. Most important, these expenditures increased the incomes of the poor and near-poor by over $20 billion, and at least part of the large Medicaid expenditure increases between 1965 and 1977 served to increase the access to health care of poor people. The food stamp program established for the first time a noncategorical welfare program entitling all Americans to a uniform, nationwide, minimum income guarantee —in food purchasing power. Medicaid established minimum standards in health benefits—albeit they varied from state to state.

Until a decade ago, welfare programs reduced benefits by a dollar for each dollar of a beneficiary's income. Since then there has been a continuing trend toward lower tax rates. Lower tax rates increase beneficiaries' incentives to work, increase the number eligible for benefits, and thereby increase the cost of these programs to middle- and upper-income families. Shifting entirely from a welfare to a universal program approach would intensify these effects.

Welfare programs have been changed in other ways as well to be more like universal programs. Benefits are based increasingly on average or presumptive need, determined principally by family size and income rather than by a detailed investigation of each family's circumstances. Caseworker discretion has given way to more automatic, impersonal entitlement rules. Assets tests, a distinctive feature of most welfare programs, have been liberalized. The value of an aged person's home, for instance, is no longer included in determining eligibility for SSI. Moreover, both the choice of name for the SSI and the choice of the Social Security Administration to administer it were motivated in large part by a desire to reduce the stigma of welfare and gain the respectability of the Social Security programs, which are universal.

All this was achieved without once raising federal taxes explicitly. Would either the poor or the nonpoor have been better off if, instead of these income-tested programs, we had enacted a children's allowance or increased some social insurance benefits by a somewhat greater amount? I do not think we can make a strong case either way. No doubt we would now have the objective of universal programs more securely in mind. But if there had truly been a fixed budget constraint, we would not have achieved as high a social minimum (defined by the basic benefit levels in our income-tested programs). Was there really an identical budget constraint during this period? Probably not. But the budget for universal programs would have had to be many times that for income-tested programs if universal programs were to provide as high a minimum as income-tested programs. Perhaps it was, but we will never know.

In short, given the political constraints of the late 1960s and 1970s the income-tested strategy probably resulted in a higher social minimum than would have resulted from a universal strategy. Had a universal strategy with equivalent basic benefits been politically feasible, I believe we would have been better off economically and socially to have pursued it.

WHITHER THE FUTURE

What should we do now, when we have a Democratic President who makes populist noises about welfare, tax reform, and justice at the same time that he says the percentage of the GNP going to taxes must not be increased?

I believe the social work profession through its formal organizations should urge President Carter and the Congress to fight for universal programs. Thus we will be helping to educate them and the American people on the issues involved in income testing. The profession should lay out a long-run agenda for reform that includes such major new programs as an age-related demogrant or credit income tax, universal programs that provide additional aid to female-headed families, and a non-income-tested national health insurance program. We should also propose short-run incremental changes that will insert more universality into the over-all system and lead us gradually into these new programs. In the current political environment, these may be critical. Finally, we must be prepared to support some reforms of existing income-tested programs even as we seek to educate the nation to the virtues of universality.

This is the context in which President Carter's welfare reform proposal should be evaluated. It represents a modest improvement in our income support system, but candidate Carter kept summoning us to something better. His reform proposal is not a big enough first step toward curing what is wrong with welfare. And we should tell him so.

The President's proposal has four major parts. First, the federal government would fund 1.4 million minimum wage jobs in an attempt to provide a job to the head of every family with children. Second, there would be a federal minimum benefit in AFDC. Third, food stamps, the only welfare program which pays uniform federal benefits based principally

on family size and income, would be replaced by a federal
cash program. Fourth, the earned income tax credit, which
increases the take-home pay of low-wage workers, would be
significantly expanded.

There are strengths in the better jobs and income proposal. The jobs program is a beginning on making good our
belief in self-reliance and independence by taking a step toward guaranteeing the opportunity to work and be self-
reliant. A federal AFDC minimum benefit would raise benefits in twelve of our poorest states, provide some fiscal relief
to all states—though not much to states with currently high
benefits—and set the stage for further federalization of the
program. Replacing food stamps with a cash program would
have virtually no effect on nutrition, but it would subject
beneficiaries to the stigma of welfare only once—when they
apply. Food stamps now stigmatize each time people buy
stamps and each time they spend them.

There are also weaknesses. We know precious little about
how to operate a massive jobs program. More important, the
federal minimum benefits in the cash program are too low—
slightly lower in real terms than the benefit levels in President Nixon's 1969 welfare reform proposal. The strengths
outweigh these weaknesses.

The principal weakness in President Carter's program—
and in alternative Congressional proposals under serious
consideration—is one of omission. Aside from expansion of
the earned income credit, nothing under discussion indicates
a desire to reduce the scope of welfare by increasing the aid
provided to the poor through universal programs.

The proposed expansion of the earned income credit is a
small step in the right direction. It would aid the working
poor without taking them into the welfare system. Because it
would also increase the take-home pay of those on welfare
who work, it would increase their chances of "making it" the
way Americans are supposed to, through hard work and sacrifice. The only way to reduce the high tax rates on the poor
and near-poor is to provide benefits or tax cuts to the lower-

middle-income group as well. To criticize expansion of the earned income tax credit as "wasting" money on tax cuts for lower-middle-income families is equivalent to saying that increasing work incentives for the poor is a waste.

But we can and should go further. As part of his income tax reform proposal, the President has proposed a nonrefundable $250 per capita credit as a substitute for personal exemptions in the federal income tax. This is a desirable reform. If the credit were made refundable it would be a universal income-support program. It could be administered the way all the other Western industrialized countries administer their universal children's allowance programs. Checks could be mailed to everyone once a month.

Another point: under current federal law, taxpayers are allowed to deduct interest and property tax payments from their gross incomes before calculating their taxes. This provision subsidizes homeowners. The rationale is that we want to encourage Americans to become property owners. The more widely property ownership is spread, the more stable and economically integrated our society will be. Whether these objectives are furthered by this tax provision or outweigh the resulting inequity between homeowners and renters is debatable. What is not debatable, however, is that under current law those with the highest incomes get the largest subsidy, and the poor, the near-poor, many lower-middle-income people—in fact, all who do not itemize deductions—get no subsidy. If these deductions were converted to refundable credits, Americans at all income levels would be encouraged to purchase homes. We would thus increase the incomes of low-income Americans, but in a way that would integrate them into the mainstream of American life rather than segregating them further.

The kind of national health insurance system we adopt will also be critical. Will it be income-tested or universal? Will it further segregate our poorer citizens or further integrate them? National health insurance proposals of the welfare type such as that proposed by President Nixon would raise tax rates on the poor and near-poor to about 70 percent. Such high rates for a large fraction of our population should be unacceptable to the Carter Administration and the American people. If initial costs must be kept lower than ultimate costs, for budgetary or political reasons, then we should begin with a national health service for all children.

Some income-maintenance experts are advising the Carter Administration and the Congress to eliminate all features of the Social Security program such as minimum benefits and benefits for spouses and other dependents that favor lower-income people. (Congress has already taken some steps in this direction.) These experts say that the objective of aiding poorer citizens can be achieved more "efficiently" through the SSI program—a welfare program for the aged. Will we follow the advice of these particular experts and push more old people on welfare? Or will we try to reduce the number of aged on welfare by, for example, increasing and rationalizing the minimum benefit so that it is a more effective and equitable way of reducing poverty?

Now is the time to move toward the goal of substituting universal for income-tested programs because doing so is the next logical step in welfare reform; because doing so would solve many of the most important problems of the welfare system; because we have probably reached the outer limits of income testing.

As noted, most of the reforms of the past decade or so have made welfare more like universal programs. Making the programs actually universal is, therefore, a logical step.

The welfare system is criticized for being too complex, an administrative nightmare. Universal programs are simple, an administrator's paradise.

Consider the apparently inconsistent criticisms that welfare is too costly and that it is inadequate. Despite the great strides we have made in humanizing welfare programs during the 1960s and 1970s, no political figure of note takes pride in the number of our welfare beneficiaries, and many say that welfare is too costly.

One way to reduce welfare costs is to expand universal programs. When President Johnson proposed a 15 percent across-the-board increase in Social Security benefits in 1967, one of his objectives was to remove 200,000 aged from welfare rolls. This objective, though not the particular strategy, should be revived. The only way to increase adequacy and simultaneously cut welfare caseloads is through the substitution of universal for welfare programs.

The welfare system is justly criticized for creating serious work disincentives. Reformers have sought successfully to reduce tax rates in several programs. But Congress has also added new income-tested programs. The tax rates in each separate program cumulate to very high rates for multiprogram beneficiaries. The best way to reduce these high tax rates is to go even further and convert from income-tested to universal programs. Then the disincentive effects of modest guarantees will be of less concern because the poor will have an opportunity to do much better than the guarantee.

The outer limits of income testing have been reached.[6] We cannot go on adding one welfare program after another without the cumulative tax rates from the combined programs becoming unacceptably high. Some of the welfare reform proposals in Congress would impose 80 percent tax rates on millions of people we expect to work. If we continue in this vein we will create a huge underclass living predominantly off transfers and irregular unreported earnings or illicit income. We will then have confirmed our worst fears about the poor—that they are lazy and dishonest. Who knows what will follow? Retrogression? Repression? Perhaps nothing more than a peaceful if belated shift to universal programs. But why take a chance?

[6] See Robert Lampman, *Scaling Welfare Benefits to Income: an Idea That Is Being Overworked*, Institute for Research on Poverty Reprint No. 145 (1975).

Personal Social Services in the United States and Canada

H. PHILIP HEPWORTH

THE UNITED STATES and Canada have many things in common—geographical, climatic, historical, linguistic, political—but all these similarities are accompanied by real differences. We are both federal states, but the United States is a republic and Canada a parliamentary democracy. The relationship of American states and the Canadian provinces to their respective federal governments is considerably different. In Canada in particular the role of the provinces fluctuates and in some real ways is still evolving. Regionally there are similarities between us. Western Canada has grown both more populous and prosperous in recent years and in this regard parallels the remarkable growth of the state of California.

ORGANIZATIONAL ARRANGEMENTS

In Canada the provincial governments have the jurisdictional and constitutional responsibility for the provision and delivery of the personal social services, of health services, of educational programs, of housing, and income-assistance programs. Collectively, I would call all of these social services. There are some federal income-support programs, such as old age security and family allowances (with a few provincial variations). We also have a Canada pension plan and a parallel Quebec pension plan.

The federal 1966 Canada Assistance Plan allowed for the

H. PHILIP HEPWORTH is Program Director, Personal Social Services, Canadian Council on Social Development, Ottawa, Ontario, Canada.

50:50 sharing of the cost of provincial income-assistance programs and related personal social services—eligibility for cost sharing being a test of economic need applied to recipients. An agreement reached in March, 1978, between the federal and provincial governments alters the basis on which the federal government will contribute to the cost of the personal social services. The linkage with the Canada assistance plan will be ended. The financial contributions will be based on an average per capita contribution, related initially to the current levels of spending on the services provided under the Canada assistance plan. The contributions will be graduated over a decade with allowance made for growth in the gross national product, so that in ten years the same federal per capita contributions will be made to all provinces.

Canadian cost sharing has been similar to revenue sharing in the United States, and some of the same problems have arisen; wealthier provinces have been more able to take advantage of cost sharing than poorer provinces, though for ideological reasons they have not always done so.[1] This latest change in Canada follows a similar change in federal contributions for health services and some postsecondary education programs. The effect of these changes is to reduce the detailed involvement of the federal government in the affairs of the provinces, a source of tension in the past. A ceiling also is placed on the level of future federal contributions, part of current federal efforts to restrain expenditures.

The role of the federal government toward the personal social services is therefore changing, perhaps drastically. In June, 1977, the federal government had, in fact, proposed a cost-shared Social Services Act designed to support the cost of services provided to a wider sector of the population than had been served in the past. This act was proposed only after prolonged discussions between the federal and the provincial governments, but became a victim of current fiscal restraints and some provincial opposition.

[1] See "General Revenue Sharing and Federalism," *Annals of the American Academy of Political and Social Science*, May, 1975.

The federal and provincial governments, however, had previously agreed that personal social services were not a fully developed and mature service sector, and it is this reality that causes concern in Canada. There are few if any strings attached to the future federal contributions, so that some provincial governments will be tempted to divert the funds for other purposes.

If the Social Services Act had become law, it would have been comparable in some respects to the Title XX program in the United States. It would have permitted planning and development of services on a more systematic basis, but this would still have been a question of provincial initiative, not a federal requirement. We have been influenced—I am not sure that "benefited" is the right word—by the American experience of so-called "uncontrollable spending"[2] on the social services.

The functional responsibility of a federal government for the personal social services is not clear. Auditing, both social and financial, of state or provincial programs requires an extensive bureaucracy at both federal and state or provincial levels. This means that an awful lot of people are ultimately involved with the services, but are very far removed from the delivery level. The over-all goals of providing services can soon get lost to sight, while the two senior levels of government argue about money.

Yet it can be argued that there should be a national interest in both the quality and the quantity of services because citizens have a right to adequate services wherever they live and because the services do perform a useful function in our respective countries. Canada and the United States are alike in acknowledging this reality belatedly and grudgingly, despite relatively large financial contributions to the services. This reluctance is, I think, a product of both history and ideology, just as the more ready acceptance and introduction of these personal social services in most European countries are also products of shared experiences and ideologies.

[2] Martha Derthick, *Uncontrollable Spending for Social Service Grants* (Washington, D.C.: Brookings Institution, 1975).

It is true that the demographic experience in some European countries has been different from that in North America, but while that may account for some of the delay in developing adequate community support services for the elderly and the handicapped in the United States and Canada, which Alfred Kahn and Sheila Kamerman[3] have suggested is such a quantitiative difference as to amount to a qualitative difference—it may reflect a difference, in fact, of attitudes and values.

Bringing about needed social changes in most countries is a complex business. It may be particularly so when the changes must take place at the local level, but the resources and initiative to make the changes possible have to come from higher levels of government. This would seem to be the case with national health insurance in the United States, to cite only one example. If we recognize that professional resistance to change is also a powerful factor in delaying the introduction of national health insurance, we begin to recognize the existence of other constraints on governmental capacity to take action.

While we must recognize that ideological, professional, economic, political, and governmental constraints exist, we do not therefore have to abandon attempts to improve the personal social services. We have to recognize where resistance lies. We have to recognize the vested interests of the caring professions, of voluntary agencies, of governments, of politicians. We should not accept without question protestations from any group that they are working for the public good. Even if they are, we must always remember the injunction that "the road to Hell is paved with good intentions." I am enjoining all of us to be skeptical both of our own motivations and of those of others. Are we really promoting the public good? This, I suggest, is the only valid criterion for assessing the work of most public services, including the personal social services. I do not think it is a particularly com-

[3] Alfred J. Kahn and Sheila B. Kamerman, *Social Services in International Perspective: the Emergence of the Sixth System* (Washington, D.C.: U.S. Department of Health, Education, and Welfare, 1977).

fortable doctrine to espouse, but it is badly needed in our complex federal societies.

SHARED CONCERNS

General issues. In Canada the provincial governments provide many personal social services themselves; some delegate this responsibility in part to regional or municipal governments, and to para-public agencies such as children's aid societies in Ontario and social service centers in Quebec. Provincial and municipal governments and para-public agencies also purchase services from private or voluntary agencies and profit-making concerns. These arrangements are not greatly different, I believe, from those in the United States.[4]

We also have common problems in our delivery arrangements. Our social agencies have developed in piecemeal fashion, and there has often been little coherent design in much of what we have. It is true that some provincial governments in Canada have attempted to introduce systems that are both comprehensive and coherent. The best example is Quebec, but British Columbia and Manitoba have moved in this direction in the past. In the case of these three provinces there has been professional and bureaucratic resistance to the proposed and introduced changes; this resistance has been joined by political resistance in British Columbia and Manitoba. Reform of service delivery systems is fraught, therefore, with problems.[5]

Similar difficulties are encountered when we consider deinstitutionalization, community care, normalization, reprivatization, and similar concepts, many of which have originated or been developed in the United States. My particular reason for discussing these concepts is that while Canada and the United States share some of these ideas at the same time, some are delayed in their transmission to Canada, and are

[4] H. Philip Hepworth, *Personal Social Services in Canada: a Review* (Ottawa: Canadian Council on Social Development, 1975–77), Vols. I–II.

[5] H. Philip Hepworth, *Community Multi-Service Centres* (Ottawa: Canadian Council on Social Development, 1976).

implemented after there may have been second thoughts about them in the United States or they may have been discarded altogether.[6] One fairly disastrous example was the introduction of community resource boards in British Columbia in 1972–75; this experiment in citizen participation and community control of social services met with considerable public apathy, and was summarily terminated with a change of provincial government in late 1975. The American experience with neighborhood service centers and other community programs during the war on poverty was a model for the British Columbia experiment, but although the American experience should have served both as a lesson and a warning I do not think it did.

Some other current American preoccupations are also relevant to Canada and will, I am sure, soon surface if they have not already done so. I am thinking of the frustration of the courts with the personal social services and the moves by judges to take over direct responsibility for treatment and placement decisions.[7] A fascinating comparison could be made with similar current concerns in the two systems for handling juvenile delinquents in England and Wales and in Scotland.

Another current American concern, which forms part of the topic of reprivatization, is the growing resistance to government standard-setting and regulation; this is of course part of the backlash to big government, but the implications for the maintenance of standards in the personal social services are important.[8]

[6] Some of the more theoretical aspects relating to the diffusion of ideas and new technologies are dealt with in Irwin Feller and Donald C. Menzel, "Diffusion Milieus as a Focus of Research on Innovation in the Public Sector," *Policy Sciences*, March, 1977.

[7] See Nathan Glazer, "Towards an Imperial Judiciary," *Public Interest*, XLI (1975), 104–23; Nathan Glazer, "Should Judges Administer Social Services?" *Public Interest*, L (1978), 64–80; Harry L. Miller, "The Right to Treatment: Can the Courts Rehabilitate and Cure?" *Public Interest*, XLVI (1977), 96–118.

[8] See articles "About Regulations" in *Public Interest*, XLIX (1977), 3–69; Francine Rabinovitz, Jeffrey Pressman, and Martin Rein, "Guidelines: a Plethora of Forms, Authors, and Functions," *Policy Sciences*, VII (1976), 399–416; William Lilley III and James C. Miller, "The New Social Regulation," *Public Interest*, XLVII (1977), 49–61.

One final example of current thinking in the United States paralleled in Canada is the preoccupation with sunset laws and the related ideas contained in zero-based budgeting.[9]

Deinstitutionalization. In the Cross-National Studies of Personal Social Service Systems and Family Policy directed by Alfred J. Kahn and Sheila B. Kamerman, we spent much time looking at residential services for children in care.[10] We came to the conclusion that only in the United States was deinstitutionalization considered to be a current major concern. Other countries did not have a history of large institutions for children, or made use of relatively small institutions and residential facilities, and regarded them as a needed part of their range of resources for helping children and young people. Canada has moved in recent years to close training schools for delinquents and large institutions for retarded children. In the process it has returned children to their home communities, or placed them in group homes or medium-sized, special-care homes.

Although this activity has been going on, I am not sure that we can be said to have created a system of community support services for children which provides a satisfactory alternative to institutional programs. To some extent we have simply created or used smaller institutions, and placed a greater burden on other traditional caring resources, such as foster homes and private families.

Deinstitutionalization can therefore be seen and used as a political slogan, but its implementation can bring about drastic changes; I think the experience with closing training

---

[9] Robert D. Behn, "The False Dawn of the Sunset Laws," *Public Interest*, XLIX (1977), 103–18; Jacob G. Birnberg and Natwar M. Gandhi, "The Accountants Are Coming! How Accountants Can Help Policymakers in Social Program Evaluation," *Policy Sciences*, VIII (1977), 469–81.

[10] Kahn and Kamerman, *Social Services in International Perspective;* H. Philip Hepworth, *Personal Social Services in Canada;* (Ottawa, Canada: Canadian Council on Social Development, 1975); Sheila B. Kamerman and Alfred J. Kahn, *Social Services in the United States* (Philadelphia: Temple University Press, 1976); Alfred J. Kahn and Sheila B. Kamerman, eds., Cross-National Studies of Social Service Systems, 6 vols. (New York: Columbia University School of Social Work, 1976).

schools in Massachussetts shows this;[11] but deinstitutionalization is not automatically accompanied by the thinking and action required to provide needed alternative resources and
adequate substitutes. Deinstitutionalization can, in other
words, be used as a short cut to economies but brings in turn
its own costs, and even eventually the return of some types of
institutions.

These considerations apply to adults as well as children. In
our wish to rid ourselves of institutions, we have not stopped
to think of some of the functions served by large institutions
in the past. For the mentally ill they provided refuge, and for
their relatives and friends respite. If we simply use the advances in modern medicine to keep the mentally ill out of
hospitals, what are the consequences going to be for families
and home communities? Almost certainly anxiety, fatigue,
and disruption, unless adequate support services are provided. We have not been very effective, I submit, in thinking
through the consequences of some of the major social
changes in our respective societies. Slogans have served to
conceal rather than illuminate some of the real problems that
face us.

Reprivatization. We have heard quite a lot in Canada about
"reprivatization"; that is, allowing private individuals or
profit-making concerns to provide services which have hith-
erto been provided by governments, para-public agencies, or
nonprofit or voluntary agencies. On the face of it, reprivatization seems to make sense; for some magical reason private
entrepreneurs have been able to provide cheaper services,
and thus fewer public dollars have been spent. This has occurred in Canada in the case of homes for the mentally ill,
group homes for disturbed adolescents, and day care centers
for children. Someone like myself reared on the history of
the Poor Law in Britain and the United States is bound to be

---

[11] Robert D. Behn, "Closing the Massachusetts Public Training Schools," *Policy Sciences,* VII (1976), 151–71; Kamerman and Kahn, *Social Services in the United States: Policies and Programs,* pp. 199–312.

fearful about this trend.[12] In has been tried during past centuries: Poor Law overseers were paid a fixed amount for the care of the people in their charge and could spend as little as possible on caring for them—the principle remains the same.

Private entrepreneurs, of course, have to be seriously corrupt before this principle fully applies. However, we do know that in day care centers staff-child ratios are eroded, staffs are underpaid, and so on. Similar considerations apply in staffing group homes, nursing homes, and so on. Physical and safety standards also suffer.

But, you may say, there is legislation on standards, regular inspections are made, and so on. I need only mention the recent problems with nursing homes and the misuse of Medicaid funds[13] in the United States to suggest that the public regulation of private, and even some public, facilities is terribly difficult and often deficient even where there is the political will to see that legislation is enforced. The point really is that one consequence of deinstitutionalization may be the confinement of many elderly people, mentally retarded or confused people, and the physically handicapped in facilities smaller than the institutions of the past, but which offer their residents a half life only and no real involvement in the community in which they are now supposed to be residing. Social

[12] Karl de Schweinitz, *England's Road to Social Security* (Philadelphia: University of Pennsylvania Press, 1943).

[13] Mary Adelaide Mendelson and David Hapwood, "The Political Economy of Nursing Homes," *Annals of the American Academy of Political and Social Science*, September, 1974, pp. 95–105; United States General Accounting Office, "State Audits to Identify Medicaid Overpayments to Nursing Homes, Social and Rehabilitation Service, Department of Health, Education and Welfare," report to the Subcommittee on Long-term Care, Special Committee on Aging, United States Senate, Washington, D.C. 1977; A. Dunn, "Growing Old in America," *New Society*, XXXIV (1975), 260–61; United States Senate Special Committee on Aging, *What Can Be Done in Nursing Homes: Positive Aspects in Long-Term Care*, Nursing Home Care in the United States: Failure in Public Policy, Supporting paper No. 6 (Washington, D.C., 1975); Bayla F. White, Prue Larocca, and Jane C. Weeks, *Conducting Community-wide Nursing Home Inventories* (Washington, D.C.: Urban Institute, 1977); John Hess, "Something Must Be Done about Our Nursing Homes," *Media and Consumer*, Vol. III, No. 2 (1975); Mary Adelaide Mendelson, *Tender Living Greed* (New York: Vintage Books, 1974); Nicholas Bosanquet, *New Deal for the Elderly* (London: Fabian Society, 1975).

workers and the personal social services have an important role to play in this area.

Child abuse. In Canada we are greatly "seized" at the moment with the problem of child abuse, which in its immediate origins is, I believe, another concern imported from the United States. I feel that this is a rediscovery of an old problem, namely, cruelty to children and child neglect. Perhaps one reason that child abuse is really being given such mileage is because this rediscovery has been made primarily by pediatricians and not by social workers. The identification of the battered baby syndrome is truly important, but I believe it is a redefinition or reformulation of an old problem with which social workers and public health nurses have had to contend for years. In the immediate postwar period we talked about "the problem family," and for years child welfare agencies, the police, and probation officers have been called upon to render help in situations of domestic violence.

I mention the medical auspices of the rediscovery of child abuse to draw attention to the somewhat clinical orientation now being adopted toward abusing parents. There is a pronounced emphasis on individual pathology, whereas the social and economic circumstances in which abuse occurs are themselves powerful predicators of the likelihood of abuse. We do not need to go so far as David Gil[14] in identifying the social ills of our societies to see that some of the more obvious remedies lie in proferring practical help for families at risk. The question that needs answering is why we are so reluctant to intervene in this way. Do we see intervention as socially justified only when it is already almost too late—and often it is? Not only that, many of the ultimate tragedies from child abuse result from our own actions in returning children to abusive families, or even in some cases placing children at risk in abusive foster homes.

Perhaps one of the lessons to be drawn from this recent rediscovery of child abuse is that it *is* a rediscovery. The phe-

[14] David G. Gil, "Unraveling Child Abuse," *American Journal of Orthopsychiatry,* XLV (1975), 346–56.

nomenon is not new, nor do we have grounds for thinking that an epidemic of child abuse is occurring. This is not to say that child abuse is not serious; but there is no need for hysteria, nor do I believe that a predominantly medical or clinical approach to the problem is particularly helpful. We should not think that we can solve "the problem." This is the danger in considering child abuse to be something of a medical epidemic rather than a more deep-seated problem of social functioning. By all means let us take advantage of the public interest in child abuse to bring about much needed improvements in public services and especially in schools. Basically, what people need to know is that they can seek help when they are in trouble. Many people become terribly isolated in our societies, and reluctant or even unable to seek help when they need it. Some prior education in schools would help.

Diversion. Another concept which has been taken up in Canada in recent years is diversion—that it is best to avoid using the criminal justice system in dealing with delinquent children and young people. Taken literally, what an indictment this is of law-enforcement agencies, courts, and correctional facilities. In effect, we are saying that these agencies do more harm than good, that they criminalize the young offender. While I feel that this is true about parts of the system, the alternatives proffered by diversion are often no more alluring. The process of diversion can itself deny important rights, incur the resentment of the young person so processed, be just as stigmatizing as any of the available alternatives, and provide treatment facilities not greatly dissimilar to those provided through the criminal justice system. We are, in other words, fooling ourselves that diversion by itself is a satisfactory alternative to our present systems.

Radical nonintervention. A more recent proposal is the concept of radical nonintervention. While this might seem to be a doctrine of despair, it does have the merit of spotlighting the pathology-inducing characteristics of some of our social institutions and helping systems. The question, of course, is:

how radical can nonintervention be in our societies as we
know them at present? My feeling is that we are most unlikely to adopt a hands-off policy with regard to juvenile offenders. After a number of years in Canada in which we
have closed training schools—partly for reasons of
economy—we are now in some provinces setting up secure
detention facilities for the really difficult or dangerous
youngsters who can no longer be contained in the community—what I would term "radical reintervention."[15] This
cycle of retribution and permissiveness endlessly repeated
may be seen in other countries, and reflects both public opinion and different schools of thought striving for dominance.

Intermediate treatment. Perhaps though, we should be seeking a balance. Perhaps the criminal justice system can be used
more constructively to set limits, to demonstrate to youngsters that there are definite limits beyond which misbehavior
will not be tolerated. Perhaps what we need are far more
thoughtful and graduated responses to the testing-out behavior of young people. In this regard the British concept of intermediate treatment warrants careful examination, even
though its implementation is still far from adequate.[16] I
suggest that slogans, panaceas, and utopian solutions are to
be distrusted. Extreme retribution and extreme permissiveness are unlikely to work. Nor should we suppose that we
can bring about character change in difficult youngsters
treated in any of our so-called "treatment facilities"; such an
objective rests more at the level of political rhetoric than as a
realistic and attainable objective.

RECAPITULATION

The federal system forces on us complex governmental arrangements and delivery systems. New policies at the senior
levels of government often become transmuted as they are

[15] H. Philip Hepworth, "Where Are We Going with Children, Prison House or
Paradise?" (paper presented at the Annual Conference of the British Columbia Association of Social Workers, 1977).
[16] Personal Social Services Council, *A Future for Intermediate Treatment: Report of the
Intermediate Treatment Study Group* (London: the Council, 1977).

implemented throughout our personal social services systems. At the same time, new ideas—or what appear to be new ideas—achieve political popularity, and are then injected into the existing service systems. The chief proponents of these new ideas themselves often become responsible for implementing them; this has been the case with deinstitutionalization, normalization, and guaranteed annual income experiments. One wonders if this process is not really a form of co-opting. In turn, these new ideas are implemented and become institutionalized, and yet another layer of bureaucracy is added.

As concepts become politicized, they also become simplified and made into slogans. An inordinate investment of resources is made in implementing these ideas at the expense of the reform of existing service systems. We prefer novelty to sober reality. We propound solutions when ultimate solutions are not possible. We seek cost effectiveness without being able to place a cost on all the elements in a social program. We introduce new budgeting systems every year, but remain little wiser at the year's end.

Perhaps what we need is a longer term perspective. In this regard some British authors provide a useful yardstick for measuring changes in social policy.[17] They differentiate among "innovation," "development," and "reform":

By innovation we mean the introduction of a policy which, although it may have been discussed and considered before, calls for the entry of the State into a new field of social action or for the creation of new kinds of services, rights or obligations. Logically, the converse process should also be included; namely the abolition or withdrawal of the State from previously acknowledged responsibilities.

By development we simply imply changes in social policy which arise from alterations in the scale or range of an existing provision. In these circumstances the State will already have embarked upon a particular programme but then accelerate or increase its commitment. Numbers grow, benefits rise or units of service multiply. Of

---

[17] Penelope Hall *et al.*, *Change, Choice and Conflict in Social Policy* (London: Heinemann Educational Books, 1975).

course, such developments go on all the time; for some to be regarded as clear changes in policy they probably have to occur rapidly or on a substantial scale. Again, the converse process of contraction falls into the same category and may be thought of as negative development.

Lastly, we consider that there are yet other kinds of changes in policies which can best be called reforms. In these cases the change is neither an entirely new departure for the State nor a development as we have defined it. It constitutes a new way of doing something with which the State is already involved. Legislation or administrative structures are literally, re-formed. We would also include in this category instances where the objectives of an existing policy are altered radically; for instance in the matter of housing subsidies. In connection with these types of changes it is especially important to make clear that we use the term reform without any necessary connotation of progress, betterment or approval.[18]

There are real difficulties in applying this type of analytical framework to the federal systems of Canada and the United States; it is not always clear which level of government has the responsibility to initiate and direct changes in social policy. However, it is possible to gain some insight into the significance of some of the concerns I have discussed.

Almost by definition deinstitutionalization implies a change in an existing system of provision. As I have indicated, it is probably a matter of opinion whether deinstitutionalization can be truly said to be a reform or a development. Moreover, a longer time perspective is required to assess the true effects of this type of change in official policy, and to see whether the change in practice is permanent or temporary.

Because child abuse has been rediscovered by the medical profession and because many new programs to combat child abuse have a medical orientation, it could be argued that an innovation in social policy is occurring. Nonetheless, the new concern with child abuse has served to focus attention on deficiencies in both the traditional child welfare services and other social programs.

The public responses to the rediscovery of child abuse may

[18] *Ibid.*, p. 19.

indicate that no true changes in social policy are occurring, that traditional programs are not being modified in ways significant enough to justify the label "development" or "reform." In other words, public concern is being absorbed through the creation of small-scale, palliative projects which in no way attack the underlying issues or problems.

We must have similar concerns about diversion and radical nonintervention. Are not these both ways of going around the criminal justice system without doing anything to reform it, or even in certain circumstances to do away with it and substitute truly innovative alternatives?

What we see, then, is how difficult it is to bring about social change in our kind of society without at the same time undermining the foundations on which our society stands. I have suggested my resistance to change simply for the sake of change. I have suggested too that we need to probe more deeply some of the ideas in vogue in both the United States and Canada. Learned journals carry a good many articles critical of fads and fashions in the social policy field. Even so, these questionable ideas travel far, once politicians and the general public become interested in them. The problem is always to sort the chaff from the wheat. Untested ideas often become conventional wisdom overnight; the task of social reform in our countries is then hindered rather than advanced. A great deal of experimentation on a project basis has taken place and this in turn has spawned what can only be called an evaluation industry in both the United States and Canada. But the dilemmas of social reform so skilfully dissected by Marris and Rein remain.[19]

The question, of course, is how far forward some of these experiments take us, and whether some of them should be undertaken at all.[20] We obviously need to think far more carefully not only about the technical merits and demerits of

[19] Peter Marris and Martin Rein, *Dilemmas of Social Reform: Poverty and Community Action in the United States* (2d ed., Chicago: Aldine Publishing, 1973).

[20] Alice M. Rivlin, *Systematic Thinking for Social Action* (Washington, D.C.: Brookings Institution, 1971); Alice M. Rivlin and P. Michael Timpane, eds., *Ethical and Legal Issues of Social Experimentation* (Washington, D.C.: Brookings Institution, 1975).

proposed projects and programs, but also much more about ethical and legal questions. Richard Titmuss is reported to have said to a friend, as he puttered about in his greenhouse one day, "You know, you can experiment with plants without hurting them; you can't do that with people."

This is a thought we should ponder as we try to work out how to reform and improve our personal social services, and consider what alternatives we still need.

An Integrated Social Service Delivery System

EUNICE B. EVANS

THE UNITED SERVICES AGENCY of Wilkes-Barre, Pennsylvania, is a demonstration agency for the Pennsylvania Department of Public Welfare (DPW) for integration of public social services. It was born in 1972 in the wake of tropical storm Agnes which caused a devastating flood, resulting in thousands of homeless residents in Pennsylvania alone and destruction of factories, businesses, and farms. So great was the devastation that usual sources of social services could not meet the overwhelming needs of the people. It was obvious that special programs and money would be needed to assist recovery efforts in the area.

Many studies made by the state government and the DPW indicated the need for a social service system which would provide easily available access to citizens and would result in a less chaotic method of service delivery than that in operation. In Pennsylvania, public assistance, Medicaid, food stamps, and other cash assistance programs are administered by the DPW. Although the DPW supervises the programs for mental health/mental retardation, aging, child welfare, drugs and alcoholism, and certain grants for juvenile probation, these programs are administered on a county level with various formulas for state and federal financing. After a joint study with HEW, it was recommended that both emergency and long-term needs of two counties, Luzerne and Wyoming, could be best met by an integrated social service agency. This

EUNICE B. EVANS is Deputy Director, Program Development, United Services Agency, Wilkes-Barre, Pa.

new agency would be designed in such a manner that fragmentation and overlap of programs would be minimized, accessibility of services would be enhanced, and public accountability would be increased.

With the availability of state legislated flood relief funds and an initial grant of $148,000 in federal project funds, the county governments of both counties were offered relief from local taxes for social services for a three-year period, and through an agreement designated the DPW to manage these services with the goal of establishing an integrated social service agency. The county public assistance offices and the local social service programs for both counties became part of the new agency. Under this agreement the county and state employees would remain on their respective payrolls, but a state management team would administer the agency.

Although there was no lead time to formulate a demonstration model, certain principles were adopted as the basis of a new human service delivery system:

1. Citizens would obtain services through single-entry service centers established in convenient population areas.

2. Case managers, called human service planners, would serve as a single point of intake for all services. Continuing services would be given by generic caseworkers retrained from specialty services.

3. The agency would be consumer-oriented, and a consumer advocacy program would be initiated.

4. The agency would establish a meaningful partnership with private social service agencies.

5. A system of fiscal management and program accountability would be initiated.

6. An advisory committee would be appointed to assure availability of services and responsiveness to community needs.

Since the inauguration of the United Services Agency, five attractive multiservice centers have been established. Centralized supporting services for housing, transportation, and information and referral/crisis intervention have given specialized assistance to area residents. Five large senior citizen centers and ten neighborhood centers to serve the elderly are in operation. A staff of more than five hundred persons has been trained in their changing functions within the system, and a training coordinator has arranged for a wide variety of courses to improve delivery of services and administrative competence.

A public-private partnership has been established, bringing together citizens and agencies concerned with social services within the service area. A system of interlocking boards and councils now involves over 250 representative citizens serving on 15 boards and committees. A committee of the United Way of Wyoming Valley brings together representatives of the public-private sector to review budgets and programs funded jointly with public and private money. The Commission on Economic Opportunity acts as advocate for consumers of the agency's services in Luzerne County and joins the agency in the provision and planning for a variety of services. Purchase-service contracts with a number of voluntary agencies help to provide a community network of services to the two-county area.

Research and evaluation have involved a number of universities and research consultants in giving the agency data for development and improvement of services. A management staff provides administration and leadership, while an integrated fiscal division and an automated management information system provide the basis for accountability for funds and social programs.

Special federal and state demonstration funds are no longer available, but each county government now pays its full share of the cost and continues its agreements with the state for management of the agency.

Since the agency's inception certain changes have been made to the original project design in response to circumstances which came about during the course of implementing the agency. Because of the absence of a research model and the management staff's conviction that no aspect of the agency is set in cement, there has been an open attitude toward change and a flexibility of administrative methodology, although basic goals have been followed. Some of the basic changes are as follows:

1. Because differences in salaries, benefits, and unionization between county and state workers caused almost insoluble personnel problems, the public assistance programs have been jointly located in the service centers, although this service remains as a valuable part of the agency system.

2. Since experimentation with the generic concept for the service workers proved to be unwieldy, a modified form of specialization has been instituted, although a generic intake through the human service planner has been maintained.

3. In Pennsylvania, funding for mental health/mental retardation programs is provided through a county administrative office. No direct service is given by that office but is provided by contracts with mental health centers and other private nonprofit agencies. The agency, therefore, did not provide direct services for these programs. Various experiments were made to resolve the dichotomy of service delivery in this area. Under contract, one mental health center was responsible for the administration of an agency center. Mental health center services were located at two agency centers, with separate intake and administration, and one center was staffed by human service planners and supervisors representing both mental health/mental retardation programs and the agency, but delivering a completely integrated intake service. This last model has proved to be most successful, and plans are underway for complete integration of intake in all the agency's centers, with mental health center services to be jointly located in all of the agency's centers.

4. Juvenile probation and detention services of Luzerne County withdrew from the agency when juvenile court judges asserted their full responsibility for supervision of these programs.

5. Certain services are delivered and administered cen-

trally. These include a housing unit with specialized staff assigned to service centers; a child abuse unit, which is required by state law to provide service through a separate administrative unit; a coordinated social service transportation service that works out of a central dispatching office; a foster home-finding unit; a nutrition service for the aging; an experimental domiciliary care program; work incentive program; children's health screening, and other parts of programs which lend themselves to more efficient central administration. However, the bulk of the service workers are employed in the multiservice centers, and access to all services, both direct and by contract, are through community centers. This provides maximum coordination of service programs.

The organizational structure of the United Services Agency consists of a small management staff including a deputy project director, a director of operations who coordinates and supervises the service centers, a director of administration, a fiscal director, a management information system manager, a director of program development and planning, and a central personnel office. Program directors and central staff for each component service are responsible for assuring that laws and regulations for their programs are followed, for supervision and direction of the service staff, for preparation of program budgets, and for advocacy for their programs. These program directors meet regularly with central office staff to make recommendations for policy and to provide coordination and interagency activities.

We believe we now have a social service system that provides maximum accessibility to consumers without the necessity for them to shop among fragmented services. We are confident that we provide a greater variety of services than is available in comparable service areas. We are eliminating duplication and overlapping of functions and instituting more accountability for the funds we administer.

Interest has been expressed in how the United Services Agency has survived as an integrated agency. HEW has spent millions of dollars to fund demonstration projects for integrated agencies. Most of these have floundered, and when federal funds were no longer available have reverted to categorical administration. Although we have had many problems in the implementation and management of this agency, we can attribute our longevity to a number of crucial factors:

1. The project director is also Regional Deputy Secretary for the DPW. Although she is no longer involved in the day-to-day operation of the agency, her enthusiasm and continued interest have provided a strong link to central office administration, which has not always adapted itself to administrative variations of demonstration programs.

2. The management staff has been knowledgeable and dedicated. The difficulties of inaugurating and administering a program such as this seems insurmountable at times, but professional dedication and ability to work together as a team have resulted in a maximum effort and a determination to resolve problems as they arise.

3. The absence of a rigid model and the willingness to be flexible as problems have arisen or when concepts have not proved out in operation have characterized this agency from the beginning.

4. The agency has been accepted by the county commissioners, who find they now have a management structure to deal with multiple programs that become more complicated and far-reaching as time goes on. They are assured of fiscal responsibility and program conformity.

5. The agency has the endorsement of community citizens who have put effort into the program and are aware that quality services are given to the community. The voluntary sector, which at first was suspicious of a "superpublic" agency, has overcome its fear and is supportive of the agency concept.

6. Encouragement by numerous consultants and researchers has given impetus to the staff to continue their work, and with a sense of accomplishment.

7. Continued support and encouragement by staff of

HEW have assisted greatly in the administration of this program.

Another important reason for survival was that we did not depend upon large sums of federal money. The project was made possible by an initial federal grant of $148,000. Later, federal project approval was given by a waiver under Section 1115 of the Social Security Act. True, we were able by this waiver to draw down 75 percent federal service funding for some functions that otherwise could not have been carried out as part of the project. Our waiver was from the requirement that the agency's services be statewide and allow all appropriate staff members of the agency to determine service eligibility. The other 25 percent was made available from state funds by the DPW. This allowed us to continue after September, 1977, on a nonfederal project basis with no serious dislocation of funding.

Our activities now have extended beyond mere survival. The requirements for the last year of our federal project were to plan for transferability of project experience and findings to other Pennsylvania counties. It was obviously not possible to apply this system statewide without further serious study and legislation. However, we devised a unique methodology to meet the requirement. With six counties and agencies in various stages of interest in integrated programs we established the Pennsylvania Integration Consortium with the goal of consulting on the integrated programs and transfer of technology regarding management information systems and other technical information required by member agencies. The approval by the DPW of a special consulting contract to help staff this program and a small federal grant have allowed us to extend the program to four additional counties. Applications to join the consortium far exceeded the number that could be admitted to membership.

Those agencies with experience in technical systems freely consult and provide technology to new agencies so that they do not need to "reinvent the wheel." Technical assistance is given in needs assessment, planning methodology, management, and structural functions. We believe that elements of the system can be easily transferred without basic administrative changes such as instituting comprehensive transportation and information and referral systems. Some counties are setting up client information and fiscal systems. Some are designing a basic structure for new departments of human services for county government. There is also participation from the private sector through health and welfare councils. Both a representative of the Community Services of Pennsylvania, our statewide health and welfare organization, and a member of the Governor's staff regularly attend our meetings. Professional satisfaction and enthusiasm characterize this organization. We feel free to share not only our successes, but also experiences that were not so successful.

We are considerably convinced, no matter how difficult the transition, that a system of service integration can maintain the program advocacy and the functioning of categorical programs, while at the same time assuring a reasonable system of accessibility and accountability to the citizens of the communities and state and local governments we serve. The concept of service integration allows for experimentation, for pooling of resources, joint planning with the private sector, and new approaches to service delivery. It provides a challenge for the reordering and rethinking of our programs, and a more flexible approach to meeting community needs.

Proprietary Social Services

DAN RUBENSTEIN, RICHARD E. MUNDY, and MARY LOUISE RUBENSTEIN

A MAJOR CONCERN in policy development and social planning is the nature of the auspice and the institutional structure for the provision of social services. The complexities of bureaucratic service and rising concern over fiscal difficulties are giving impetus to a crescendo of protest of the management by "big government and federal programs." Thus, conservative expression is calling for greater efficiency and efficacy toward the reduction of financial costs. Inherent in these mini-maxi (minimum costs for maximum service) efforts is the recurrent theme of *marketplace* utilization.

Since a service market is generally conceived to consist of all the buyers and sellers of a particular service who deal with one another,[1] there is an expectation that with the provision of social services on the open market, the competitive process of free enterprise will inherently bring about the most qualitative service at the most reasonable price. The more competitive, the more efficiently and equitably it will perform.[2] It is also generally understood that this concept is feasible because the private-for-profit service agency is more viable, for it is answerable neither to membership nor to clientele but rather

DAN RUBENSTEIN is Professor, Syracuse University School of Social Work, Syracuse, N.Y.
RICHARD E. MUNDY is Associate Professor, Syracuse University School of Social Work, Syracuse, N.Y.
MARY LOUISE RUBENSTEIN is Executive Director, Onondaga County Child Care Council, Syracuse, N.Y.

[1] Louis W. Stern and John R. Grabner, Jr. *Competition in the Marketplace* (Glenview, Ill.: Scott, Foresman & Co., 1970), p. 11.

[2] *Ibid.*, p. 5.

to entrepreneurs or corporate boards of organizations that seek profit or personal economic gain.

Today more than ever we are hearing that there is a public works mentality which wants government to finance and operate "everything." This supposedly discourages private sector responsibility and private sector jobs, while encouraging public works, public employment, public debt, and more taxes.[3] We also are reminded by entrepreneurs that this is an era when social problem-solving has begun to look away from government control and responsibility and tax-based financing of social services.[4] Reichert reminds us that currently "the balance seems to be shifting toward entrepreneurialism in ideology and in the operations of the health and welfare system,"[5] while Kahn queries, "Who would have predicted in 1960 that a society with increasing social welfare commitments would, a decade later, be giving major attention to market models?"[6]

But human services as programs that provide rights, benefits, entitlements, and security from risks have always been made available by nonmarket criteria and mechanisms. The encouragement and enhancement of human development, the implementation of social justice concepts, and the helping and rehabilitating of those in need were never functions of the marketplace and the capitalistic economic system. To the contrary, Weber explains, our spirit and practice of capitalism "would both in ancient times and in the Middle Ages have been proscribed as the lowest sort of avarice and as an attitude lacking in self-respect."[7] Why is there the persistent

[3] New York *Times*, October 8, 1978.

[4] *Protective Services for the Elderly*, prepared for the Special Committee on Aging, United States Senate (Washington, D.C.: U.S. Government Printing Office, 1977), p. 129.

[5] Kurt Reichert, "The Drift toward Entrepreneuralism in Health and Social Welfare: Implications for Social Work Education (paper presented at the Annual Program Meeting, Council of Social Work Education, 1977).

[6] Alfred J. Kahn, *Social Policy and Social Services* (New York: Random House, 1973), p. 148.

[7] Max Weber, *The Protestant Ethic and the Spirit of Capitalism*, tr. Talcott Parsons (New York: Charles Scribner's Sons, 1958), p. 52.

refusal to accept the reality of the statement that no one goes into business to make a better world but only to make money? Why cannot we accept the rationale of Marx that

The need for money is the real need created by the modern economy, and the only need which it creates. The *quantity* of money becomes its only important quality. Just as it reduces every entity to its abstraction, so it reduces itself in its own development to a quantitative entity. Excess and immoderation become its true standard. . . . Private property does not know how to change crude need into human need; its idealism is *fantasy, caprice* and *fancy.*[8]

If this abstraction does not seem plausible, let me cite a case in point. A young lady enrolled in a Packard Stereodyne-contracted Jobs Corps Center desired an abortion. The abortion could have been provided legally and safely, and neither the policy nor the convictions of the staff and administration opposed this action. Yet it was decided not to support the abortion because the cost (approximately $250 for transportation and medical fee) would have diminished the corporate profits that the stockholders were entitled to. Weber articulates the principle as:

The important fact is always that a calculation of capital in terms of money is made, whether by modern bookkeeping methods or in any other way, however primitive and crude. Everything is done in terms of balances: at the beginning of the enterprise an initial balance, before every individual decision a calculation to ascertain its probable profitableness, and at the end a final balance to ascertain how much profit has been made.[9]

However, the young lady's need for an abortion was met. A social worker on the staff of the Job Corps Center solicited the funds from her friends and colleagues.

Despite the priority given to profit-making, the case for private proprietary institutions is made in terms of their inherent superiority over public institutions; that is, private services are of higher quality and efficient and public services

---

[8] Frederic L Bender, ed., *Karl Marx: the Essential Writings* (New York: Harper & Row, 1972), p. 101.

[9] Weber, *op. cit.,* p. 18.

are bureaucratically slow, poor, and inefficient. The case for the private service includes rationales such as: personal responsibility; protection of professional freedom; a continuity of past established wisdom and freedom for creativity and innovation; and "diversity, free choice, heterodoxy."[10] But let us look at these attributes of quality and efficiency that are held to be superior in proprietary services. To the contrary, we are finding in the health services fraudulent entrepreneurs and providers of substandard care. In New York, as in other states, special legislation has been found necessary to require adherence to decent standards of care by proprietary institutions.[11]

The AFL-CIO[12] in its national study urged a halt to nursing home profits because of abuses. In New York State the Legislature found

that there are severe deficiencies in the level of care provided in proprietary nursing homes. Also, that the elderly are subjected to greater degradation within proprietary nursing homes than necessary in an institutional atmosphere. The Legislature further finds . . . . that the profit motive in the nursing home industry is inducive to create situations which permit fraud and the improper use of Federal and State money; and further, that proprietary nursing homes outnumber voluntary nursing homes two to one, thereby dominating the industry.[13]

Also in New York State, Dr. Stephen Rose, in a most thorough research effort into an examination of the service to deinstitutionalized former mental patients, concluded that "we know of no evidence anywhere which suggests that these groups of people, those most likely to be placed in profit-motivated group residences, have benefited materially, so-

[10] Alan Pifer, "The Jeopardy of Private Institutions," the 1970 Annual Report, Carnegie Corporation of New York, p. 5.
[11] Community Service Society Legislative Memorandum No. 3, February, 1977.
[12] *America's Nursing Homes: Profit in Human Misery* (Washington, D.C.: AFL-CIO, 1977).
[13] Assembly Bill 1772, Andrew J. Stein (D-Manhattan), 1977. See also Moreland Commission Report, and U.S. Senate Special Committee on Aging, Introductory and nine additional reports (Washington, D.C.: U.S. Government Printing Office, 1974).

cially and/or psychologically."[14] In these instances, not only do we find that the quality of care is less than superior, we find that the quality of care is substandard.

Are the private proprietors of human services efficient? The 1977 audit report released by the Office of New York State Comptroller Arthur Levitt[15] documented alleged abuses ranging from luxury cars and international travel for private school officials to artificially inflated salaries, tuition, fees, and profits for the schools and their operators. The audit report says that millions of dollars in overpayments were made to three profit-making and one "nonprofit" school over the past several years. No such problems were found at four other nonprofit schools studied by the auditors.

By what standards do we want to measure efficiency? A dispute over the enforcement of a federal regulation intended to control soaring medical costs has threatened to close the country's second-largest blood dialysis center, a Queens facility where 250 people receive life-sustaining treatment three times weekly. The operator of the center, an eminent physician who is also the president of a chain of eighty-two dialysis centers in the country, has warned that he will close the Queens facility if he is forced to provide cost data on his financial operations.[16]

How efficient was a private utility company in its treatment of an individual with a kidney problem?

Mrs. Norton, a 65-year-old widow, receives both Social Security and Medicaid, but they cover only a portion of her [kidney] dialysis cost. Her own home has neither heat nor hot water, so three times a week she trudges to her son's home where the machine is kept. Her son and his wife have six children, and although Mr. Norton works, his job is marginal. The younger Mrs. Norton prepares all

---

[14] Stephen M. Rose, "Contradictions in Deinstitutionalization Policy and Program," testimony prepared for the New York State Assembly Subcommittee on After-Care, November 9, 1977, p. 2. See also comments by Wilma Donnahue, Kleeburg Memorial Lecture, Gerontological Society, San Francisco, 1977 (unpublished).

[15] "Auditors Criticize Spending on Handicapped Schooling," Syracuse (N.Y.) *Herald Journal*, December 16, 1977.

[16] "Facility in Queens Threatens to Close 'Kidney' Machines," New York *Times*, March 19, 1978.

her mother-in-law's meals in addition to those of her own family. This year, the Nortons couldn't afford winter clothes for their children. With the burden of a sick, elderly woman, the Nortons found their lives unmanageable and they went deeply into debt.

When they fell behind in their electric bill, CVPS (the utility company) promptly turned off the electricity. The utility knew of the dialysis machine and, indeed, told the Nortons that was the reason their bill was so high. By way of a grace note, CVPS informed the Nortons that, should they desire to have their service restored, they would have to pay both a $20 disconnection fee and a $20 reconnection fee.

The first question that comes to mind is this: considering the severity of the situation, the absolute life-and-death need for kidney dialysis, couldn't CVPS have worked out some arrangement with the Nortons to keep the electricity on?

The answer is: No, they don't have to. CVPS is interested in only one thing, getting its money. No ledger book has a column for abstractions like "the quality of life." Charity is only a public relations function.[17]

From these situations it must be recognized that the efficiency is in making money not in providing services.

The Committee on Aging and Health of the Community Service Society in New York City opposed certification of profit-making home health care agencies because studies and reports in other states revealed that such enterprises have engaged in dubious practices and seldom locate in underserviced areas.[18] Opening the door to proprietary interests without rigid control and adequate surveillance could well create

[17] *Yankee*, January, 1977, p. 64.

[18] This selection of service area is one of the many forms of "creaming." "Creaming," a process of selecting the easiest clients to serve, has long been recognized as a practice in human services which increases at an inverse ratio to the relationship to public responsibility. In the fields of medical and mental health services voluntary agencies have "creamed" patients from the standpoint of the severity of problems that patients present and in relation to the patients' capacity to pay for service. The most hopeless and the most indigent patients wind up in state hospitals, county homes, and correctional institutions. The proprietary hospital, nursing home, day care center, or special school is least willing to serve the troublesome, the handicapped, the chronic patient. The reason for this reluctance is the profit motive.

The more complex a client's problem is, usually the more specialized equipment and highly trained personnel may be needed for proper care and treatment. As the cost for care rises, generally the profit margin drops. The most severely ill mental patients are thus likely to be found under care of the state just as the preschool handicapped youngster will find a place in public subsidized programs, but rarely in proprietary nursery schools.

the same potential for abuse of tax dollars that occurred in the nursing home industry.[19]

Efficiency in the private sector appears to be synonymous with the conventional capitalistic attitude which recognizes and accepts the *"appetitus divatarum infinitus*—the unlimited lust for gain."[20]

Do you sometimes wonder what the Minnie Pearl Fast Food chain knows about day care, what Upjohn Chemicals knows about home health care, what realtors know about nursing homes? Is their expertise in the human services?

MARKET MECHANISMS

Let us explore in more detail some of the components and mechanisms of the capitalistic entrepreneurial system of social services, such as vouchers; performance contracts; contracts for, and purchase of, service; grants of capital; consumer sovereignty; the value of competition; and the phenomenon of supply and demand.

The voucher[21] as a marketplace mechanism is frequently discussed as a reaction to the frustration and oppression of the bureaucratic service. Bureaucratic rigidity and institutional conservativism can readily be faulted for not providing adequate service. The advocates and protagonists, or the self-serving consumers of service, after repeated experiences of service denial and rejection are continuously reinforced in their belief that bureaucracy is incapable, inept, and inadequate and that some other means for service fulfillment and delivery need be found.

Here, then, comes the cry for the voucher, which is imagined to be an instrument that will redistribute power. It is felt that the consumer will be able, as an equal in the marketplace, to use this voucher as an instrument of power that will cause or condition providers in the market to conform to the wishes of the purchaser. It is then supposed that

---

[19] Community Service Society, Legislative Memorandum No. 10, May, 1977.

[20] R. H. Tawney, "Introduction," in Weber, *op. cit.,* p. i (e).

[21] Kahn, *op. cit.,* p. 113. Kahn discusses another facet of the voucher—the one for in-kind service. This voucher is sometimes referred to, by others, as "funny money." While "funny money" is also a market mechanism, it is not discussed here.

play in the market would bring about competition among providers, and thus it is believed that competition will cause providers to give a better quality of service in an effort to seek the voucher. Through this competitive process, the flow of vouchers would seek the better service, and the inadequate service would not survive. The less qualitative or poorer service will be forced out of the market, and subsequently we will have developed a quality market. It is expected that this marketplace will then maintain a high standard of service, since the consumer, with the power of the voucher, will be ever present as a safeguard of quality and will get what he wants.

With these perspectives, it can be readily seen why the voucher concept is so much more desired as a service modality than the present bureaucratic service system that is neither accessible nor responsive. Why do we not find this market mechanism operational? The reasons are obvious: (1) the insensitivity and misguidedness that are consistently oppressive and debilitating to those in need in the government bureaucracy are equally present in the bureaucracy of the corporation; (2) markets do not exist; (3) the self-regulatory process does not take place; and (4) the purifying process of competition is in reality a myth.

The performance contract is a market mechanism to provide incentives to stimulate greater production for the same or less cost. If the contractor succeeds he makes a profit, if he fails he does not get paid. Through this mechanism the performance does not emphasize process but output—what you will get for your money. While the performance contract has a high appeal for service efficacy, and you will get what you pay for, it has little appeal to the entrepreneur, for the risk is too great. Performance contracting was field-tested in education by the Office of Economic Opportunity.[22] They found that "this form of performance contracting [improving read-

[22] Office of Economic Opportunity, *A Demonstration of Incentives in Education,* OEO Pamphlet 3400-7, Office of Planning, Research and Evaluation, Executive Office of the President, Washington, D.C., p. 2; *An Experiment in Performance Contracting: Summary of Preliminary Results,* OEO Pamphlet 3400-5 (Washington, D.C.: U.S. Government Printing Office, 1972), p. 31.

ing and mathematics skills] did not seem to be successful." In
absolute gains the results were equally disappointing. It was
also found that a representative group of private education
firms under the performance contracts did not perform significantly better than the more traditional school systems.
The contracting for, or the purchasing of, services is a widely
used market mechanism encouraged by the government sector or categorical grants and most recently by the provisions
of Title XX of the Social Security Act. The worthwhileness of
these mechanisms is expressed in the contentions that: (1) it
is more cost efficient to utilize established organizations than
to establish new organizations; (2) the experience and expertise in the marketplace cannot be replicated; and (3) by being
part of the capitalistic, competitive, business system you are
supporting tested American traditions. Needless to say, there
is growing doubt about these stated rationales. The numerous studies of the delivery of services under Title XX
persistently question the efficacy of this mechanism; and the
American Public Welfare Association has appointed a national committee to explore the nature of contract for services in public welfare. The case of the Job Corps Centers
(mostly operated by private corporations), a persistent recipient of large contracts for service, is commonly noted as a
program that is what Lofton calls "a loser, a revolving door
that wastes the tax payers money."[23] The private sector is
most creative in its efforts to secure the public dollar. Most
recently, a working paper for the U.S. Senate Special Committee on Aging[24] urged a private sector approach for protective services to the elderly. But how responsible are these
entrepreneurial efforts toward the need for, and provision
of, humane social services? It has been said that:

The modern corporation is not and cannot be expected to be a
"responsible" institution in our society. For all the self-congratula-

[23] John D. Lofton, Jr., "Job Corps Good Money After Bad," syndicated column,
Syracuse (N.Y.) *Herald Journal,* March 29, 1977.
[24] Special Committee on Aging of the United States Senate, "Protective Services
for the Elderly," 95th Congress, First Session Committee Print (Washington, D.C.:
U.S. Government Printing Office, 1977), Appendix 5, p. 122.

tory handouts depicting the large firm as a "good citizen" the fact remains that a business enterprise exists purely and simply to make more profits—a large proportion of which it proceeds to pour back into itself. Corporations, like all businesses whether large or small, are in the primary business of making money; indeed, they do not even exist to produce certain goods or services that may prove useful or necessary to society. If Eli Lilly or Searle and the other drug companies discovered that they would chalk up larger profits by getting out of vaccines, and manufacturing frozen orange juice instead, they would have no qualms or hesitation about taking such a step.[25]

One of the most avant-garde attempts to inculcate the human services into the capitalistic market system is the effort made by Fisher in his unorthodox conceptualization of a mechanism devised as a grant of capital to replace the Social Security system. While the greater business community seeks the demise of the system as a means of eliminating Social Security taxes to increase the corporate profit, Fisher's scheme is not thus motivated. Fisher is a firm believer in the productivity of capital when he proposes:

Instead of supporting elderly people by grants of income at the end of life it would be cheaper, easier, and less disagreeable in many ways to give each American a grant of capital at the beginning of life instead. Suppose that every American received at birth a sort of "national inheritance"—a gift of capital in the amount of $1400. The gift would be surrounded with many restrictions. It could never be spent, loaned, borrowed, alienated, expended, or employed as collateral in any way. This capital sum would be invested—perhaps in a savings account, or in government securities. The money would not be taxable. It would be left to earn compound interest until the infant who originally received it reached the age of sixty-five. At 8 percent, over sixty-five years, the original $1400 would grow to $225,000![26]

After pages of convincing rationality, there is an admission of weakness: it is noted that inflation could destory the plan.

[25] Clarence C. Walton, *Corporate Social Responsibility* (Belmont, Calif.: Wadsworth, 1967), p. 2.
[26] David H. Fisher, *Growing Old in America* (New York: Oxford University Press, 1977), p. 204.

Inherent in the utilization of market mechanisms are the activities of consumer sovereignty, the purifying influence of competition, and the phenomenon of supply and demand that are inexorably interrelated and interdependent. Consumer sovereignty signifies that the consumer is in fact supreme and that the market is ultimately oriented toward meeting his needs and wants—to permit consumers to select from an array of types or kinds whatever they happen to prefer.[27] To the contrary, it is most difficult to find a market performance response to consumer demand. Lewis, Fein, and Mechanic observe that:

In medicine the impact of consumer sovereignty appears to be particularly weak. A number of studies have indicated that, to a significant extent, physicians control and determine demand for their services and that patterns of third-party coverage have insulated the consumer and his utilization decisions that impel him in other economic activity.[28]

This most desired state of freedom of choice is vague, ambiguous, and unfounded. The extent to which consumers can truly be sovereign is questionable,[29] and the concept appears to be more mythical than real.

The purifying influence and cost benefits of competition appear to be another myth uncovered in the search for rationales of private entrepreneurial social service:

The classic concept of competition begins with an ideal world in which many small enterprises manufacture a given product. In this "forest of firms," each enterprise is so small, relative to the total market for the product, that neither the individual producer nor the purchaser can influence the general level of prices. However much the producer manufactures, and regardless of whether a purchaser buys or does not buy, the unseen hand of the market de-

---

[27] Melvin Webber, "Planning the Urban Environment," in Robert Mayer, Robert Moroney, and Robert Morris, eds., *Centrally Planned Change* (Urbana, Ill.: University of Illinois Press, 1974), p. 47.

[28] Charles E. Lewis, Rash Fein, and David Mechanic, *A Right to Health* (New York: John Wiley & Sons, 1976), p. 263.

[29] Jerome E. Rothenberg, "Consumers' Sovereignty Revisited and the Hospitality of Freedom of Choice," in Lee E. Preston, ed., *Social Issues in Marketing* (Glenview, Ill.: Scott, Foresman & Co., 1968), p. 260.

termines the price. Producers and consumers make an infinite number of such decisions, these constituting the market. Supply and demand move constantly back and forth, and the price level continuously adjusts to meet these shifts.[30]

Where do we find this process in social service or in trade and commerce? Higher profits for the individual enterprise are more often achieved by limiting competition. Warren,[31] in a number of his writings, bemoans the development of trusts, cartels, mergers, and other devices as forms of maintenance and control by social service agencies that impede valid and qualitative service. Thayer states it pointedly:

The assumptions that competition produces benefits for all of us and that our economic system cannot function without it are so widely accepted that even those who worry most about our worship of the Gross National Product overlook the possibility that the logic of any competitive economic system (socialist or capitalist) compels the producers within it to behave in ways which achieve results precisely the opposite of those proclaimed by conventional wisdom.[32]

But what is more real and inherently dangerous is that when the theory of economic competition is stripped of its pretense

[30] Gardner C. Means, *Pricing Power and the Public Interest* (New York: Harper Brothers, 1962), chap. 9.

[31] This classic concept is expressed more popularly as: many sellers compete for the consumer's dollar, and consumers, in turn, buy the best products at the lowest prices. By "voting" with dollars, the consumer determines the types, quantities, and prices of goods to be produced. The result is that economic resources are allocated among users to maximize consumer satisfaction. Sellers who want to survive the competitive struggle must constantly increase their efficiency and seek out product innovations. "The unrestrained interaction of competitive forces," summarized the Supreme Court as early as 1904, "will yield the best allocation of our economic resources, the lowest prices, the highest quality and the greatest material progress." Mark J. Green, ed., *The Closed Enterprise System: Ralph Nader's Study Group Report on Antitrust Enforcement* (New York: Grossman Publishers, 1972).

This concept in a more limited sense is also referred to as the classic price theory where the automatic adjustment of supply and demand, with price fluctuating accordingly, constitutes a mechanism that it is claimed will maximize the distribution of resources and awards. Roland Warren, "Concerted Decision-making in the Community," in *The Social Welfare Forum, 1965* (New York: Columbia University Press, 1965), p. 159.

Roland Warren, "The Decartelization of the Human Services" (unpublished paper, Brandeis University [n.d.]).

[32] Frederic C. Thayer, *An End to Hierarchy! An End to Competition!* (New York: New Viewpoints, 1973), pp. 81–82.

it is "the equivalent of a political theory of anarchy, but it is doubly dangerous because policies derived from it forcibly prevent sensible planning or collective decision-making."[33] Competitive strategies have never been known to support co-operative and coalitional efforts.

As we have noted, we are devoid of market models that incorporate the free-flow dynamics of interactional supply and demand. The private entrepreneurial social service market reflects a demand devoid of real need, but a demand of needs that are artificially created and developed to provide markets to support private gain. Conspiring vendors and unaware consumers give lie to the concept. Surely you have heard that "the health care business turns the normal supply and demand equation upside down. Medical supply creates the demand. An empty hospital bed will attract a patient regardless of whether that person needs a hospital bed."[34]

REGULATION AND THE PROFIT MOTIVE

The historic tension between industrial profit-makers and governmental regulators for the protection of labor and consumers is well-known and understood. The public, however, is much less aware that an identical situation exists in the proprietary operation of human services.

When scandals arise in fraudulent billing for purchase of services or gross violation of standards for care, such as have occurred in the nursing home industry and in Medicaid, citizens are temporarily appalled and there is a call for action. The continuing effort of the proprietary service provider to water down regulations, however, is rarely recognized publicly for two reasons. Organized proprietary care-givers keep a low profile with their litigations and lobbying efforts because they do not wish to appear to advocate less than top-quality care. At the same time, professionals and governmental licensing units also seek a low profile when advocating high standards because high standards of care drive up

[33] *Ibid.*, p. 83.   [34] Syracuse (N.Y.) *Herald Journal*, March 22, 1978.

the purchase of service cost for both government and private consumers.

The result of this conspiracy of silence between consumer advocates and profit-makers in human services is a long, grinding process of bargaining, stalling, and accommodating in the setting of standards for care. The classic example right now is the Federal Interagency Day Care Regulations, commonly known as FIDCR. Efforts to revise these 1968 standards first began in 1971 when the federal government began to realize how expensive child care was becoming and at the same time private providers began effective and continuous pressure upon their local legislators for dilution of the standards. Since that time HEW has spent untold dollars on conferences, commissioned expert documents and reviews to develop new, less costly standards for child care. As of March, 1978, when the latest HEW reports were issued, no definitive recommendations for change had evolved because no one, indeed, could say that the 1968 standards were not basically good standards for the care and protection of children.

Yet through this long-ranging dispute the profit-makers have won time by the continued postponement of implementation by the United States Congress. At the state level, proprietary child care lobbyists are winning as well. In New York State, where state licensing standards were early written to match the proposed federal regulations, a powerful Long Island group of proprietors has been in litigation for several years, claiming exemption from New York State licensing regulation on grounds that they have no welfare children and, therefore, should not have to meet FIDCR which are essentially payment standards.

In Massachusetts, efforts to revise state day care regulations began in 1970. Top child development experts, as well as proprietary and nonprofit providers, were involved in the draft stage. When the first hearings on the draft were held on Beacon Hill, however, the fight was already on. Legislators from across the state had been primed by proprietary

day care providers to block any strengthening of standards.
That block held firm. Seven years have passed, and the proprietary providers are less worried today about regulations
than they were in 1971.

The day care story is not unique. The effort of the proprietary human service provider to keep regulations to a
minimum is paralleled in every service area. It is simply good
business to be free to operate at the lowest cost level with all
options open on what program elements will be offered and
how a service will be given. Thus, it becomes apparent that
the profit motive itself is incompatible with regulation. Yet
regulation is the community's response to protect the vulnerable consumer who may be too young, too old, too ill, or too
disabled to protect him/herself.

The fact that the community pays the bill for human services either through taxes, insurance, or private payments
places the vulnerable service consumer in jeopardy. Public
unwillingness to pay for quality services supports the unconscionable profit-makers in the same way that the public supports the bootlegger in business. One of the more complex
and inhumane results of the unconscionable relationship between profit-making in human services and regulation can be
seen in the interstate commerce of children. Kenneth
Wooden has documented the searing facts of child abuse in
Texas proprietary institutions that receive children by the
thousands from Illinois, Louisiana, and New Jersey.[35]

During the early 1970s states such as Illinois established
standards for acceptable institutional care in their own states.
But these same states then chose to ship their children to
Texas where they could pay less for their care because standards were both lower and less rigorously enforced. Thus,
says Wooden, state legislators supported a system of double
standards and contributed to high personal profits at the expense of helpless youngsters. As long as profit-making continues in human services the "at-risk" consumer is in double

[35] Kenneth Wooden, *Weeping in the Playtime of Others* (New York: McGraw-Hill,
1976).

jeopardy—from poor service that violates standards of care and from service that meets inadequate public regulation.

THE MARKETPLACE

It is acknowledged in the field of human welfare service that the market seldom, if ever, operates fairly or distributes resources in an equitable or optimal fashion. We know, as Warren states, that

There are many important types of goods and services that are best distributed on some other basis than the price that individual consumers can and will pay for them in a free market. In such areas as police and fire protection, education, highways, probation services, vocational training programs, costs of medical care, and family casework services, price as the resultant of demand and supply in a free market is largely irrelevant.[36]

Yet the call continues for the utilization of the capitalistic entrepreneurial marketplace system and, paradoxically, with the constant reminder that it must be watched closely, kept under control with specific restrictions to limit the freedom to abuse, misuse, and exploit for personal gain. Why is there this rational demand for irrational service?

The functional incompatibility tends to convince us that we are dealing with more than the concept of marketplace and competition. These are merely components of the so-called "free enterprise" entrepreneurial industries of the economic system of capitalism. Weber's definition of capitalism includes: "enterprises, namely, which are carried on by private entrepreneurs by utilizing capital (money or goods with a money value) to make a profit, purchasing the means of production and selling the product,"[37] and the traditional character that is inherent in the capitalistic enterprises. This traditional expression of the spirit of capitalism is used to describe that attitude which seeks profit rationally and systematically. This is justified by the historical fact that the attitude of the mind has on the one hand found its most suitable

[36] Warren, "Concerted Decision-making," *op. cit.*, p. 149.
[37] Weber, *op. cit.*, p. 64.

expression in captialistic enterprise, while on the other, the enterprise has derived its most suitable motive force from the spirit of capitalism.[38] It does appear that we are historically and culturally affected by the intangible and irrational spirit of capitalism.

With this desire to maintain the spirit of capitalism we get caught up in an overzealousness to explain and confirm scientifically and intellectually, the rightfulness of our actions. What we then develop in the spirit of capitalism is the misuse of science[39] or misdirection of intellectual conceptualism, just as Spencer and Sumner *et al.* inappropriately transferred Darwin's theory of human evolutionary development from the biophysiological sciences to the realm of social sciences in an effort to create a theory of Social Darwinism. The protagonists for social services in the marketplace of capitalism are likewise injudiciously attempting to provide a good fit of economic theories into the realm of social service provision. Titmuss summed it up when he complained about the "Philistine resurrection of economic man in social policy."[40]

CONTRADICTIONS

Amitai Etzioni, discussing his brief tenure as a staff director of the Moreland Commission in New York State, suggested that the Commission had neglected two important questions:

First, can human services really generate a legitimate profit without skimping on quality or quantity, without weeding out the really ill and giving unnecessary services to the relatively healthy? And, realistically, could the standards of service among for-profit homes be brought up to a reasonable level, given the profit picture and the ethics characteristic of many of the owners involved in this "industry"?[41]

---

[38] *Ibid.*, p. 65.
[39] Ethel Tobach, "Social Darwinism Rides Again," in Ethel Tobach *et al.*, *The Four Horsemen* (New York: Behavioral Publications, 1974), pp. 99–123.
[40] Richard M. Titmuss, *The Gift Relationship* (New York: Pantheon Books, 1970), p. 14.
[41] Amitai Etzioni, "What to Do about the Nursing Homes," *Juris Doctor*, September, 1976, p. 26.

The answer to both questions, we believe, is *no*. There is an inherent contradiction between the purposes of human service delivery and the profit-making goal of entrepreneurship. Each has its place in the institutional fabric of a democratic capitalist society, but they are not the *same* place. Attempts by one organization to "have it both ways" lead inevitably to systemic conflict: the entrepreneur in human services must violate one or the other of the sets of principles he purports to combine. Analysis of the structure of the business and service endeavors reveals the logic of this assertion; a growing body of empirical evidence supports its validity.

The goal of social welfare services is to meet human needs, both residual and developmental,[42] to see that dysfunctions of the total social system are not perpetuated at the cost of human deprivation, both by meeting needs that are otherwise left unmet—"picking up the pieces"—and by correcting the society's institutional dysfunctions which bring about the need for such "residual" services. The shared aim of those service organizations which make up the total social welfare institution, therefore, is to increase investment in resources and services and/or improve their effectiveness so that the aggregate of unmet needs will be reduced. The criterion of success in the operation of this social institution is the *reduction* of demand (or need) for its services. The societal instrument for realization of its citizens' right to welfare is the allocation of adequate and appropriate resources to this purpose.

In contrast, creating the *opposite* circumstance is the goal of the business institution in relation to the marketplace. The condition most favorable for profit-making is imbalance, in which demand for goods is continually greater than supply: unsatisfied want is the impetus for consumers' bidding up the price that will be paid for goods and services. The profit imperative compels the marketer to charge as much as the market will bear, while at the same time investing as little as

[42] Harold L. Wilensky and Charles N. Lebeaux, *Industrial Society and Social Welfare* (New York: Free Press, 1965), pp. 138–40.

possible in the material and human resources which make up
the cost factors in the computation of profit: the net difference between aggregate price and aggregate cost of production and marketing. Maximizing profit is the business of
business, the aim of the economic process. But as Marshall
observes:

> In contrast to the economic process, it is a fundamental principle of
> the Welfare State that the market value of an individual cannot be
> the measure of his right to welfare. The central function of wel-
> fare, in fact, is to supersede the market by taking goods out of it, or
> in some way to control and modify its operations so as to produce a
> result which it would not have produced itself.[43]

The result to which Marshall refers can best be seen in
terms of the individual beneficiary of welfare operations—a
person who is entitled to the benefits of whatever services will
improve his status and satisfactions in life, assuring his dignity and equity of opportunity for human fulfillment. He is
generally referred to as a client, implying that he receives his
services in a transaction with a professional, a human service
practitioner who takes responsibility for delivering services in
a manner consistent with the purposes of the social welfare
system. This professional's practices are, therefore, guided
by ethical standards which are a rational blend of welfare
purposes with knowledge of the potentialities of material and
human resources for effective use for human betterment.

As Levy points out, it is especially crucial that human services be delivered in accordance with such standards because
of the peculiar vulnerability of the recipient:

> These persons may need the help so badly that they may not even
> be in a position to judge whether they are being given short shrift.
> In fact, they may be in such dire straits that they become easy
> marks for, and quite helpless when confronted with, social workers
> who have any inclination toward negligence, laziness, or sheer ex-

[43] T. H. Marshall, "Value Problems of Welfare Capitalism," *Journal of Social Policy*,
I, No. 1 (1972), 19–20.

ploitation for the sake of their own personal gain, gratification, or self-aggrandizement.[44]

Herein lies the ultimate contradiction in the introduction of the profit motive in the delivery of human services. The business manager is committed, by virtue of his contractual obligation to investors, to use the service recipient in the role of customer, not client. The customer's role in the business system is as the sole source of the business income—the amount of which must be as much in excess of costs as the businessman can achieve. Producing a profit is the ultimate purpose for which all factors in the business process, including the customer, have to be exploited. Exploitation, whether hardened by cynicism or softened by sentimentality, is the antithesis of what we mean by human services. What we are arguing is that the incidence of abuses is not accidental but a predictable effect of the unrealistic expectation that, by some kind of magic, mutually inconsistent purposes can be served consistently by the same organization. Kurnburg sums this up when he explains that "they make tallow out of cattle and money out of men."[45] Weber further explains that "the peculiarity of this philosophy of avarice appears to be the ideal of the honest man of recognized credit, and above all, the idea of duty of the individual toward the increase of his capital, which is assumed as an end in itself."[46]

CONCLUSION

The delivery of the human services is more efficient and expeditious outside the marketplace. Alvin Schorr supports this contention when he explains that:

Most significant attempts at pioneering in the social services during the 1960's [innovative juvenile delinquency programs, community action, new service initiatives under Social Security amendments, community care of the mentally ill, model cities] were largely in-

[44] Charles S. Levy, *Social Work Ethics* (New York: Human Sciences Press, Inc., 1976), p. 19.
[45] Weber, *op. cit.*, p. 51.   [46] *Ibid.*, p. 51.

spired and set in motion by government. Thus the decade's major examples of pioneering have marginal connection with voluntary [or proprietary] social service or owe it nothing.[47]

In the same vein Titmuss[48] has shown that altruism may assure a higher quality product than do market incentives. He demonstrated that in an examination of methods of providing blood for transfusions the nonmarket system produces a more reliable supply of blood with less waste and administrative red tape than does the market system.

We therefore conclude that human social welfare services must be perceived and developed not through the economic process of the capitalistic marketplace but as Gilbert and Specht do in the "context of a benefit-allocation mechanism functioning outside the marketplace."[49]

We are not in agreement that the complexities of our democratic society and its problems of distributive justice call for the resolve in a pluralism of service that is inclusive of the proprietary role. To the contrary, we find proprietary social services to be deficient, discriminatory, and dehumanizing. Social welfare service for profit is neither humane nor social, even its service is misdirected.

May we suggest and encourage that our social policy planners and service providers give up the spirit of capitalism and recognize, in the words of Stretton, that:

Multiple problems of justice and social cohesion are forcing each national society whatever the color of its government, to take public control of its resources and [through price and income policies] its inequalities. The public control is inevitable. But its methods and purposes are wide to choice.[50]

[47] Alvin Schorr, "The Tasks of Voluntarism in the Next Decade," in Kahn, *op. cit.*, p. 52.

[48] Titmuss, *op. cit.*

[49] Neil Gilbert and Harry Specht, *Dimensions of Social Welfare Policy* (New York: Prentice-Hall, 1974), p. 28.

[50] Hugh Stretton, *Capitalism, Socialism, Environment* (London: Cambridge University Press, 1976), p. 1.

Jobs: One Kind of Work in America

FREDERICK A. ZELLER and WIL J. SMITH

O̲STENSIBLY, THE PURPOSE of discussing work and its changing meaning in the United States is to permit consideration of the practices of the social work profession against a backdrop such as might thus be provided in order to identify strengths and weaknesses of current and future program administration and other operations.

Seemingly, this should not be a difficult task. One could present data related to: the changing composition of the labor force; the ever-changing occupational structure; changing wage and other benefits levels; patterns of, and changing relationships between, the proportions of time devoted to paid work and leisure; as well as other kinds of data. Our research has led us to the conclusion that this focus would not contribute very meaningfully to the more vital needs and interests of the likely audience. This conclusion follows from the fact that social welfare practitioners have been given a great deal of responsibility for significantly changing the essential life styles of a large number of people. We are referring, of course, to the tasks associated with the term "workfare"; that is, changing the status of people from social dependence to gainful employment.

It is realized by even the most socially conservative persons that adverse physical and mental characteristics preclude

FREDERICK A. ZELLER is Professor of Economics and Industrial Relations, West Virginia University, Morgantown.
WIL J. SMITH is Associate Professor of Economics and Industrial Relations, West Virginia University, Morgantown.

some people from full participation in the nation's labor market. However, even among the more liberal thinkers, there frequently seems to be a gnawing suspicion that the numbers of people who could be liberated from welfare are much larger than the numbers of successes with past policies and programs, and that failure to "save" these "question-ables" is due primarily to inept program operation combined with benefit levels which are a disincentive to sincere job search efforts.

Then, too, still another stream of thought, although not widespread, appears to be growing in importance. This holds that the whole workfare-welfare debate may be misdirected; that for some people employment as conventionally defined may be far less important in the future than in the past. Margaret Mead claims that: "The idea that each individual buys his way to food and shelter, education and safety, by holding a job is terribly new and was characteristic of the Industrial Revolution with which we have now more or less finished."[1] Positions such as these, which have not been taken very seriously, imply criticism of welfare programs and their staffs for buttressing an allegedly outmoded economic system.

Because of these and other points of view, as well as data that suggest the possibility of growing problems associated with affirmative action, higher than normal (or acceptable) unemployment rates in otherwise prosperous periods, and the large influx of white women into the labor force, we concluded that we should focus on the nature and meaning of work and jobs and the public policies intended to affect them in one way or another. The authors hope that this presentation will clarify the complex nature of work in America (or in any society, for that matter) and that this clarification may enable social workers to gain a more insightful perspective

[1] Margaret Mead, "The Changing Cultural Values of Work and Leisure," Seminar on Manpower Policy and Programs, Manpower Administration, U.S. Department of Labor, 1967, p. 8.

about what they are doing or being asked to do, and the probability for succeeding in their efforts.

WORK AND JOBS DEFINED

Much of the controversy surrounding discussions of public welfare and other human resources programs can be traced to definitional problems with two key terms: "work" and "jobs." It seems possible to circumvent this difficulty to a great extent by defining the terms more explicitly so that they refer to two different things. "Work" is used here as "a general term which is closely linked to one's approach to life, which may or may not parallel job demands."[2] In other words, work is the physical and mental activity required for adaptation to one's physical and social environment. On the other hand, "job" is used here to refer to work made up of task functions or operations as defined by organizations and situations.[3]

These definitions are helpful in immediately disposing of several issues. First, while people who prefer unemployment to employment may be described as lazy, even lazy people cannot avoid "working" except by dying. A brief elaboration on the nature of work as we use the term here in a generic sense might be useful.

It is hard to think of an effective argument against the following proposition: On the average, man is born with the instinct to become something other than what he is at any given moment. For example, when he is younger he longs to become older, and he strives to become wealthier, more powerful, less hungry, less tired, less in pain, happier, more prestigious. Man is never (or at least seldom ever) content with what he has or what he is. His mind is forever on what he *will become* relative to his fellow man and his total environment.

His planning period for *becoming* may be short, particularly

[2] Donald W. Tiffany, James R. Cowan, and Phyllis M. Tiffany, *The Unemployed: a Social Psychological Portrait* (Englewood Cliffs, N.J.: Prentice-Hall, Inc., 1970), p. 17.
[3] *Ibid.*

if he is starving or afflicted with terminal illness. Or it may be infinite even if he is starving or fatally ill, if he believes in life after death. His plan for becoming something other than he is may depend on physical or spiritual achievement. The methods he uses to accomplish that plan may contribute to the welfare of others, to the frustration of the plans and hopes of others or to both.

The process of man's becoming is, however, regulated. On the one hand, it is regulated by what he is and what he can become by virtue of his given (and acquired) physical, mental, and social attributes. In part these are a function of his socialization, and in part they are a function of his personality, or individual autonomy, which that socialization both permits, encourages, and condones. On the other hand, man is regulated by his society and by his physical environment, although the boundaries of the physical regulation can be removed by technology through the exploitation of natural resources even if never very far or for very long.

With this conception of man on earth and in society, we have identified three interrelated elements which determine the process of becoming: physical environment, social structure, and personality. Work is the physical or mental activity required for integrating these three elements into a series of experiences which move man from one state and/or level to another. In this sense work is common to all men and all historical epochs and will ever be so. And the quality and quantity of the pleasure and pain associated with it always have been and always will be functions of the smoothness of the fit of the integration of physical environment, social structure, and personality.

These factors are variable both among societies and within societies. Consequently, some resource-rich societies are poor and some resource-poor societies are rich; some societies have not defined wealth in ways which consider solely (or even largely) their economic resources; some rich societies are becoming poor while some poor societies are becoming rich; and within the same society philosopher kings may be equally as happy or as unhappy as slaves. But the variation which is identifiable has more to do with certain kinds of outcomes rather than whether or not man works. Man's inherent, unavoidable nature is to become something else than what he is, and for the most part he will use his mental and physical capabilities to strive toward that goal whether he is on a job, in prison, in a hospital, at home, or on welfare. Work, hence, is adapting to opportunities to change, and hence its study and discussion per se (as we have defined it) are relatively uninformative to social workers, although for historians, anthropologists, and biologists this may not be the case.

Thus, our real concern is with job structures—that is, a certain kind of work—and the ease or the difficulty of fitting people into them. A useful way of approaching this matter is to look at the functions performed by occupational structures.

THE MEANING OF "HAVING A JOB"

In 1966 the sociologist Harold Wilensky identified the importance of jobs by reference to how they have been described by prominent thinkers of the past. It seems clear that the particular emphases uncovered are all more or less relevant to present job analyses. We simply were centuries in discovering the implications and ramifications of what we have been doing or what has been done to us. Before quoting Wilensky we should point out that in every instance where he refers to or actually uses the word "work," we have substituted "job." According to Wilensky (with the modification in brackets):

Why is man a [job holder]? First of all, of course, man [has a job] to sustain physical life—to provide food, clothing and shelter. But clearly [the job] is central to our lives for other reasons as well. According to Freud, [the job] provides us with a sense of reality; to Elton Mayo, [the job] is a bind to community; to Marx, its function is primarily economic.
Theologians are interested in [the job's] moral dimensions; socio-

logists see it as determinant of status, and some contemporary critics say that it is simply the best way of filling up a lot of time. To the ancient Greeks, who had slaves to do it, [the job] was a curse. The Hebrews saw [the job] as punishment. The early Christians found [the job] was being praised as a natural learning and contemplation. During the Reformation, [the job] became the only way of serving God. Luther pronounced that conscientious performance of one's labor was man's highest duty. Later interpretations of Calvinistic doctrine gave religious sanction to worldly wealth and achievement. This belief, when wedded to Social Darwinism and laissez-faire liberalism, became the foundation for what we call the Protestant ethic. Marx, however, took the concept of [the job] and put it in an even more central position in life; freed from capitalist exploitation, [the job] would become a joy as workers improved the material environment around them.[4]

Stating the matter more succinctly, and changing his reference to "work" to "job" as we did with Wilensky, the astute rural sociologist Walter L. Slocum maintains that [jobs] in the modern industrial society provide the following: source of subsistence; regulation of activities; patterns of association; identity; meaningful life experiences; and social status.[5]

Think about these attributes of job-holding and ask these two questions of yourselves: Even if welfare benefits were substantially higher, how could being voluntarily unemployed possibly be as rewarding as having even a poorly paid job, considering that the unemployed is often regarded with contempt? To what extent is it reasonable to expect people with jobs but without power to control their continued employment to encourage potential competitors to enter the labor force? Clearly, the job status quo is surrounded by extensive minefields, and its attackers have been ill-equipped for their mission and have made advance preparations for

[4] *Work in America*, report of a Special Task Force to the Secretary of Health, Education, and Welfare, prepared under the auspices of the W. E. Upjohn Institute for Employment Research (Cambridge, Mass.: MIT Press, 1973), p. 1; acknowledged to be based on Harold Wilensky, "Work as a Social Problem," in Howard S. Becker, ed., *Social Problems: a Modern Approach* (New York: John Wiley & Sons, 1966), pp. 117–66.

[5] Walter L. Slocum, *Occupational Careers: a Sociological Perspective* (2d ed.; Chicago: Aldine Publishing Co., 1974), pp. 26–28.

their repulsion. Still, there have been extensive labor market changes in the past, and undoubtedly there will continue to be changes for some time in the future. Indeed, the prospect of changes has drawn much attention in recent years.

RECENT LABOR MARKET CHANGES

A key indicator of change in labor market analysis is the labor force participation rate, the proportion of the population (or some group in the population, such as blacks, women) sixteen years or older which is employed or unemployed. In other words, these are the people who are competing for the stock of jobs at any given time (either through being employed or through actively seeking employment).

Whereas the total labor force participation rate increased only from about 59 percent to about 61 percent between 1960 and 1976, the changes are somewhat more pronounced when they are analyzed by sex. During that period the male labor force participation rate declined from 82 percent in 1960 to 77 percent in 1976, with the greater declines experienced by older males. In contrast, the female labor force participation rate increased from 37 percent to about 47 percent, with the increase spread across all age groups except those sixty-five years or older. There were, of course, important differences in the amount of increase from one age group to another.

During the same period, the nonwhite female labor force participation rate, always high compared to that of white females, increased only from about 47 percent to about 50 percent, while the nonwhite male labor force participation rate decreased sharply from about 80 percent to about 70 percent.

In addition to the changing age and sex composition of the labor force, and undoubtedly contributing to those changes, the distribution of employment by occupational group also is changing significantly. According to estimates of the United States Department of Labor, cited by Sanford Cohen, workers in the white-collar occupations are expected to constitute

53 percent of the total employment in 1985 compared to 43 percent in 1960.[6] Declines in the proportion of workers in blue-collar occupations from 36 percent to 32 percent and farm workers from 8 percent to 2 percent are also expected. Relatively little change is expected in the proportion of service workers.

It is important to consider one other labor market indicator—the unemployment rate. The unemployment rate has been particularly high in recent years. In 1975 the rate was 8.5 percent, in 1976 it was 7.7 percent, in 1977 it was 7.0 percent, and in March, 1978, it was 6.2 percent. Generally during periods of comparative prosperity, such as we are experiencing now, the unemployment rate has been less than 6 percent, and in three years of this decade it has been less than 5 percent.

What do these and similar kinds of data tell us about the changing character of jobs in America? In a very general way, they tell us that the society is responding to changing markets occasioned by technological changes, changes in natural resources costs, changing tastes and preference, changing public policies and the like, though, as gauged by recent levels of unemployment, not as smoothly as one might prefer. However, the interpretation of those changes varies with the interpreter.[7]

Some people are optimistic about the effect of the changes, citing the decreasing need for manual labor and the greater equality of competition for labor market employment and, ostensibly, opportunities for self-fulfillment. Others are more pessimistic. They cite the substantial and persistent unemployment for large numbers and underemployment for even larger numbers of the labor force; the fact that some manual and otherwise unsatisfactory labor is still and probably always will be required; and that equal-opportunity programs have not yet produced, and indeed may never produce, ideal re-

---

[6] Sanford Cohen, *Labor in the United States* (4th ed.; Columbus, Ohio: Charles E. Merrill Publishing Co., 1975), p. 35.

[7] For a good discussion of this matter see Denis F. Johnston, "The Future of Work: Three Possible Alternatives," *Monthly Labor Review*, May, 1972, pp. 3–11.

sults. Our position on the matter is unimportant, since reaching any position at all is possible only by the liberal application of value judgments. However, several interesting points have been made by a number of knowledgeable persons.

With respect to the kind of jobs found in society, referred to as "work" by the author, Walter S. Neff observes that "it is not work itself which is degrading but the power relationships and social structures which surround it."[8] Much the same point could be made with respect to the status of unemployment or being on welfare. Neither of these conditions is in itself degrading, nor does it indicate freedom from "work," as the term is used here. The unemployed and/or the welfare recipient are degraded by a society which will accept nothing less than job employment (a job in the traditional labor market) for social approval even though there may not be sufficient jobs to go around and even though there may not be great economic demand (or need) for some jobs. Little wonder, then, that in his review of the Work in America Task Force report Harold Wool concludes: "The most important single set of measures which can contribute to improvements of *quality* of work [jobs] in America are . . . those designed to increase the *quantity* of work [jobs] in America."[9] While Wool may be correct, we feel compelled to point out that such a strategy could destroy itself if it results in the serious depletion of high quality, fairly accessible, natural resources. Already we are being warned about future shortage of fuel and energy supplies and their sharply rising prices relative to most other prices, including the price paid for labor or human energy—that is, income (wages).

DISCUSSION

The problem with work in America is that it has become almost impossible to "work" without having a "job." There are many reasons for this, including the economic efficiency

---

[8] Walter S. Neff, *Work and Human Behavior* (New York: Atherton Press, 1968), p. 43.

[9] Harold Wool, "What's Wrong with Work in America? A Review Essay," *Monthly Labor Review*, March, 1973, pp. 39–44.

achieved through specialization, organization, cost accounting and accountability, standardization and uniformity, and
scientific management which requires a scientific human to
manage, among other reasons as well. Having a job is seemingly valued above all else in America: it is better than being
on welfare, better than being a housewife, better than early
retirement, better than being a student, and better than almost any other status one can think of. There are expanding
job opportunities in the United States, and we are not aware
of a single study which has not established that workers
prefer suitable, meaningful employment to unemployment.
However, there is trouble in Paradise. While welfare in
America is intimately bound up with having a job, some
Americans sometimes do not have jobs and some of them
may never have jobs—at least suitable, permanent jobs. In
some cases there are no jobs available, and in other cases the
jobs are available but the unemployed do not fill them for
one reason or another.

By its very nature, the welfare profession is involved with
both the temporarily unemployed and the more or less permanently unemployed. When the difficulty is simply a lack of
jobs, the welfare professionals can do little except administer
available programs as efficiently as possible. When jobs are
available, somewhat more latitude is possible in arranging
programs to achieve employment of clients.

However, given the complex nature of job employment
and the preparation for employment in a job, this task is almost inordinately difficult to accomplish. In either case, people in the welfare profession are apt to turn in disappointing
records in the eyes of the general public and in the eyes of
the clients they seek to serve. In some cases, the clients are
physically or mentally incapacitated, some temporarily, some
permanently. For some there will be no accession to paying
jobs, and for others the rate of accession will be under the
control of multiple forces which can at best be only partly
managed. In other cases, the people on welfare for "no good
reason" are there because powerful forces have led them to

reject the "good life" of this society and the means of acquiring and enjoying it. If the goal is to place these people on "jobs" as defined in the traditional labor market sense, then invective and instruction are not likely to be very effective in accomplishing this goal. The solution to the so-called "welfare problem," if indeed there is one, might possibly (though perhaps not probably) come through the application of powerful, rational, individualized, public policies and programs combined with the willingness of broad sectors of the public to make them (or let them) work.

The Earnings Test in Social Security

MARTHA N. OZAWA

RUMBLINGS OF TROUBLE in the financing of Social Security have already been heard, and although Social Security taxes have been increased, the basic problem remains. The trouble has been building up because the elderly have increasingly been retiring earlier than 65, working less, and living longer than earlier generations. But major shocks are likely to be experienced when the imbalance between the working population and the retired population grows even more pronounced around 2005 when the postwar baby-boom generation starts to retire.

Can the system survive and still maintain present benefit rates?

Since the changing demographic composition strongly affects the economics of Social Security—and will affect it still more profoundly within a score of years—the time seems ripe for a critical review of the earnings test, a factor that has a significant influence on early retirement and retirees' participation in the labor force. The test is one of the most controversial features of the program for it tends to contravene the work ethic and work incentives generally valued by Americans. The pertinent provisions in the Social Security amendments are debated in almost every session of Congress, now that the wisdom of early retirement is questioned.

MARTHA N. OZAWA is Professor, George Warren Brown School of Social Work, Washington University, St. Louis.

EMERGING PROBLEMS

When the Social Security Act was passed in 1935, we were in the midst of the great depression. Social Security was designed to provide income support to workers who retired. It was meant to be an earnings-replacement program, not an annuity. This was an important reason for incorporating the earnings test (or retirement test).

A secondary objective was to open employment opportunities to younger workers. The Social Security Act established 65 as the official retirement age. Many employers followed suit in their pension programs. The 1956 amendments to the Social Security Act lowered the minimum retirement age for women to 62, with actuarially reduced benefits; the 1961 amendments lowered the minimum retirement age for men.

The rate of male participation in the labor force by those 65 and over declined from 45.8 percent in 1950 to 20.3 percent in 1976, while that for females declined from 9.7 percent to 8.2 percent.[1] In 1965 only 31.7 percent of retired workers were receiving reduced benefits; by 1975, the proportion reached 56.5 percent.[2]

Quite suddenly, Congress and the public have seen a potential problem in the declining labor force participation among the elderly and are aware of an impending crisis in financing Social Security for a proportionately greater number of retirees in the next century. Because of the declining birth rate following the baby boom, each 100 workers in 2030 will have to support 45 retirees; currently, the ratio is 100 to 30.[3]

The 1974 Quadrennial Advisory Council on Social Security reported that 65 percent of the estimated future deficit could be attributed to the demographic shift. One third of

[1] *Employment and Training Report of the President, 1977* (Washington, D.C.: U.S. Government Printing Office, 1977), p. 143, table A-4.

[2] *Social Security Bulletin: Annual Statistical Supplement, 1975*, p. 127, table 95.

[3] *Reports of the Quadrennial Advisory Council on Social Security*, 94th Congress, 1st session (Washington, D.C.: U.S. Government Printing Office, 1975), p. 49.

the deficit would be due to a flaw in the 1972 amendments which allowed future benefits to be adjusted not only for the cost-of-living increase in the benefit formula but also for the increase in taxable wages.[4] The 1977 amendments corrected this double adjustment. Thus the bulk of future deficits will be attributable almost solely to the demographic shift. How much will payroll taxes have to be raised if the present system of financing Old-Age, Survivors, and Disability Insurance (OASDI) is continued in the next century? The projected expenditures during the period 2027–51 will require payroll taxes at 16.69 percent, while the projected tax income under the 1977 amendments during this period will be only 12.40 percent of taxable payroll, creating a deficit of 4.29 percent.[5]

Faced with the increasing problem of financing, it is reasonable to expect that policy-makers will wish to change the policy in regard to retirement. Logically, they would favor flexible retirement, which encourages the elderly to work beyond age 65.[6] It takes a long time to change public attitudes toward retirement. It seems desirable, therefore, to change the policy now so that the elderly in the next century will in fact prefer late retirement.

Studies indicate that the earnings test has a lot to do with the issue of whether the elderly should or should not be encouraged to retire. Furthermore, the earnings test is interrelated with economic conditions and society's economic need for the elderly to stay in the labor force.

LEGISLATIVE DEVELOPMENT

The 1939 amendments to the Social Security Act included the first provision for the earnings test, which allowed the retired beneficiary to earn no more than $14.99 per month

[4] *Ibid.,* p. 50.

[5] A. Haeworth Robertson, "Financial Status of Social Security Program after the Social Security Amendments of 1977," *Social Security Bulletin,* XLI, No. 3 (1978), 27.

[6] Juanita M. Kreps, ed., *Employment, Income, and Retirement Problems of the Aged* (Durham, N.C.: Duke University Press, 1963), p. 163.

without losing benefits; earnings in excess of $14.99 subjected the beneficiary to the entire loss of that month's benefits. The 1960 amendments provided, for the first time, an implicit tax rate on a certain range of earnings in excess of an annual exempt amount, thus correcting the all-or-nothing situation. Legislative efforts since 1939 have focused on either increasing the annual exempt amount or lowering the implicit tax rate on earnings. Currently, retired beneficiaries can earn up to $4,000 a year without reducing their benefits. Excess earnings are subject to a 50 percent implicit tax rate; that is, each additional $1.00 earned beyond $4,000 a year reduces benefits by $.50.

Between 1955 and 1974 average wages increased by 115 percent, but the annual exempt amount by only 100 percent.[7] The 1977 amendments provided that the amount would rise from $3,000 to $4,000 in 1978 and by $500 each year until 1981, and thereafter in accordance with the rise in wage levels.[8]

The implicit tax rate of 50 percent still acts as a disincentive to work. Not only do working retirees lose benefits, but they also have to pay Social Security and income taxes. A certain range of earnings is therefore subject to a cumulative tax rate that may be even higher than 70 percent.

The 1977 amendments made two other related changes. These amendments eliminated the monthly measure of earnings, except during the first year in which a beneficiary is entitled to benefits, to calculate reduced benefits. Thus, any reduction in benefits will be calculated solely on the basis of annual earnings. The new provision eliminates the unfair advantage previously enjoyed by retirees who could earn a sizable income during a part of the year and still draw full monthly benefits during the rest of the year. Also, the age at which the earnings test no longer applies will be lowered in 1982 from 72 to 70.

[7] Robert J. Myers, *Social Security* (Homewood, Ill.: Richard D. Irwin, 1975), p. 115.
[8] The annual exempt amount for those aged 62–64 was frozen at $3,240.

THE EARNINGS TEST AND RETIREMENT INCENTIVES

The decision to retire is a complex one. Some workers have to retire because of poor health, compulsory retirement policies, or other reasons. Some respond to incentives built into the Social Security program and private pension programs. For some, compulsory retirement policies or poor health may interact with retirement incentives.[9]

Bowen and Finegan investigated factors associated with the marked difference in the rate of labor force participation—a 33 percent difference—between men aged 65 and 67.[10] Their multiple regression analysis indicates that, controlling for other variables, over one third of the difference in the rate of labor force participation between men aged 64 and 67 can be attributed to income other than earnings. Social Security benefits constitute the largest portion of "other income" for the majority of the elderly.[11] Therefore, one can conclude that Social Security benefits are strongly associated with decisions to retire. However, other income, such as pensions, is often linked to compulsory retirement policies in many firms. Also the Social Security benefit depends on the degree of labor force withdrawal, or the level of earnings. Simply put, then, the other income is an endogenous variable of retirement. Therefore, it is wrong to say that the retirement decision is influenced solely by the effect of other income.[12]

[9] For research findings on the interaction between limitations in health and level of retirement income in the decision-making process see Joseph F. Quinn, *The Early Retirement Decision: Evidence from the 1969 Retirement History*, Staff Paper No. 29 (Washington, D.C.: Social Security Administration, Office of Research and Statistics, 1978).

[10] William G. Bowen and T. Aldrich Finegan, *The Economics of Labor Force Participation* (Princeton, N.J.: Princeton University Press, 1969), p. 282.

[11] For those who retired during January–June, 1970, Social Security benefits constituted between 40 percent and 48 percent of "other income," depending on marital status and sex. See Alan Fox, "Income of New Beneficiaries by Age at Entitlement to Benefits," in *Reaching Retirement Age: Findings from a Survey of Newly Entitled Workers, 1968–70*, Research Report No. 47, U.S. Department of Health, Education, and Welfare, Social Security Administration (Washington, D.C.: U.S. Government Printing Office, 1976), p. 99, table 8.2.

[12] For detailed discussion see Quinn, *op. cit.*, pp. 2–5.

Boskin's study focused on the effects of the earnings test and the benefit level on the probability of the worker to retire.[13] It used net earnings as a proxy independent variable for the earnings test. Net earnings refer to earnings after the deduction of the earnings-tested loss in Social Security benefits. He found that net earnings and Social Security benefits were the two most statistically significant predictors for probability of retirement. Boskin estimated that a $1,000 increase in net earnings reduced the annual probability by about 60 percent and that an increase in Social Security benefits per couple from $3,000 to $4,000 per year more than doubled the annual probability. Furthermore, he estimated that a decrease in the implicit tax rate involved in the earnings test from one half to one third could reduce the annual probability of retirement by 50 percent.[14]

A 1963 study by the Social Security Administration indicated that the rates of labor force participation among those aged 63 to 72 noticeably declined when earnings exceeded the exempt amount.[15] The implicit tax rate at this point increases from zero percent to 50 percent. However, the study found that no sudden decline in the rates of labor force participation occurred when the implicit tax rate increased to 100 percent.[16] Another study by the Social Security Administration indicated that about one half of the men who received benefits in 1969 and worked at the same time kept their earnings within the annual exempt amount of $1,680.[17]

These empirical studies show that the earnings test and the level of income available after retirement are two strong incentives for a worker to retire. Retirement income makes

[13] Michael J. Boskin, "Social Security and Retirement Decisions," *Economic Inquiry,* XV, No. 1 (1977), pp. 1–25.

[14] *Ibid.,* p. 13.

[15] Kenneth G. Sander, "The Retirement Test: Its Effect on Older Workers' Earnings," *Social Security Bulletin,* XXXI, No. 6 (1968), 3–6.

[16] In 1963 when the data for this study were collected, benefits were reduced $1 for each $2 of earnings from $1,200 to $1,700, and $1 for each $1 for earnings in excess of $1,700.

[17] Virginia Reno, "Retirement Patterns of Men," in *Reaching Retirement Age,* p. 32.

leisure a less expensive commodity. This is especially true when the replacement ratio of retirement income to preretirement income is high. Then retirement becomes less economically painful.

In addition to these built-in incentives, the way in which the benefit formula is developed discourages postponing retirement. Although a worker who retires between 62 and 64 years of age receives actuarially reduced benefits, postponing retirement does not provide adequately increased benefits that an actuarial calculation warrants. Under the 1977 amendments, if a person retires at an age later than 65, his benefits will be increased by 3 percent for each year of postponed retirement; however, such an increment is still short of an actuarially warranted increase, which is about 10 percent.[18]

Thus it is clear that, in concert, the earnings test, Social Security benefits, and the benefit formula are strong economic incentives for a worker to retire, possibly earlier than age 65, and not to postpone retirement beyond 65. Downgrading the benefit levels probably would not be politically feasible unless the benefit structure were radically changed. However, a policy change in the earnings test to boost work incentives and a policy change in benefit formula to encourage late retirement would seem to be acceptable to the majority of the public and the policy-makers in Washington. Improvement would greatly ameliorate the financing of OASDI in the next century.

THE EARNINGS TEST: PRO AND CON

Since the earnings test is linked with incentives to retire early, the way seems open for considering repeal. However, policy issues related to repeal involve much more than the work disincentive.

Arguments for the test. A study by the Social Security Administration indicates that retirees who forego total Social Se-

---

[18] Alicia Munnell, *The Future of Social Security* (Washington, D.C.: Brookings Institution, 1977), p. 79.

curity benefits are highly paid professionals.[19] Probably the strongest argument for retaining the test is that highly paid workers would receive windfall benefits if it were abolished.[20] A part of this argument is that repeal would increase OASDI expenditures by approximately $3 billion a year.[21]

Another argument for the test is that retirement opens up opportunities for younger workers. However, available data seem to indicate that the rate of unemployment is not related to the rate of retirement.[22]

Still another important argument concerns the basic objective of Social Security as a partial replacement of earnings lost because of retirement. It is also pointed out that a sizable portion of Social Security benefits was not paid for by the retired population but is being financed by the working population, and this portion represents "intergenerational transfers."[23] These two factors together provide convincing evidence that Social Security is not an annuity duly paid for by the retiree. This argument inevitably goes on to say that repeal of the test would accentuate the intergenerational transfer component—or, as some call it, the welfare component—of Social Security. Increasing that component would seem unfair to the working population, especially low-wage earners. Social Security taxes are regressive and hit such workers hard.

Arguments against the test. In the main, these arguments emphasize the adverse economic and social effects of the test on the elderly themselves and its adverse impact on the economy.

It is said that—while keeping the cost of Social Security down by a few billion dollars and also keeping off the benefit rolls the few high earners among the elderly—the earnings

---

[19] Reno, *op. cit.,* p. 35, Table 3.10.
[20] Rita Ricardo Campbell, *Social Security: Promise and Reality* (Stanford, Calif.: Stanford University, Hoover Institution, 1977), p. 210.
[21] Munnell, *op. cit.,* p. 79.   [22] Kreps, *op. cit.,* p. 144, table 1.
[23] For a detailed discussion see Martha N. Ozawa, "Individual Equity versus Social Adequacy in Federal Old-Age Insurance," *Social Service Review,* L, No. 2 (1976), 209–23.

test is forcing a sizable portion of the elderly to retire or curtail their work effort substantially, against their will.[24] Furthermore, those who work less because of the test tend to be low-wage retirees.[25] They typically are the persons who especially need to supplement their meager Social Security benefits.[26] Research findings indicate that earnings are a decisive factor in lifting elderly persons out of poverty.[27] Staying longer in the labor force would also assure that the income level of the elderly would not lag so far behind that of the general population in the future as it does at present.[28] Moreover, work helps the elderly maintain the social contacts and involvement that they need to keep their sense of self-esteem and self-identity as members of the community.

Another argument points out the inequity in the way that earned income and unearned income are treated. Retirees— typically high-income retirees—who do not work but derive income from such sources as rent, interest, and dividends are not affected by the earnings test, but those who work are affected. However, the issue involved here goes right back to the basic objective of Social Security: a partial replacement of earnings lost because of retirement.

Some argue that imposed retirement and/or reduced working are bad for the economy. Keeping as many people as possible off Social Security could, they say, channel funds to other uses—to capital formation, for instance, or to stimulation of industries that produce hard commodities. The elderly, too, would continue to participate in producing goods and services. On the other hand, workers forced out of the

[24] Richard J. Zeckhauser and W. Kip Siscusi, "The Role of Social Security in the Income Security of the Elderly," in Michael J. Boskin, ed., *The Crisis in Social Security: Problems and Prospects* (San Francisco: Institute for Contemporary Studies, 1977), p. 59.

[25] Reno, *op. cit.*, p. 38, table 3.16.

[26] Virginia Reno and Carol Zuckert, "Income of New Beneficiaries by Size of Social Security Benefit," in *Reaching Retirement Age*, p. 131, table 9.7.

[27] For example, of the couples newly entitled to Social Security benefits during January–June, 1970, only 8 percent of those who reported earnings had income below the poverty line, compared with 41 percent of the couples without earnings. See Fox, *op. cit.*, p. 150, table 8.7.

[28] Kreps, *op. cit.*, pp. 204–5.

labor market become full-time consumers, mainly of "soft commodities" such as social services and medical care.[29] Impact on economic growth is less favorable than it would be if the elderly were allowed to stay in the labor force as long as possible.

POLICY OPTIONS

How should the earnings test policy be changed in order to mitigate the problem of retirement incentives? That question is difficult to answer. If, for example, we are seeking ways both to remove work disincentives among middle- and low-wage earners and to prevent high-wage earners from receiving windfall benefits, then we should improve the earnings test but not eliminate it altogether. If we are to keep the basic structure and maintain the objective of partially replacing lost earnings, we have to resort to an incremental approach. On the other hand, if Social Security were radically transformed into an annuity, repeal of the test would be justified. If this change were made, all those reaching age 65 would simply get back, in the form of benefits, the investment (or annuity) value of their past contributions.

An incremental approach. The earnings test could be improved in two ways: one would be to upgrade the annual exempt amount, and the other to lower the implicit tax rate on excess earnings. Since the annual exempt amount is expected to increase substantially, thanks to the 1977 amendments, additional action seems unnecessary now. But the implicit tax rate could be further liberalized. Currently, earnings in excess of $4,000 are implicitly taxed at a 50 percent rate. The policy-maker might adopt the recommendation made by the 1974 Quadrennial Advisory Council on Social Security: that a 33 percent tax rate be applied to earnings in excess of the annual exempt amount but less than twice this amount, and a 50 percent tax rate to earnings in excess of twice this amount.[30]

---

[29] *Ibid.*, p. 163.
[30] *Reports of the Quadrennial Advisory Council on Social Security*, pp. 22–23.

What would be the effect of upgrading the annual exempt amount and lowering the implicit tax rate on a lower range of excess earnings? First, the break-even point, at which the beneficiary ceases to receive Social Security benefits, would be higher than at present. Liberalizing the earnings test according to the council recommendation would also mean that a relatively low level of excess would be subject to the lowered implicit tax of 35 percent. This would boost work incentives of low- and middle-wage earners who are now adversely affected by the earnings test.

In addition, the policy-maker could boost the work incentive by providing actuarially increased benefits to those who retire after age 65. This would correct the built-in bias that favors early retirement.

The policy-maker might also look into the exemption of workers aged 65 and over from OASDI payroll taxes, as proposed by Pechman, Aaron, and Taussig.[31] This would mitigate the problem of the high cumulative implicit tax rates imposed on earnings above the exempt amount. It would also then be economically more attractive to hire elderly workers, since employers as well as workers would be exempt from Social Security payroll taxes. And what about the equity of the situation? Is it fair—on the one hand—to tax the aged who continue to work and do not receive Social Security benefits and—on the other hand—*not* to tax the aged who stop working and receive their benefits? It seems not.

A radical approach. As stated, it seems clear that the earnings test can be eliminated only if the Social Security program is transformed into an annuity. An annuity benefit formula could be developed so as to return to the retired worker the investment value of his past contributions, carrying a reasonable amount of real compounded interest.

The elderly worker, having "fully paid for" the benefits so calculated, could justifiably start receiving benefits at 65

---

[31] Joseph A. Pechman, Henry J. Aaron, and Michael K. Taussig, *Social Security: Perspectives for Reform* (Washington, D.C.: Brookings Institution, 1968), pp. 144–45.

whether or not he continued full-time work. Thus the earnings test would be neither necessary nor justified.

Transforming Social Security into an annuity would produce positive side effects. First, basing benefits on the investment value of past contributions would eliminate the prevailing inequity in treating earnings attained during different periods of the working life. Indeed, the effect would be similar to, but more equitable in calculating benefits than, indexing earnings in relation to the rise in average wages.[32] Second, calculating benefits on the basis of the investment value of contributions would eliminate the unfair advantage currently accruing to those who join the Social Security system only a few years before retirement. Indexing taxable wages, which is provided under the 1977 amendments and becomes effective in 1979, still cannot completely eliminate this injustice. Third, this model would also eliminate the relative advantage in the benefits to a disabled worker compared with those provided to a retired worker.

Thus it is clear that transforming Social Security into an annuity would make the program more rational and equitable. However, since current retirees are receiving benefits much greater than the investment value of their past contributions, their benefits under the revised scheme would be smaller. A "guesstimate" based on a previous study is that the retired worker in the high-wage bracket, who has contributed the maximum amount, would receive benefits only one-third as large as those now received, and the retired worker in the low-wage bracket, who has contributed half the maximum or less would receive benefits only one fourth as large as at present.[33]

To ameliorate this problem the policy-maker could introduce another layer of benefits, providing a modest

---

[32] The 1977 amendments introduced for the first time the indexing of taxable earnings, which will become effective in 1979. An important difference between benefits strictly based on the investment value of past contributions and benefits based on average wage-indexed monthly earnings is that the latter still fail to take into account the different tax rates used under the OASDI programs over the years.

[33] For a detailed discussion see Ozawa, *op. cit.*

amount of flat benefits to all beneficiaries regardless of wage levels. In essence, Social Security would become a double-decker system, composed of contribution-related benefits and universal pensions. Operationally, benefits received by the worker aged 65 and over would reflect two components: one representing the investment value of past contributions; the other, flat-amount intergenerational transfers paid by the working population. Since, in absolute terms, high-wage retirees are currently receiving a larger amount through intergenerational transfers, they probably would lose under the revised system. Low- and middle-wage retirees might or might not lose, depending on the amount of the flat benefit that the Congress decided to provide.

Flat-amount benefits, however, represent intergenerational transfers which the revised scheme attempts to deemphasize. But, since the conception of flat-amount benefits to all retired workers opens the way toward the infusion of general revenues to finance Social Security, it is expected that political resistance will be less than that to the present intergenerational transfer component of the program.

The development of such a double-decker system would offer flexibility for upgrading either the flat benefits or contribution-related benefits, or both, depending on legislative intent at a given time. If, for example, Congress decided to raise the minimum floor of benefits, only the flat benefits would have to be increased. Thus fiscal resources would be utilized more efficiently. The customary proportional increase in benefits to upgrade the minimum floor would be more costly than a flat-amount increase. With respect to financing Social Security, the proposed system would open the door to the use of general revenues, especially for improving the flat benefits. If general revenues were so used, the system would gradually mitigate the regressivity of current payroll taxes.[34]

---

[34] See Martha N. Ozawa, "Social Insurance and Redistribution," in Alvin L. Schorr, ed., *Jubilee for Our Times: a Practical Program for Income Equality* (New York: Columbia University Press, 1977), p. 167.

From a philosophical point of view, developing a double-decker system would enable the policy-maker to separate the benefits clearly into benefits warranted by the principle of individual equity and benefits reflecting the principle of social adequacy or the welfare objective. Under the present formula, there is no way to see explicitly where individual equity ends and social adequacy begins, although these components are incorporated in the program. Worse yet, there are two kinds of widespread conventional wisdom: (1) implementing social adequacy always erodes individual equity; (2) social adequacy is implemented to benefit low-wage beneficiaries, eroding individual equity for high-wage beneficiaries. Both are generally based on either one of the following facts: (1) Social Security provides a higher internal rate of return to low-wage beneficiaries in terms of benefits; (2) the replacement ratio of benefits is higher for low-wage beneficiaries. But the alternative logic may convince the reader otherwise.

Suppose one operationalizes individual equity as a return of the investment value of contributions with, say, 3 percent real compounded interest. Then, it is clear that Social Security is currently providing benefits larger than individual equity warrants. That is, the program is implementing social adequacy *in addition* to individual equity. Furthermore, over and above the return of the investment value of their contributions, high-wage beneficiaries receive larger benefits through intergenerational transfers than low-wage beneficiaries receive. These transfers represent the social adequacy component of Social Security which can best be assessed in absolute terms because it is a welfare provision. Both facts convince one that social adequacy is implemented in favor of high-wage earners.

The proposed model would make it possible to distinguish between individual equity and social adequacy and to quantify each component. As a result, Congress would be better able to control Social Security expenditures, especially with respect to the social adequacy or welfare component. The model also would permit Congress to shape the distributive pattern of that portion of benefits which represent the principle of social adequacy. Flat-amount benefits are one option that may be considered by the Congress.

Another way to supplement the envisioned annuity program is to use SSI for providing an adequate minimum income to those whose income is considered inadequate. However, since SSI is an income-tested program, the improvement in work incentives brought about by transforming Social Security into an annuity and eliminating the earnings test would be undone by bringing more Social Security beneficiaries under SSI. Therefore, using SSI to supplement the annuity is objectionable because this would defeat a major aim of the radical change proposed in the Social Security program.

If it seems desirable to change the social policy to encourage the elderly to stay in the labor force, the policy-maker can either liberalize or eliminate the earnings test. Liberalizing the test has been a continuous effort of the Congress. This could be further pursued incrementally without reforming Social Security radically. However, if the choice is to eliminate the earnings test, Social Security must be changed from an earnings-replacement program to an annuity. This opens up the opportunity to develop Social Security into a double-decker system, including both contribution-related benefits and universal pensions. Such a system would bring more flexibility in increasing the benefits and in financing the program; it would also make for a higher degree of individual equity and rationality in distribution of benefits. In short, the repeal of the earnings test not only would improve work incentives among the elderly but also would bring an opportunity to reform the entire Social Security system.

Empowering Minority Youth

JUDY PRINCE BRETZ

A FAMILY SERVICE agency, a group of inner-city minority youth, and ultimately a city government engaged in a joint five-year struggle which resulted in personal growth, social change, and enhancement of the quality of life for all those involved. Here we shall discuss trends in the social work profession and the family service field which permitted this movement; the social and political context in which it developed; the human service action program itself; and a challenge to those who are delivering services in the 1970s.

Professional social work has had much role transition through the years in relation to its place in delivering services to people. There have been periods when there was over-identification with social reform, and other trends have focused services almost exclusively on intrapsychic functioning of individuals. Jane Addams and Mary Richmond demonstrated the ability to combine concern for "the environment" and "the personality."[1] Even though agencies' bureaucratic systems and professionals' search for prestige[2] currently do not encourage modeling services after the pioneers, different needs within the social structure suggest that some linkage with "foreparents" could be helpful professionally.

In recent years the profession has answered somewhat the cries of minority colleagues. Both education and practice

JUDY PRINCE BRETZ was formerly Counselor/Coordinator of Family Enrichment and Advocacy Services, Family and Child Services, Birmingham, Ala.

[1] Jane Addams, *Twenty Years at Hull House* (New York: Macmillan Co., 1910); Carol H. Meyer, "Purposes and Boundaries—Casework Fifty Years Later," *Social Casework*, LIV (1973), 269.

[2] Richard A. Cloward, "Social Class and Private Agencies," in *Education for Social Work, Proceedings of the Eleventh Annual Program Meeting* (New York: Council on Social Work Education, 1963), pp. 123–44.

have given more emphasis to the needs of black individuals and families. At this point romanticism with black struggles has declined, leaving a more realistic basis for developing new avenues for addressing institutional racism. The complex structure of the urban situation for blacks, other racial and ethnic groups, and whites today emphasizes the need for personal and social change efforts to be directed toward involvement of "the whole" in human service delivery. If professionals do not view a social agency as "a static organization with no play of internal forces," [3] there is currently potential within these systems for the utilization of professional knowledge and skill to bring people together. This is particularly a challenge for family service agencies, with most agencies having clients from all income levels, while many of the management-level jobs and board positions are controlled by the values of the white, middle class.

The energies of management and board are usually directed toward policy decision-making and program maintenance and development rather than to direct involvement with minority struggles. The casework agencies' clients are usually viewed as "recipients of service." Professionals fail to recognize the therapeutic and enrichment value to clients of different socioeconomic backgrounds when opportunities are presented to them to cooperate in social change projects and group experiences. This oversight has resulted in clients being labeled "one of the most neglected sets of human resources in the system." [4] With many mental disorders in urban America currently being associated with boredom and loss of a sense of purpose, a linkage of these individuals could promote opportunities for inner growth and attitudinal change, and aid in the appreciation of the participatory role in a larger and more personal community.

[3] William Schwartz, "Private Troubles and Public Issues: One Social Work Job or Two?" in *The Social Welfare Forum, 1969* (New York: Columbia University Press, 1969), p. 34.
[4] Elliot Studt, "Organizing Resources for More Effective Practice," in *Trends in Social Work Practice and Knowledge* (New York: National Association of Social Workers, 1966), p. 91.

SOCIAL AND POLITICAL FORCES IN THE INNER CITY

Social workers, other helping professionals, and the general public increasingly recognize that urban areas need some type of "help." During the past decade inner-city youth in particular have been viewed as explosive elements by some, while others completely ignored their existence due to the polarization in society. The youths themselves have not been encouraged to value "primary group relationships" (peer group and immediate neighborhood)[5] in their developmental tasks. They have encountered traditional institutions which were more interested in conformity and adjustment to the system than in meeting their needs for stimulation, power, intimacy, interdependence, and "anger outlets." It was only when they turned to instant gratification of those needs through violent actions, drug misuse, and sexual activity that they experienced "concern" from the larger society. Then the available "helping" monies were channeled into band-aid treatment programs or punitive measures. Present dysfunctioning institutional systems and the developmental needs of youth emphasize that intervention strategies must be developed at the individual and agency level as well as at community and societal levels for primary prevention purposes.

Additional crippling factors for these youths were that they were black in a nation with a history of racism; residents of a taxpayer-subsidized housing project; and lived near their peers who had "social utilities" [6]—more specifically, a city-financed recreation facility in their project. Their early socialization processes had conditioned them to believe that they had little control over circumstances affecting their lives. The civil rights movement had given hope to some that change was possible.

[5] Harold L. Wilensky and Charles N. Lebeaux, *Industrial Society and Social Welfare* (New York: Russell Sage Foundation, 1958), chap. 5.
[6] Alfred J. Kahn, "New Policies and Service Models: the New Phase," *American Journal of Orthopsychiatry,* LXV (1965), 658.

In the political arena in this urban area, there had been some shifts in interaction between blacks and the white power establishment since the racial conflicts of the 1960s. While "the commercial-civic elite," protectors of the status quo,[7] continued to control much of the behavior of city administrators, elected officials were at least listening to the needs of black residents. Their ears, however, were mostly tuned to leaders of the black community who were either ministers, persons who were well-established economically, or those who had political aspirations. A grass-roots organization composed of nonvoting age, public housing residents was a new experience both for elected officials and for black leaders. However, with "white flight" to suburbia and the trend in citizen participation shifting away from involvement only of "the elite" who were thought to be "fit to govern," [8] the time was appropriate for any group of residents to find an audience.

HUMAN SERVICE ACTION PROJECT

The Martin Luther King, Jr., Recreation Center opened in Birmingham in the summer of 1977. The physical structure itself symbolized the growth of a group of minority youth, a family agency, and a city. In the early 1970s the family service mobile outreach services moved into the Avondale community because the housing project area had the largest number of children per block of any area of the city; unlike all other housing projects, it had no planned social or recreational services. Because of rivalry between residents of this project and a neighboring one, the youths feared to venture "over there" for recreation, as had been suggested for years by housing officials.

The agency's work in this community was organized somewhat along the same lines as early settlement house pro-

---

[7] Blaine A. Brownell, *The Urban Ethos in the South, 1920–30* (Baton Rouge, La.: Louisiana State University Press, 1975), pp. 47–60.

[8] Helen Harris Perlman, "Social Work Method: a Review of the Past Decade," in *Trends in Social Work Practice and Knowledge*, p. 88.

grams. Community workers recruited teen-agers for two groups which were designed to offer enrichment and educational activities, and possibly social action endeavors, if the group members decided there was a community need. The group leader used weekly discussion sessions to explore personal issues and community concerns. Because most of these youths lacked conviction that they had the power to influence anyone, it was conceivable to the outreach team that using peer discussions about everyday concerns, exposing the young people to new opportunities, and broadening their information base could promote changed attitudes about themselves and different behavior in relation to community systems. This was first realized through an effort which involved them in documenting their exclusion from certain school courses and from extra grade points in required courses because they were unable to pay school fees. After the outreach team had confronted the local principal with the students' problem, he agreed to resolve it for them. However, to assure that their new freedom did not result in increased pressure on other students to help fund the public school system, the outreach team involved the agency's advocacy committee (board, staff, and volunteeers) in a broader strategy which ultimately linked them with the state attorney general's office in order to eliminate the discriminatory—and unusual—practice of charging fees in public schools throughout the state.

The teen-agers also took a trip to a national park where they learned from an agency volunteer that "this land is our land." With such activities their sense of isolation and powerlessness diminished, and they developed a group perception that change could be possible through united action. At the completion of the group discussions, they decided to band together with a few parents to let others know their need for a place to play, setting a comprehensive recreation program as their ultimate goal.

Within the context of community change strategies studied by Perry, this minority group used a mixture of cooperation and conflict.[9] Initially, their approach was one of cooperative action (petitioning, telephoning, and writing officials). Even the choice of organizational name—Pushers for Recreation for Avondale Youth (PRAY)—denoted that they did not wish to alienate those "in control" but neither were they to be considered "pushovers." After they were shuffled for months from one city administrator to another, with "no funds" and "no land" ringing in their ears, they began to recognize the technique of "passing the buck." They finally decided to keep pursuing their game strategy, hoping that other persons would eventually recognize the absurdity of the situation. They also accepted the promises of the housing management to designate a vacant apartment as a recreation center. However, that solution did seem inappropriate for 1,000 kids, and they resented such measures which were designed to divert them from their comprehensive plan. This was particularly felt when a newly arrived housing administrator offered to give them tennis lessons and simultaneously suggested that they refrain from further agitating about their rights. PRAY members also experienced the disappointment of the news media's failure to keep their promise to assist them in dramatizing their plight—an overcrowded apartment/recreation center with only a few table games.

When they took their case to the City Council, they were again referred to heads of city departments; but they recognized a commitment on the part of some council members to equitable distribution of resources and a desire for city agencies to integrate services. One black council member came to a PRAY strategy meeting, at their request, and advised and encouraged them to keep pushing. When the council told PRAY that a recent city-financed recreation study indicated that the Avondale community had a declining rate of population, the teen-agers documented the fact that the housing project area had been overlooked in the main study but had

[9] Lorraine R. Perry, "Strategies of Black Community Groups," *Social Work*, XXI (1976), 210–15.

been included (via the outreach team) as a priority in another section of the study's recommendations.

The frustrations of dealing with bureaucrats and the political process were educational as well as supportive of group cohesion and stimulated creative thinking. PRAY considered such disruptive techniques as bouncing balls in City Council chambers until their message was heard. When they attended a city meeting to help develop a comprehensive citizen participation plan, PRAY distributed a flier designed to counter a rumor that they were "a bunch of loud children without a leader" by identifying themselves as representing "families from which come our leaders."[10]

PRAY had regular meetings, which included at least one representative from the agency, to evaluate its activity, analyze social and political dynamics, and plan its next strategy. To build individual self-confidence and develop appreciation for each other's abilities and limitations, the group sessions utilized a shared decision-making approach. There was equitable distribution of tasks (the chair position rotated monthly). When individuals (such as a community resident with political aspirations) attempted to impose plans for action, the group politely explained their philosophy of utilizing democratic procedures in pushing for change.

Pressing for a recreation center was not PRAY's only activity. There was collaboration with various disciplines (law, business, teaching, recreation, and the humanities) in order to promote group solidarity, meet immediate needs of members, and offer enrichment activities for their neighborhood. For instance, they sponsored a carnival which included production of a skit, "Know Your Rights with the Police." An attorney from the Civil Liberties Union of Alabama followed up with a discussion whose purpose was to promote individual rights, to bridge the gap between the criminal justice system and minorities, and to use the arts as a creative means of

[10] From flier which was produced by PRAY and distributed at the Municipal Auditorium, Birmingham, April 1, 1974.

expressing feelings. Some PRAY members did volunteer work at a recycling center, joining forces with environmentalists who were also trying to gain support from the city. The young people also participated in voter registration; elected one of their members to a new neighborhood committee which was to have an impact on planning for use of federal community development monies; served as inner-city resources for a federal recreation agency; helped to document managerial problems within the housing authority for the family agency's coalition; and one member was elected to the agency's board.

PRAY began to consider itself as performing a "watchdog role"[11] over city government (discovering from the Department of Housing and Urban Development that the housing authority had misled tenants for years about their "play eligibility" in the neighboring project). PRAY recognized that the City Council was learning to value that watchdog role when it discovered that over five hundred thousand unspent dollars had been returned to the city by the housing authority in 1956, at the time the Avondale project had been constructed. It was out of these funds that the council decided that PRAY's community would get a recreation program. The new building would also allow the neighboring elementary school to receive accreditation and the project residents to have a rental office in their area.

However, at the completion of their struggle PRAY continued to have "image" problems with parts of the "outside" world. When the city decided to seek help from PRAY and black leaders in planning the opening ceremony for the center, a PRAY member overheard remarks from the leaders that they should not be at city hall when school was in session. There was also a rumor that the recreation department thought it would have problems staffing the center in such a "bad" neighborhood. In sorting through both concerns in

[11] Daniel Thurz, "The Arsenal of Social Action Strategies: Options for Social Workers," *Social Work*, XVI, No. 1 (1971), 33.

their final group meeting, it was decided that they could deal with both issues in their official statements on opening day. They did so by paralleling their struggle with that of Martin Luther King's and stressing that it was through his earlier "example of hope" and their "youthful determination" and continued "commitment to nonviolence" that they were able to present the facility to their community.[12]

During the PRAY struggle the family agency took a behind-the-scenes role, providing consultation and tangible support. This included serving as the group's broker; mobilizer of resources; printer; interpreter of social and political changes; transporter to meetings; group facilitator, on request; and counselor for individuals. This was accomplished by the outreach team's expanding its resources by securing help from board members, agency consumers, and persons from other disciplines. The outreach team met weekly, drawing heavily on the Barker and Briggs model of team service delivery.[13] The team meetings also included the agency executive and the program supervisor for outreach projects in order to integrate various activities, to assist all in maintaining "a feeling knowledge"[14] of the situation for minorities, and to promote consistency in goals. This "street learning" with minorities was transmitted to the agency's casework program, which had simultaneously experienced an increase in requests for help from minorities. The casework clients who chose to support PRAY's efforts were inspired by the group's creativity and "fidelity,"[15] thus enhancing their own effort at personal change. Therefore, this experience, which brought together and strengthened the agency's casework, enrichment, and advocacy efforts, also

[12] Remarks made by William Thigpen, Keith Durden, and Wayne Dansby, members of PRAY, at the opening ceremonies of the Martin Luther King, Jr., Recreation Center, Birmingham, July 3, 1977.

[13] Robert Barker and Thomas Briggs, *Using Teams to Deliver Social Services* (Syracuse, N.Y.: Syracuse University Press, 1969).

[14] Perlman, *op. cit.*, p. 91.

[15] Erik Erikson, "Youth: Fidelity and Diversity," *Daedalus*, XCI (1962), 15–27.

improved social relationships between individuals in an agency and in a community—giving all involved a larger voice in community affairs.

CHALLENGE TO HUMAN SERVICES

In the experience of the Birmingham family service agency, the type of social work practiced in empowering this group of minority youth was effective in benefiting the youth themselves, the sponsoring agency, and the community at large. This model, which demonstrates the value that advocacy can have when it draws on, and contributes to, existing services to individuals and families has several implications for the field of human services. Social workers and other helpers need to recognize and develop interventive measures to utilize the multiple resources of human energy which are available to them. Along with the appreciation of diversity and flexibility, they need skill in facilitating a process which promotes the interdependence of many individuals and service disciplines within agencies and the broader community. This calls for a reaffirmation of self-determination as a major factor in planning and delivering services, and an ability to maximize opportunities in exploration of alternatives so that persons involved can choose with integrity their own way of attaining their own ends. At this time of broad social changes and problems within traditional institutions, helping disciplines must assist individuals, families, and organizations to use citizen participation to its fullest potential. The creation of new arrangements is necessary to humanize urban society. Such arrangements should support rather than constrict on-the-spot creativity; enable any individual to perform a participatory role in community life; assist in the completion of developmental tasks; and connect individuals with the total human family.

Juvenile Delinquents After Release

WILLIAM H. BARTON

WHAT HAPPENS TO young people who have spent time in a juvenile correctional program? If the rehabilitation and social protection goals of these programs are being met, the youths should fit into the mainstream of society, lead productive, satisfying lives, and, presumably, cease engaging in troublesome or law-violative behavior. How can we tell if these goals are being met? One way is to conduct extended, longitudinal, follow-up research with youths released from juvenile correctional programs. Such research would ideally focus on all aspects of the youths' lives in an attempt to measure their over-all adjustment.

RECIDIVISM AS AN OUTCOME MEASURE

Longitudinal research would be lengthy and prohibitively expensive, even assuming that one could adequately put it into operation and isolate the variables which would reflect the effect of the juvenile correctional programs. Consequently, most attempts to evaluate the programs have relied on recidivism as a simple indicator of success or failure. Recidivism data get right to the heart of the public concern for delinquency control and are relatively easy to obtain from police records.

WILLIAM H. BARTON is a Teaching Assistant, School of Social Work, University of Michigan, Ann Arbor.

The original research from which this follow-up study was derived was the National Assessment of Juvenile Corrections, Robert Vinter and Rosemary Sarri, co-directors, completed under grant numbers 75 NI-99-0010 and 76 JN-99-0001 from the National Institute of Law Enforcement and Delinquency Prevention Operations Task Force, both in the Law Enforcement Assistance Administration, U.S. Department of Justice. The follow-up was directed by Rosemary Sarri. Points of view or opinions expressed are those solely of the author.

Concern with recidivism also reveals an implicit assumption that the causes of delinquency, or deviance in general, inhere in the individual. In one version of this assumption, deviance is seen as something the individual has, like a disease, perhaps as a result of personality defects or inadequate socialization. Juvenile correctional programs, then, are designed to resocialize the youth into conventional patterns of behavior. From this perspective, a subsequent appearance on police records indicates a failure of that enterprise: the "patient" has not been "cured". Another version suggests that the deviant individual is morally deficient. Juvenile correctional programs are thus viewed not so much as treatment facilities, but as just punishment designed to exact penance from offenders and deter others who might be tempted to stray from the moral path. Recidivism thus indicates that the sinner has not been sufficiently penitent. Although admittedly exaggerated here, the idea of the delinquent as patient or sinner is reinforced by the emphasis on recidivism data in program evaluation.

Limitations of recidivism. Usually, recidivism means that an individual has been adjudicated by social control personnel as having committed more than one offense. If we ignore for the moment the occasional false arrest, recidivism means that offending behavior has been committed by the individual, has been detected, has been judged sufficiently troublesome to warrant official action, and has resulted in a formal disposition. Clearly, recidivism is determined by a complex interaction of the behavior of witnesses or victims, police, and judges as well as that of the offending individual.

It is equally clear that not every instance of offending behavior results in an official record of delinquency. From a national survey, Williams and Gold[1] presented data which indicated that about 80 percent of all youths engage in at least some form of delinquent behavior, but only a small percentage become officially delinquent. Furthermore, those who

[1] Jay Williams and Martin Gold, "From Delinquent Behavior to Official Delinquency," *Social Problems,* XX (1972), 209–29.

become officially delinquent are not a random sample of those who engage in delinquent behavior. To be sure, the more frequent and serious the behavior, the more likely it is that a person will become officially delinquent. However, other factors, such as sex, race, and social class, may also affect the process of transforming delinquent behavior into official delinquency.

It is not unreasonable to suggest that an individual's prior correctional history may influence the behavior of other people at various points in the process. This is one of the key propositions of the labeling theory of deviance. Given the knowledge that an individual has just been released from a juvenile correctional program, others, such as the police, may watch that person closely, thereby increasing the probability of detection of delinquent behavior. They may also interpret instances of delinquent behavior as more serious than they would otherwise be interpreted, thereby increasing the probability that the behavior will lead to formal processing. Similarly, judges may view such behavior as indicative of a pattern consistent with the prior disposition, thereby increasing the probability of subsequent assignment to a correctional program. In other words, a youth released from a correctional program not only has to be "good," he has to be "better" than most of his peers in order to avoid recidivism.

Recidivism, then, is an inadequate measure of program effectiveness because it is determined by a complex set of factors many of which are independent of the program itself. In addition, the effects of the experience may operate at cross purposes. On the one hand, the program may reduce an individual's propensity to engage in delinquent behavior but at the same time may affect the behavior of others, making it more likely that they will judge the individual as delinquent in the future and restrict the opportunities available to him. Recidivism data are also inadequate because, in themselves, they give us no suggestions for programs and policies which might lead to improved outcomes.

Alternatives to recidivism. Instead of, or in addition to, focusing upon the subsequent offending behavior of youths released from correctional programs, we can look at adjustment more broadly. In what kinds of living situations do released youths find themselves? Are they in school? If so, how are they faring? Do they have jobs? If so, what kinds of jobs? The answers to these kinds of questions would provide a good indication of the immediate environment. It may be hypothesized that it is the nature of this immediate environment that will affect their subsequent engagement in delinquent behavior more importantly than the more remote nature of their correctional experience. Of course, that experience may facilitate or hinder their over-all adjustment. The answers may also provide clues as to the kinds of programs and policies that might best serve youth and society. These are the questions we asked in a follow-up study in a national sample of juvenile correctional programs.

THE FOLLOW-UP STUDY

Between 1973 and 1975 the National Assessment of Juvenile Corrections (NAJC) research project, directed by Robert Vinter and Rosemary Sarri, selected forty-two juvenile correctional programs in sixteen states throughout the country. Details of the sampling procedure may be found in NAJC reports.[2] These programs included institutions, group homes, and day treatment programs. Although many other kinds of data were also collected, we are mainly concerned here with information obtained from the 1,837 youths who completed an extensive questionnaire. Most of them (81 percent) voluntarily provided an address where they thought they could be reached at a later date. In early 1976 an attempt was made to make contact with these young people for a follow-up study. As might be expected, given the passing of time and the high mobility of that age group, relatively few could be reached. Follow-up questionnaires were sent to 383

[2] Robert Vinter, Theodore Newcomb, and Rhea Kish, *Time out: a National Study of Juvenile Correctional Programs* (Ann Arbor, Mich.: University of Michigan, National Assessment of Juvenile Corrections, 1976).

youths whose addresses were verifiable. As in the original study, they were assured of the confidentiality of their responses. Only 192 returned questionnaires were sufficiently complete to be used.

Although this return rate represents merely 12 percent of the original sample, it was felt that analysis of the data would be worthwhile for several reasons. To begin with, it is so rare to have access to a national sample that any data should be of some interest. Second, there is reason to believe that the subsample who returned follow-up questionnaires was reasonably representative of the original sample. Using data from the original questionnaire, we compared this subsample with the youths for whom we had no follow-up data on a number of variables which one might expect to be predictive of future adjustment. Those who returned follow-up questionnaires did not significantly differ from the rest in race, sex, or age. Nor did they differ on measures of prior delinquent behavior or prior contact with the juvenile justice system. Finally, all of the forty-two programs were represented by at least one follow-up response, and the same percentage of youths (78 percent) who returned follow-up questionnaires had been in institutions (as opposed to group homes or day treatment programs) as was true of the rest of the youths. (A more detailed account of this comparison as well as a more extensive report of the follow-up study may be found in Barton and Sarri.[3])

Selected results. Our first question concerned the living situations of the youths at the time of the follow-up. Fifty-eight percent lived with one or both parents, relatives, or foster parents. Twenty-four percent were living more independently, with spouses, friends, or alone. A few, 5 percent, did not respond to the question. Finally, 13 percent were still or again in institutions or group homes. These latter youths are excluded from the rest of the analyses, leaving 159 youths

---

[3] William H. Barton and Rosemary Sarri, "Where Are They Now? A Follow-up Study of Youth in Juvenile Correctional Programs," *Crime and Delinquency* (forthcoming).

who were not in correctional programs at the time of the follow-up.

Concerning the major conventional activities for this age group, 28 percent of the released young people reported that they were in school, 40 percent had a job, and 16 percent were in a job-training program. Several were involved in more than one of these activities. Most important, fully 38 percent were neither in school, in a job-training program, nor working. Let us refer to these youths as *unoccupied* and the others as *occupied*.

Considering the occupied youths first, we may ask about the quality of their work or school experiences. Most of those who had been released, nearly 70 percent, have been employed, either full time or part time, at least once since their release. About half of these (34 percent of all released youth) have had two or more jobs. Since only 40 percent were employed at the time of the follow-up and so many have had more than one job, we can conclude that their job situations tend to be unstable. In addition, few appear to have jobs that show much promise for the future. The most commonly mentioned full-time jobs were factory work, waiter, waitress, and construction work. The most frequently mentioned part-time jobs were waiter, waitress, and babysitter.

Nearly two thirds of the youths who are in school claim that their grades are better than before they went to their correctional program. Forty-two percent of those in school say that they plan to go to college within the next two years. Yet 40 percent report that they have been suspended from school at least once since they have been released, and about one in four claim that they have skipped school ten or more times. Thus, many youths continue to find school a difficult or unrewarding experience after release.

Although their work or school experiences may leave much to be desired, the occupied youths at least have some connection to conventional society. What about the unoccupied youth? Their status is not a side effect of the length of time since their release. Both the occupied and the unoccupied respondents averaged about twenty months between release and the follow-up contact. Nor are these unoccupied youths simply lazy. Only 10 percent report that they have not tried to get a job. On the other hand, unoccupied youths are twice as likely to say that they have had trouble getting a job. More than half have had at least part-time employment since their release, but the fact remains that at the time of the follow-up they were not working. Lack of motivation or lack of effort does not appear to explain their unoccupied status.

When unoccupied and occupied youth are compared in terms of a number of background variables, delinquent behavior items, and correctional contact items, a disturbing pattern begins to emerge (see table). Unoccupied youths are significantly more likely than their occupied peers to be nonwhite and to have been released from a closed institution. The two groups do not differ in terms of self-reported engagement in delinquent behavior prior to going to the correctional programs in which we first got in touch with them. They do differ in the amount of previous correctional contact they reported, with unoccupied youths reporting significantly more times in jail and in court. However, there was no difference between the groups in the percentage committed for relatively serious offenses to person or property. Since their release, more unoccupied youths report that they have gotten high on drugs or run away from home, but the groups do not differ in other forms of delinquent behavior. Differences in amount of correctional contact continue to be observed after their release, as significantly more of the unoccupied youths report being arrested and appearing before a judge.

Unoccupied youth do not seem to be "harder core" in terms of their past behavior or commitment offenses than the occupied youth. They have had as much time as occupied youth to find jobs, have tried to get them, but have experienced more difficulty obtaining them. Since they are more likely to be nonwhite, to have been released from institutions, and to have had prior correctional contacts as well, one is

Comparison of Occupied and Unoccupied Youth

	Percent	
	Occupied	*Unoccupied*
Background Characteristics		
Male	61	67
Nonwhite	34	52 [a]
Lower class [b]	53	67
Program Type		
Institution	71	87 [a]
Prior Delinquent Behavior		
Robbed someone	43	43
Been suspended from school	45	50
Ran away from home more than once or twice	61	66
Prior Correctional Contact		
Been in jail more than twice	22	35 [a]
Been in court more than twice	59	71 [a]
Reason for Commitment to Correctional Program		
Person or property offenses	49	49
Delinquent Behavior in Last Month		
Got high on drugs	42	72 [a]
Hurt someone physically	23	32
Shoplifted or stole	21	26
Ran away from home	2	15 [a]
Correctional Contact Since Release		
Been arrested	32	49 [a]
Been before a judge	34	56 [a]
Been convicted of a crime	23	35
N (in range) [c]	(74–98)	(48–61)

[a] $p < .05$, tested by chi-square.
[b] Social class measured by father's occupation.
[c] The number of responses varies greatly across items.

tempted to conclude that stigmatization based upon race and/or reputation may have played a role in determining their unoccupied status. The fact that they continue to be more likely than occupied youths to report correctional contact after their release, when the only behavioral differences concern victimless, retreatist activities, suggests that these unoccupied young people are being harassed by agents of social control.

Results such as those reported here underline the inadequacy of simple recidivism data for program planning and evaluation. It is quite likely that the unoccupied youths will show higher recidivism rates than the occupied ones. Yet it appears that neither the youths themselves nor the specific correctional programs can be cited as the source of such recidivism, which means that neither the disease nor the sinner model is applicable. Rather, the recidivism would appear to be the result of a combination of past and concurrent labeling of these youths by their social environment.

Such results reinforce with data what many people already know by intuition. Programs must be developed in communities to assist released youths in their attempts to develop nondeviant patterns of behavior. They cannot be expected to leave a juvenile correctional program and successfully adapt to school or work settings without assistance and continued support.

It is recommended that programs try to obtain the kinds of follow-up data discussed here on a continuing basis to assist in planning and evaluation.

Pennsylvania's Mental Health Procedures Act and Children's Services

SUZANNE STENZEL and ANITA BRYCE

In RESPONSE TO litigation and the national trend stressing deinstitutionalization and procedural due process safeguards,[1] Pennsylvania revised its mental health act after ten years and passed the Mental Health Procedures Act, which became effective in October, 1976. The *Bartley* v. *Kremens* case was still pending, and the new act reflects the concern with children's rights regarding involuntary commitment procedures, the primary issue raised by *Bartley* v. *Kremens*.[2]

Events which have significantly affected the mental health delivery system for children fall into three broad and interrelated contexts: funding, legal development, political support.

FUNDING

A review of the funding for mental health services begins with the termination of federal staffing grants to community mental health centers and the failure of state or county funds to replace the loss. The loss of federal funds precipitated the

SUZANNE STENZEL is Director, Continuing Education, School of Social Work, University of Pittsburgh, Pittsburgh.
ANITA BRYCE is Social Worker, Children's Inpatient Unit, St. Francis Hospital, Pittsburgh.
[1] John P. Panneton, "Children, Commitment, and Consent: a Constitutional Crisis," *Family Law Quarterly*, X (1977), 295.
[2] *Ibid., p.* 299.

cutback in prevention services and reversed the trend toward decentralization of services within catchment area programs.[3] The cutback in prevention services has reduced the opportunity for early detection and intervention which can be of particular benefit to mentally ill children.[4] Reversal of the decentralization trend reduces the accessibility of services and falls more harshly on children, who are less mobile than adults.

Funding at the state level is equally disappointing. The allocation for mental health has not kept pace with the rising cost of service delivery. Pennsylvania's mental health allocation has been at a standstill for the last five years. In 1978 catchment area programs suffered additional cutbacks in funding, with losses as high as 8 percent of the 1977 budget. Similar cutbacks for county-wide special services for children range from $30,000 to $100,000 losses which have forced the furloughing of staff. Simultaneously, the new act prescribes functions such as court hearings, treatment planning and evaluation, and case monitoring which either add to the cost of providing service or force the reduction of time and staff available for direct treatment. The Mental Health Procedures Act did not include appropriations for the added functions it mandated for both the mental health and the justice systems.[5] The new act requires that both systems do more with less. The funding picture reflects the political context.

Essentially, the political situation in Pennsylvania reverberates with the familiar refrain of a legislature facing an election year, and therefore the legislators are campaigning on the basis of their refusal to pass a tax increase.[6] The state budget was delayed for months. When it was finally passed a small tax increase was necessary in order to maintain existing services. The only strong political initiative in the mental health arena was the active support for legal procedural re-

---

[3] Interviews with catchment area personnel.

[4] James W. Ellis, "Volunteering Children: Parental Commitment of Minors to Mental Institutions," *California Law Review*, LXII (1974), 840, 908.

[5] Paul A. Lundeen, "Pennsylvania's New Mental Health Procedures Act," *Dickinson Law Review*, LXXXI (1977), 627.

[6] Speech by Senator Coppersmith.

form of the state's 1966 Mental Health Act. The legal reforms instituted by the new act are neither new nor innovative from either a national or a state perspective. Similar acts
exist in other states, and piecemeal revisions of Pennsylvania's 1966 act began as early as 1971 through departmental
regulations and the court's decision in *Dixon* v. *Commonwealth
of Pennsylvania*. The new act is to some degree consonant
with the hold-the-line budget strategy of the legislature in
that the law makes it more difficult to get into the state's
mental health hospitals, limits commitments to the hospitals
to ninety days, and reduces the number of groups previously
included under the act's coverage. The new act excludes the
senile, the drug dependent, and the alcoholic. To some extent, then, the new act can be read as a strategy to reduce
state spending for mental health services.[7] This strategy is
particularly detrimental to the community program because
institutionalized patients are discharged into the community
with greater frequency. From the perspective of the community mental health program it is interesting to compare the
1966 act with that of 1976. There is a major difference in
emphasis. The 1966 act was concerned with establishing an
array of community-based services. The major values
stressed were accessibility, availability, and continuity of
care.[8] The 1976 act stresses the procedures which determine
who shall receive care, under what conditions, where, by
whom, for how long, and under what criteria.[9]

The legal context includes the debate over children's rights
when the loss of liberty is possible. The debate has gathered
momentum since *in re* Gault was decided by the Supreme
Court in 1967.[10] In Pennsylvania added emphasis in the new
act of 1976 was further accentuated by the fact that *Bartley* v.
Kremens was awaiting Supreme Court review. The major
changes in Pennsylvania's new act with respect to children's
services are as follows:

[7] Lundeen, *op. cit.*
[8] Mental Health and Mental Retardation Act of Pennsylvania, 1966.
[9] Mental Health Procedures Act of Pennsylvania, 1976.
[10] Ellis, *op. cit.*, p. 849.

1. The age at which a juvenile may request, on his/her own initiative, voluntary admission to an inpatient facility has been lowered from eighteen to fourteen.

2. The criterion of possible danger to self or others within the past thirty days has been substituted for that of mental illness as the basis for determining the necessity for involuntary commitment.

3. Procedural due process safeguards all juveniles fourteen years of age or older. The procedural protections include:

a) Timely notice
b) The right to a hearing in Juvenile Court
c) The right to independent counsel
d) The right to an independent psychiatric evaluation
e) The right to present evidence and testimony
f) The right to cross-examination
g) The right to a copy of the written decision and the reasons supporting that decision.

4. Other major changes limited the role of psychiatrists in commitment decisions and increased the role of lawyers, clients, and the court.

5. The new act seeks to organize the flow of service to clients in a time-limited sequence: "emergency detention (3 days); inpatient (20 days); institutional commitment (90 days)."[11]

The broad policy trend embodied in both judicial decisions and in the deinstitutionalization movement is the protection of personal liberty. Legal impetus for this trend has come from the decisions of cases (*in re* Gault, *Donaldson* v. *O'Connor, Bartley* v. *Kremens,* and *Lessard* v. *Schmidt*) as well as from legislation like the Lanterman-Petris-Short Act and Pennsylvania's Mental Health Procedures Act.[12] A somewhat balancing and a somewhat conflicting trend can be seen in the legal decisions of cases such as *Wyatt* v. *Stickney* which stress the

---

[11] Mental Health Procedures Act of 1976.
[12] Robert Roos and Terri Ellison, "The Mentally Ill Juvenile Offender," *Juvenile Justice,* XXVII (1976), 4.

right to treatment.[13] The issue of balance and/or conflict is also reflected in the policy statement of the new act which asserts that the purpose of the act is to provide adequate care in the least restrictive setting possible and to provide procedural safeguards to those facing the prospect of involuntary commitment.[14] These two goals inevitably conflict as lawyers seek to preserve liberty and physicians seek to provide care. The legal balancing act is dynamic and not yet fully resolved by a decisive Supreme Court holding which sets forth the limits of the state's duty to provide treatment as against its obligation to protect liberty.[15] Under Pennsylvania's law it is quite possible to process mentally ill children with the correct legal protections fully observed and still produce anomalous results from the perspective of the child's mental health needs. Thus the conflict between liberty and treatment is not resolved, it is simply deferred. This result is most starkly apparent with children who are mentally ill but not dangerous. The struggle between the legal profession and the medical profession in the mental health arena involves a clash of values and the differences in training of the two professions. Defense of freedom vs. delivery of service is not an easy either/or choice. Lawyers are trained to protect liberty beyond doubt; psychiatrists are trained to treat children with an eye to prevent future deterioration.

DATA PRESENTATION

Methodology. The data presented here come from the case records of children and adolescents treated at the short-term inpatient units of St. Francis Hospital in Pittsburgh. St. Francis has the largest of the two children's inpatient units in the Allegheny County mental health system. Since Act 143 was implemented in October, 1976, seventy-nine children ages two to twelve have been treated in the unit at St. Fran-

[13] Alexander D. Brooks, *Law, Psychiatry, and the Mental Health System* (Boston: Little, Brown, and Co., 1974), p. 845.

[14] Lundeen, *op. cit.*

[15] Alan A. Stone, "Overview: the Right to Treatment; Comment on the Law and Its Impact," *American Journal of Psychiatry*, CXXXII, No. 11 (1975), 1129.

cis. Information was collected from these case records and compared with the records of the seventy-nine children treated at the same facility immediately prior to implementation of the act. The ages of the children, area of the county from which they were referred, and the treatment dispositions were analyzed to ascertain any significant differences in the two populations.

In the adolescent unit at St. Francis 127 cases have been treated since the implementation of the act. Data collected from these clinical records were compared to the data from the 127 cases treated immediately prior to implementation of the act. St. Francis has the only short-term inpatient unit for adolescents in Allegheny County. Again the ages, area of referral, and treatment dispositions were analyzed to ascertain significant differences in the two populations. There were no significant differences in the ages of the children or the adolescents or in the area of referral.

Five types of disposition plans are available to those who are discharged from the St. Francis facility:

1. Discharge from inpatient unit and admission to the partial hospitalization program
2. Discharge to the child's home with referral to a specialized class within the community public school system or special mental health system educational classes
3. Discharge to a child welfare facility, such as a group home, institution, or shelter which has a therapeutic emphasis
4. Discharge to a state hospital for longer-term inpatient care
5. Discharge against medical advice (A.M.A.). The hospital has no further involvement with the child or family following an A.M.A. discharge.

Data. The results of the information regarding discharge decisions obtained from the 156 children's records examined for 1975 and 1976 are seen in Table 1.

Table 2 summarizes the data on dispositions gathered

Table 1

Children's Discharge Dispositions

	Partial	Home/Special Class	Child Welfare	State Hospital	A.M.A.
Before Act 143	43	20	7	4	4
After Act 143	44	11	15	5	3

from a review of 256 records of adolescents seen prior to and after Act 143 on the St. Francis unit.

As can be observed from Table 1, there has been a doubling of the discharges that were made to child welfare prior to Act 143. There has also been a significant increase in the number of adolescents (Table 2) committed to a state hospital—the number has more than doubled. There has been an increase in the number of adolescents referred to a child welfare facility, but perhaps most disconcerting is the drastic increase in the number of adolescents discharged A.M.A. These discharges represent adolescents exercising their new rights to sign themselves out of the hospital against their psychiatrist's advice. It should be noted in regard to Table 1 that only one state facility that provides long-term care to children is available to Allegheny County residents. This facility is always full and has a substantial waiting list as do the two St. Francis units. There are countless unrecorded treatment dispositions based on the knowledge that the units at St. Francis are full, as is the only children's long-term care facility. We are aware of these dispositions, openly regarded as less than ideal, as a result of many interviews conducted with children's unit outpatient staff. There is only one other chil-

Table 2

Adolescents Discharge Dispositions

	Partial	Home/Special Class	Child Welfare	State Hospital	A.M.A.
Before Act 143	54	43	15	9	6
After Act 143	49	23	24	19	14

dren's short-term inpatient facility in Allegheny County, but changes in program, area of referral, and staffing changes precluded obtaining comparable data. Moreover, foster placements for mentally disturbed children and adolescents are unavailable in Allegheny County. This alternative is desperately needed, in the opinion of many children's clinicians.

TREATMENT ISSUES AFFECTED BY THE ACT

The criticisms most frequently leveled against the new act by clinicians are that the commitment criterion of dangerousness is irrelevant to many mental illnesses like autism suffered by children, that the commitment procedures neglect any consideration of child development, and finally, that granting procedural due process rights to adolescents fails to consider the complexities of mental illness coupled with the already difficult process of adolescent rebellion against parental control. Clinicians frequently point out that explaining the rights available to adolescents frequently means that their right to be discharged A.M.A. is exercised but that its meaning and consequences are not fully understood. Several clinicians admit that their use of coercive tactics increases in their efforts to retain adolescents in treatment. Another factor that concerns clinicians is that parents will be less likely to seek treatment for mentally ill adolescents now that adolescents have legal rights independent of their parents. Clinicians point out that while the act covers the suicidal or threatening child and adolescent, it does not cover the needs of the phobic, severely depressed, or delusional child suffering from one or another form of schizophrenia. While there is no data base to demonstrate the extent of still another unfortunate by-product of the act, clinicians report that children and adolescents who "belong" in the mental health system wind up in the juvenile justice system because of the lack of early intervention services and because of the financial and legal barriers to short- and long-term care. Finally, clinicians report that the suicidal and homicidal content of children's fantasies, delusions, and verbalizations is increasing. They seriously wonder if this simply means a change in the kind and quality of mental illness occuring in Allegheny County, or whether it is a reflection of the old principle that people's behavior changes on the basis of how it is evaluated. There is no answer at present to this haunting question.

The decision of what to do with children who are mentally ill is not easy or simple to make. Institutionalization can involve stigmatization, dehumanization, loss of liberty, and reinforce sick role behavior.[16] Institutionalization, whether in a local hospital inpatient unit or in a more removed and larger state hospital, cannot guarantee cure of mental illness.[17] The freedom to refute the necessity of commitment, however, may be an empty protection if it means simply the freedom to deteriorate to the point of becoming actually dangerous. Without funding to establish additional community facilities, the freedom of choice available to the most conscientous decision-makers robs this freedom of significant meaning.[18] Dangerousness and procedural due process are standards borrowed from the criminal justice system. Though loss of liberty is possible in both systems, perhaps the transplant is less than appropriate, particularly when applied to children. Advocates for children's mental health services do not necessarily promote the use of the adversary process as a therapeutic tool except in instances of child abuse. Advocates of children's rights are correct in wanting to protect children from abuse and from unnecessary or inappropriate commitments. The issue at hand is whether public policy should lean in the direction of providing adequate care or in the direction of preventing unnecessary commitments. Deinstitutionalization is a substantive goal currently stalled by the lack of funding; it should not be perverted to mean that institutionalization should be made more difficult for those who

[16] Leon Ginsberg, "Civil Rights of the Mentally Ill: a Review of the Issues," *Community Mental Health Journal*, IV (1968), 246.

[17] Carl Buxbaum, "Second Thoughts on Community Mental Health," *Social Work*, May, 1973.

[18] Ellis, *op. cit.*, p. 893.

need it. Legal decisions continue to stress the requirements of due process safeguards, patients' rights, and the standard of dangerousness, yet the most treatable children and adolescents are those who are not dangerous.[19] The law "protects" those most likely to benefit from treatment from securing it, and requires treatment for those most unlikely to benefit from what the treatment system has to offer.

Historically this country has abridged the freedom of individuals and systematically substituted paternalism in the instances of children and the mentally ill on the basis that these individuals are unable to decide rationally for themselves.[20] Have our mentally ill children suddenly become able to exercise rational judgment independently, or do we expect too much of children when we ask them to decide if and when and for how long they might like to be treated?

The mental health system has a long way to go before it lives up to its title; it remains a system of managing illness.[21] Mental illness in children and adolescents produces substantive incapacities that are not cured or ameliorated by granting them rights to safeguard their liberty. The mental health system can be controlled through the law or through the profession of medicine.[22] Underdiagnosis should not be substituted for overdiagnosis as a lesser evil.[23] Either model or profession may gain control of the system, substitute its criteria for decision-making and its reasoning to support and provide the rationale for the systems procedures. The system will survive lawyers and the criminal model as well as it will survive psychiatrists and the medical model. The unresolved issue is whether children, adolescents, and families can continue to look to themselves for answers to the question of what to do with mentally ill juveniles. Who should decide, and what the structure of choice is that confronts those who decide, illustrates the fact that the mental health system for children is still in its infancy.

[19] Stone, *op. cit.*, p. 1131.   [20] Panneton, *op. cit.*, p. 296.
[21] Conversation with Professor Charlotte Dunmore, University of Pittsburgh.
[22] Brooks, *op. cit.*, p. 614.   [23] Ellis, *op. cit.*, p. 865.

Women in a Changing Society

VERONICA G. THOMAS

IN THE LAST fifty-five years one of the most dramatic changes in the American economy has been the increasing number of women entering the labor force. During this period the number has risen from one out of five to two out of five workers. Nearly thirty-seven million women work—that is, 48.8 percent of all American women or approximately 41 percent of the total labor force.

WHY WOMEN WORK

Like men, most women work for economic reasons. Statistics from the U.S. Department of Labor[1] suggest that decisions of individual women to seek employment outside the home are usually based on economic reasons. More important, data suggest that most women in the labor force work because they or their families need the money they can earn. Some women work to raise family living standards above the level of poverty or deprivation; others, to help meet rising costs of food, education for children, and medical care. Relatively few women have the option of working solely for personal fulfillment. Simply put, women work to improve or maintain their standards of living for themselves and their families.

Recent data support this reasoning. Because of rising divorce rates, greater life expectancy, and decreasing real family income, women are forced to assume an even greater economic role. For instance, female-headed families have

VERONICA G. THOMAS is a graduate student, Howard University, Washington, D.C., and an intern, U.S. Department of Labor Job Corps.
[1] U.S. Department of Labor, Employment Standards Administration, *Why Women Work* (Washington, D.C.: U.S. Department of Labor, Women's Bureau, 1976).

increased from 12 percent of all families in 1975 to 14 percent of all families in 1977. Coupled with the fact that only 29 percent of all female-headed families receive some form of public assistance, it implies that the vast majority of these women must work. Moreover, in 1976, 6.9 million women who were either widowed, divorced, or separated from their husbands were compelled to work. The number of working wives increased from 44.4 percent in 1975 to 46.6 percent in 1977. Equally important, nearly 25 percent of their husbands had incomes of less than $10,000.

When marital status is considered by race, the trend is more apparent. Minority wives were more likely to be in the labor force (54.9 percent) than were single minority women (48.5 percent) or those who were widowed, divorced, or separated (45.7 percent). For white women, the trend is somewhat different. The white working wife was less likely to be in the labor force (44 percent) than was the single white woman (61.2 percent), but surprisingly, more likely than the white woman who was divorced, widowed, or separated (39.8 percent).[2] Thus, no matter how it is considered, financial needs remain among the strongest factors that cause women to enter the labor force. Still other reasons have been cited, such as "desiring self-fulfillment" or "desiring to achieve." However, no more than 20 percent of all working women, particularly married women, cited social or psychological reasons.[3]

WOMEN AND JOBS

Despite changing needs and political movements, women are still concentrated in relatively few occupations. For example, in 1973 more than two fifths of all women workers were employed in ten occupations, e.g., secretary, retail sales-

[2] U.S. Department of Labor, Employment Standards Administration, *Minority Women Workers: a Statistical Overview* (Washington, D.C.: U.S. Department of Labor, Women's Bureau, 1977).

[3] Sandra L. Bem and Daryl J. Bem, "Training the Woman to Know Her Place: the Social Antecedents of Women in the World of Work" (Bureau of Instructional Support Services, Pennsylvania Department of Education, 1973).

worker, bookkeeper, household worker, elementary school-
teacher, typist, waitress, cashier, sewer/stitcher, and regis-
tered nurse. Other statistics prepared by the Women's
Bureau of the U.S. Department of Labor indicated that over
three quarters of all women workers were employed in fifty-
seven occupations. Of this total concentration nearly 53 percent were classified as white-collar workers, 25 percent as service workers, and 22 percent as blue-collar workers and/or
farm operatives.

For men, the occupational concentration was significantly
less. The ten occupations in which men were mostly employed accounted for only 20 percent of the total male labor
force. Only 52 percent of the total male labor force were
employed in the fifty-seven largest occupations. Moreover,
78 percent of all women as compared to 40 percent of working men were employed in clerical, service, or factory work
in 1973. In other words, women are still twice as likely to be
crowded into certain industries and/or occupations than are
men.

Recent statistics compiled by the Department of Labor
show that trends in occupational concentration of women
have not changed much. In 1977 women filled at least 80
percent and as much as 99 percent of jobs such as library at-
tendants, secretaries, telephone operators, nurse aides, and
bank tellers. Women remain five times as likely as men to
work in clerical positions and twice as likely to be service
workers outside the home. Women account for nearly 42
percent of all professional and technical workers. However,
this can be misleading. The majority of the women classified
in these categories are teachers and/or health workers. Even
where this is not the case, these women are in low-paying,
entry-level positions with little if any chance for upward mobility.

In sum, the data suggest that although women are increasingly entering the labor force, they are concentrated in low-
status, dead-end jobs and not professional occupations with
well-defined career ladders. Because of socioeconomic fac-

tors attached to women workers, they are forced to accept jobs that are less prestigious and more routine.

Despite these dim facts, there has been a gradual shift by women from so-called "traditional" to "nontraditional" jobs. Typically, traditional occupations are defined as those with more than a 50 percent concentration of women and include elementary schoolteachers, health and clerical workers. Nontraditional occupations are usually defined as those where 30 percent or fewer women are employed. Included in this category are plumbers, carpenters, doctors, and lawyers.

Data from the U.S. Department of Labor indicate that between 1960 and 1970 employment of women increased in almost all of the skilled trades: construction, mechanics and repair, and supervisory blue-collar occupations. In 1970 almost half a million (495,000) women were working in the skilled occupations (crafts and kindred work), up from 227,000 in 1960. In some skilled trades the numerical increase was greater than that for men. For example, the employment of women carpenters increased by nearly 8,000 compared with a growth of fewer than 6,000 male carpenters. The number of women plumbers rose from about 1,000 to 4,000 (0.3 percent to 1.1 percent). Women tool and die makers rose from about 1,100 to 4,200 (0.6 percent to 2.1 percent). Similar gains in employment were made in other skilled trades, such as electricians (0.1 percent to 1.8 percent), auto mechanics (0.4 percent to 1.4 percent), and painters (1.9 percent to 4.1 percent). Women also made some minor gains in predominantly male professions. Employment of women lawyers grew from less than 5,000 (2.4 percent) to more than 12,000 (4.7 percent) between 1960 and 1970. Similar gains were found in the medical profession. From 1960 to 1970 the number of women physicians rose from about 16,000 (0.07 percent) to nearly 26,000 (0.09 percent). Women dentists increased from about 1,900 (2.3 percent) to more than 3,100 (3.4 percent) of all dentists.

The 1977 Household Data Annual Averages compiled by the Women's Bureau of the U.S. Department of Labor in-

dicate that this moderate increase of women in nontraditional occupations has not continued to rise drastically from
the gains of 1970. The number of women physicians, dentists, and related practitioners was only 10 percent in 1977.
Probably the most significant gain was in the legal profession.
In 1977 women were 9.3 percent of all lawyers as compared
to 4.7 percent in 1970. While there has been a modest shift
to nontraditional, higher paying jobs within the last ten
years, these gains were not sufficient to get the majority of
working women out of the low-paying and low-mobility jobs.

FACTORS THAT DIFFERENTIATE TRADITIONAL
AND NONTRADITIONAL WOMEN

In recent research, particularly on professional women, there
have been attempts to identify the factors that differentiate
traditional and nontraditional occupational aspirations.[4]
These studies suggest that women in traditional and nontraditional careers are quite distinct from one another. In
fact, the literature strongly indicates that the characteristics
that differentiate them are mostly personality and motivational. In Tangri's research, the role innovators, as she referred to the nontraditionals, were more autonomous, indi-
vidualistic, and motivated by internally imposed demands to
perform to capacity. Tangri's study also indicated that the
role innovator relies on her own opinions, considers herself
unconventional, and has others depend on her. Almquist
found that nontraditionals differ predictably from tradi-
tionals in terms of familial influences, work values, work experiences, role model influences, and collegiate activities.

[4] Elizabeth M. Almquist, "Sex Stereotypes in Occupation Choices: the Case for the
College Woman," *Journal of Vocational Behavior*, V (1974), 13–21; Elizabeth M. Almquist and Shirley Angrist, "Role Models Influence on College Women's Aspirations,"
Merill Palmer Quarterly, XVII (1971) 263–379; Eva Chunn, "Black Females' Choices
of Traditional and Nontraditional Careers as It Relates to Personal Sex Role Ideology, Perception of Significant Males' Sex Role Ideology, and Perceived Socioeconomic Status" (master's thesis, Howard University, 1976); Martha S. Mednick and
Gwendolyn Puryear, "Motivational and Personality Factors Related to Career Goals
of Black College Women," *Journal of Social and Behavioral Sciences*, XXI (1975), 1–30;
Sandra Tangri, "Determinants of Occupational Role Innovation among College
Women," *Journal of Social Issues*, XXVIII (1972), 177–200.

The nontraditional woman does not show evidence of having identified with her father in preference to her mother as previously suspected[5] or fit the stereotype of a social misfit lacking companionship and uninvolved in "feminine pursuits."[6]

While social class is an important but not a determinate variable accounting for occupational choices among women, its importance varies according to race. For white women, social class was shown to have positive influences on their choices of nontraditional occupations. In general, middle- to upper-income white women were more likely than low-income white women to choose nontraditional jobs.[7] For black women the outcome was somewhat different; that is, social class was not so important in influencing occupational aspirations of traditional and nontraditional careers.[8] Yet despite relatively few differences, Gurin and Epps argue that black and white women are more alike than different in their intentions of working and in the kinds of jobs to which they aspire.[9] On the basis of data, they suggest that only sex-role demands, socialization practices, and patterns of sex discrimination determine "role-appropriate" educational and occupational choices among all women regardless of color. Yet, is this really the case?

HOW DOES THE BLACK WOMAN FIT IN?

Black women are most typically at the very bottom of the occupational pyramid. They earn less than white women, who, in turn, earn less than men either white or black. For black women, race as well as sex composition enters into their definition of traditional and nontraditional careers.[10] While an

[5] Tangri, *op. cit.*, p. 7.   [6] Almquist, *op. cit.*, p. 7.
[7] Almquist and Angrist, *op. cit.;* Tangri, *op. cit.*, p. 7.
[8] Chunn, *op. cit.;* Mednick and Puryear, *op. cit.*, p. 7.
[9] Patricia Gurin and Edgar Epps, *Black Consciousness, Identity, and Achievement* (New York: John Wiley and Sons, 1975), p. 182.
[10] Chunn, *op. cit.*, p. 7; Cynthia F. Epstin, "Black and Female: the Double Whammy," *Psychology Today*, VII, No. 3 (1973), 57–61; Cynthia F. Epstein. "Positive Effects of the Multiple Negative: Sex, Race, and Professional Elites," *American Journal of Sociology*, LXXVIII (1973), 912–35.

occupation such as that of airline hostess is nontraditional for black women, it is traditional for white women.[11] In American society, sex and racial status have cost black women prestigious and high-paying jobs because women and blacks are judged not to be high in potential and/or mental capacity. Thus, they are restricted to "black" and/or "women's" work.

Despite this multiple negative, black women were more likely to be represented in some nontraditional professions in greater proportion to their race than white women. For instance, in 1960 only 7 percent of all white physicians were women while black women accounted for 9.6 percent of black physicians. By 1970, white women accounted for 8 percent of all white physicians while black women were 13 percent of black physicians. Similarly, in 1960, black women made up 8 percent of all black lawyers while white women made up only 3 percent of white lawyers. By 1970, black and white women, respectively, accounted for 11 percent and 5 percent of lawyers in each case. Since blacks, both male and female, have been denied access to professional occupations, race still emerges as the crucial variable that determines the socioeconomic position of black women.

Although black women have more discrimination barriers to overcome to acquire jobs, certain psychological barriers appear to be less evident for black women than for white women when they are pursuing a professional career. One of the typically psychological barriers faced by women is the feeling that one cannot have a career and be a successful woman simultaneously. In other words, a competent and motivated women is caught in a "double bind" which few men have ever faced. If she succeeds in her career, she is judged not to be living up to the social standards of a feminine woman. Defined by Horner as "fear of success"[12]—an expec-

---

[11] Martha S. Mednick, *Motivation and Personality Factors Related to Career Goals of Black College Women* (Springfield, Va.; Manpower Administration, U.S. Department of Labor, 1973).

[12] Matina S. Horner, "Sex Differences in Achievement Motivation and Performance in Competitive and Noncompetitive Situations" (doctoral dissertation, University of Michigan, 1968).

tancy that success in competitive situations would lead to negative consequences—this variable was thought to play an important role in the lives of women but not men. The theoretical connections of fear of success in women have been summarized thus:

Success requires achievement behavior, achievement behavior requires competitive behavior, competitive behavior is a "sublimated" form of aggressive behavior, but aggressive behavior is negatively sanctioned in this society as unfeminine; this conflict thus leads to anxiety and avoidance behavior in situations involving present or future success.[13]

Thus, repression of aggression is part of the gender role socialization of all women, thereby resulting in fear of success.

Defining fear of success as an expectancy that success would lead to negative consequences, Horner argues that such consequences would be reflected in fear of social rejection by both men and women. This conflict was strikingly revealed in a study that required college women to tell a story based on the following cue: "After first-term finals, Ann finds herself at the top of her medical school class."[14] Over 65 percent of the college women either portrayed Ann as anxious or guilty or predicted that her success would have negative consequences, such as loss of femininity and social rejection. In a comparable group of college men responding to a similar cue ("After first-term finals, John finds himself at the top of his medical school class"),[15] less than 10 percent expressed negative themes. The theoretical connections of this argument are unresolved and continued to be researched within the psychology profession after Horner's original study.[16]

[13] David Tresemer, *Fear of Success* (New York: Plenum Press, 1977), p. 35.
[14] Horner, *op cit.*, p. 12.   [15] *Ibid.*
[16] Thelma G. Alper, "Achievement Motivation in College Women: a Now-You-See-It-Now-You-Don't Phenomenon," *American Psychologist*, XXIX (1974), 194–203; Carolyn Breedlove and Victor G. Cicirelli, "Women's Fear of Success in Relation to Personal Characteristics and Type of Occupation," *Journal of Psychology*, LXXXVI (1974), 181–90; Lois W. Hoffman, "Fear of Success in Males and Females: 1965 and

Examining racial differences, Weston and Mednick[17] found that black women showed less fear of success than white women. It is suggested that the high fear of success found in white women was due to the aggressive overtones of intellectual competition needed for success in male-dominated professions, and since aggression has been socially linked to lack of femininity, success in such professions is seen as leading to negative consequences for women. Speculating that success in intellectually competitive situations does not elicit similar fear in black women, Weston and Mednick argue that this may be related to the different sex-role patterns. Because of historical reasons related primarily to racial conflict, black women have had to assume a more dominant role in society in general, and in their families in particular, than white women. For example, a black woman who is a successful wage earner tends to be less fearful of social rejection by men than her white counterpart. More pointedly, because of high unemployment rates and low incomes among black men, black women have a larger share in the economic obligations of the family than do white women. This can be observed on two counts.

First, black women have historically had a higher labor force participation rate than white women. In 1976 the white women's labor force participation rate was 46.9 percent, while the minority women's (89 percent of whom are black women) labor force participation rate was 50.2 percent. As of February, 1978, the white women's labor force participation rate was 48.8 percent, while the participation rate of minority women was 51.9 percent.[18] Examination of these statistics

---

1971," *Journal of Consulting and Clinical Psychology,* XLII (1974), 353–58; Adeline Levine and Janice Crumrine, "Women and the Fear of Success: a Problem in Replication," *American Journal of Sociology,* LXXX (1975), 964–74; C. Tomlinson-Keasey, "Role Variables: Their Influence on Female Motivational Constructs," *Journal of Counseling Psychology,* XXI (1974), 232–37.

[17] Peter Weston and Martha S. Mednick, "Race, Social Class and the Motive to Avoid Success in Women," *Journal of Cross-cultural Psychology,* I (1970), 284–91.

[18] U.S. Department of Labor, Employment Standards Administration, *Women in the Labor Force: February 1978–1979* (Washington, D.C.: U.S. Department of Labor, Women's Bureau, 1978).

also indicates that the differential gap between white women and black and other minority women participation rates in the labor force is gradually closing.

Second, the earnings of black women account for a substantial portion of the total income of their families. For instance, in the last five years, black women contributed at least 33 percent to the total family income, while white women contributed about 25 percent. In short, a successful black woman is an economic asset and thus is attractive rather than threatening to a black man.

In a more recent study[19] on fear of success, the results indicated that fear of success imagery is associated with occupational choices of black women. The purpose of this study was to examine black college women's perceptions of traditional and nontraditional career choices as a function of fear of success imagery, delay of gratification, and risk-taking under two different contexts. Participants were 132 black undergraduate women at Howard University. It was found that black women who exhibited a low fear of success imagery aspired to more nontraditional careers than those who exhibited a high fear of success imagery. This difference expressed itself in the participants' perceptions of the traditionality or nontraditionality of their career choices. It is noteworthy to mention that the over-all level of fear of success imagery of the participants in this study was quite low.

PSYCHOLOGICAL AND SOCIAL IMPLICATIONS

Even if we were able to turn the corner on sex discrimination in the labor market, for example with passage of the Equal Rights Amendment, only half the battle would be won. Discrimination against women represents only a fraction of the problem confronting them in the labor force. The total socialization of the American woman closes off options for her in certain areas. The female role is typically characterized as

---

[19] Veronica G. Thomas, "Black Women's Perceptions of Traditional and Nontraditional Career Choices as a Function of Fear of Success, Delay of Gratification, and Risktaking" (master's thesis, Howard University, 1978).

being oriented toward people, being solicitous, appealing, understanding, and seeking pleasurable responses by giving pleasure to others. This suggests that the woman becomes aware, very early in her life, that if she must work, she should choose an occupation (nurse, elementary school-teacher, social worker) that is consistent with the role that society has designated as "female-appropriate."

Psychologists suggest that between the ages of three and seven a girl has sufficient intellectual development to realize that she is female, and at that point she wishes to act the way females are "supposed" to act. The child does not have to be taught this literally, she figures it out by observing the world about her. Thus it may be argued that the gradually changing roles of women as portrayed in the media may be influential in the adult sex-role ideology of the female child of today.

Not only the sex-role ideology of women needs to be reoriented, but much of the thinking of the many professionals who may be called upon for assistance in this endeavor. Some contemporary clinicians even believe that a healthy women is, among other things, submissive, dependent, noncompetitive, and unaggressive.[20] In order to have careers, women need to become more dominant, independent, adventurous, aggressive, and objective. One should note that in a male, all these qualities would be considered positive traits, yet the same traits in a female bring disapproval from society. Thus, an end to sex discrimination in the labor force is not enough. The psychological and motivational effects of sex-role ideology date much too far back in our society to end so abruptly.

The social implications of women in the work force are massive. Since women are crowded in the lower-paying, entry-level jobs, they are forced to work harder and longer to support themselves and their families. In many instances, women must rely on public assistance to supplement their in-

[20] Inge K. Broverman *et al.*, "Sex-role Stereotypes and Clinical Judgments of Mental Health," *Journal of Consulting and Clinical Psychology*, XXXIV (1970), 1–7.

come in order to meet the rising cost of living. Although this is especially true of minority women, white women are not in much better shape. Many women, especially single parents, have to work part time because of family responsibilities. A possible solution to this problem is the organization of efficient, well-run, well-staffed, child care centers operating twenty-four hours a day and equipped to accept newborn infants, and even sick children. Although this would be a rather expensive solution, it would probably be less expensive than forcing women on public assistance.

The policies and/or strategies for combating the socioeconomic and psychological factors of discrimination are complex. They include governmental and group efforts to eliminate juridical sexism in American society. A major social policy strategy to liberate women is to combat sexism in American education. Schools train people to fit into this society as it exists; therefore their courses reflect the traditional subservient roles that women are expected to play.

From preschool to postgraduate work, girls get a different education from that of boys. They play with dolls more than blocks; they learn to be passive and docile in elementary and secondary school; they are channeled into traditional occupations in high school and college; and they are often passed over when it comes to graduate fellowships. Stacey, Béreaud, and Daniels state in their Introduction:

Schools cannot create a nonsexist world. They can join in the struggle or continue to thwart it. They can either continue to perpetuate the old roles and relationships between women and men, or they can begin to free girls and boys from the rigid and stunting identities that have been imposed by our culture.[21]

Girls must be trained to believe that to be intellectual is not unfeminine. This can only be done by retaining teachers who will treat boys and girls identically when they engage in intellectual and competitive tasks. Teachers, principals, and educators must be aware that they are guilty of "feminizing"

[21] Judith Stacey, Susan Béreaud, and Joan Daniels, *And Jill Came After: Sexism in American Education* (New York: Dell Publishing Co., 1974), p. 29.

girls. A firm commitment should be made to do away with rigid sex distinctions and to make the school experience livelier and more rewarding for all children.

Research suggests that counseling procedures, job recruitment, hiring, and reward systems are eminently structured to discourage women from entering certain occupations. Black women, especially, engender additional discrimination when seeking employment outside the home. Fortunately, women, both black and white, are beginning to demand efforts to end discrimination against them in the labor force. It is time for our society to stop forcing women to think about their inefficiencies as women and encourage them to realize their potentials as human beings. This should be realized not only as an effort to benefit women, but as a concentrated effort to achieve a better society for all Americans.

Ethnic and Racial Variations in Aging

PAULINE K. RAGAN

THERE IS VERY little good research data on the minority aged; even census data leave much to be desired when it comes to studying groups such as the black and Mexican American aged. A research team at the Andrus Gerontology Center, University of Southern California, compiled a bibliography which includes close to every available reference on black and Mexican American aging. The paucity of research data on the Mexican American aged, as reflected in that bibliography, is even more discouraging than that on black aging.[1] Nevertheless, attempts are made in social policy and service delivery to take into account racial differences among the aged, and decisions are based on whatever information and impressions are at hand.

There are at least two hazards in generalizing about the minority aged. First, we often overromanticize the advantages of growing old in a culture, or subculture, that is thought of as more traditional and family-oriented than our own, glossing over the real hardships involved. The second hazard is just the opposite: it is the problem of focusing on

PAULINE K. RAGAN is Research Associate, Andrus Gerontology Center, University of Southern California, Los Angeles.

Data reported here are from the University of Southern California Social and Cultural Contexts of Aging research project (Vern L. Bengtson, Principal Investigator; Pauline K. Ragan, Project Director). This research was supported by grants from the National Science Foundation's (NSF) RANN program (#APR 21178) and by the 1907 Foundation of the United Parcel Service. Conclusions are those of the author and do not necessarily reflect the views of NSF or of the 1907 Foundation.

[1] Pauline K. Ragan and Mary Simonin, *Black and Mexican American Aging: a Selected Bibliography* (Los Angeles: University of Southern California Press, 1977).

the problems and deprivations of the minority aged and
overlooking the resources that they may bring to their aging
experiences.

A selection of recent survey findings may illustrate the corrections that are necessary to both these tendencies. Some of
the findings surprised the researchers. The survey involved
interviews with a probability sample of middle-aged and
older (aged 45 to 74) black, Mexican American, and white
residents of Los Angeles County; the sample of 1,269 was
about evenly divided among these three subpopulations. The
survey was carried out in 1974 by a research team at the Center, in conjunction with a group of minority representatives
who participated in the planning throughout the project.[2]

UNDERESTIMATED PROBLEMS

Our data confirmed the harsh facts about minority aging that
most of us are familiar with: the problems of poverty, housing, transportation, and health. It was in the area of attitudes
and feelings that the survey turned up some unanticipated
problems.

It is frequently suggested that older Mexican Americans
may enjoy some of the advantages of aging in a more traditional subculture in which elders are honored and strong
family ties provide emotional support. In contrast, out of all
the race-by-sex categories in our sample, it was the Mexican
American women (aged 45–74) who were the unhappiest.
More than any other group, they reported feelings of sad-
ness, feelings that life is not worth living, that life is hard. We
tend to expect Mexican Americans in Los Angeles to share
the values about aging of the Mexican culture, in which *los
ancianos* are honored and respected and perform important
roles in the family and community. Nevertheless, on a measure of positive images of aging, although the blacks reported more positive images, Mexican Americans and whites

---

[2] Pauline K. Ragan and Vern L. Bengtson, "Aging among Blacks, Mexican Americans and Whites: Development, Procedures and Results of the Community Survey,"
final report to the National Science Foundation RANN Program, 1977.

were about the same. The statements that made up that measure were:

In most jobs, older people can perform as well as younger people.

Older people can learn new things just as well as younger people can.

People become wiser with the coming of age.

Older people are valuable because of their experiences.

Similarly, on a measure of feelings about one's own aging, Mexican Americans were the least positive; only half as many of the older Mexican Americans (aged 65–74) expressed positive feelings about growing old as older blacks and whites.

The measure of feelings about one's own aging included these questions:

As you get older, do you feel less useful?

Compared to your life today, how happy do you think you will be five or ten years from now?

Compared to your life when you were younger, would you say you feel happier now, not so happy, or about the same?

The empty nest period in the lives of women is often discussed in terms of loss and adjustment, although those assumptions are under reexamination. The corollary assumption is that women in an environment in which important motherly roles are not interrupted will show fewer problems of adjustment. We found that the Mexican American women in our sample indeed were much more likely to have a child under eighteen in the home with them.[3] Middle-aged Mexican American women have had more children than white women and have continued to bear them at later ages, so some of the young children still in the home were theirs. About half of these "full nests," however, were so defined by the presence of grandchildren, nieces, nephews, and children of relatives and friends. The Mexican American women were not happier than the white women, and were somewhat

[3] Teresa Bremer and Pauline Ragan, "A Study of the 'Empty Nest' Patterns in the Lives of Mexican American and White Women" (paper presented to the Western Gerontological Society, 1977).

less happy in certain respects; there was no clear association between the empty nest and morale in these two groups. The highest percentage of Mexican American women reporting that they felt less useful as they grew older was actually found among those older (aged 65–74) women with a child in the home. We were down to small samples at this point in the analysis, but the eight women in this category tended to be Mexican-born, Spanish-speaking, widowed women of low education and income, in poor or fair health, who lived in the homes of their children and grandchildren. Middle-aged and even older Mexican American women were indeed less likely to face the empty nest, but this did not seem to provide a buffer against unhappiness.

Although one third of these individuals had had a parent or parent-in-law living with them at some time, one in four of *these* individuals reported that this was a less than satisfactory arrangement. Ninety percent had seen at least one of their adult children within the previous week, but one third did not see their adult children as often as they would like to; 58 percent did not see their grandchildren as often as they would like. Living arrangements and stated norms about family ties did indeed reflect a closer familial system among the older Mexican Americans, but we should not presume that this system does away with disappointment and unhappiness in old age.

OVERLOOKED RESOURCES

There is no denying the problems that aging blacks are especially faced with, problems such as low income, poor health, poor housing, and the results of a lifetime of discrimination. Nevertheless, to portray the older black as despairing in old age misses some evidence to the contrary. On many measures our middle-aged and "young-old" black respondents reported a comparatively positive outlook.

We asked people what they liked about being the age they were, and distinctive ethnic patterns emerged. Among the older segment of the sample (aged 65–74), typical answers of the Mexican Americans centered on relaxation, home, and family; the mention of "tranquillity" was notable and typified the general pattern of responses. Older whites tended to mention independence, retirement, children, and recreation such as travel; several said that they like "nothing" about this age. On the other hand, a striking and almost stereotypical response among older blacks was satisfaction at having reached this age. One out of five black men and one out of three black women said something like: "God let me stay here as old as I am, strong, being as well as I am. It's a beautiful age, and I'm proud of it." We can appreciate this expression of having survived to old age against greater odds than most of us face. The theme of active involvement also characterized older blacks' responses to this question.

On the measure of positive images of aging, older blacks were more likely to state positive and optimistic views (66 percent) than older Mexican Americans (48 percent) or older whites (41 percent). About two thirds of the older blacks (62 percent) and older whites (63 percent), compared to one third of the older Mexican Americans (34 percent) expressed positive feelings about their own aging.

A number of questions were asked to try to measure morale, or life satisfaction. Blacks in the 45-to-74-year span showed high morale, compared to Mexican Americans and whites of the same age, on questions regarding: feeling that life is not worth living; worrying so much one can't sleep; feeling afraid; and feeling bored.

On the other hand, blacks showed similar or greater problems on questions of: feeling sad; feeling lonely; getting upset easily; things keep getting worse as one gets older; and life is hard. Some of the items on which blacks showed lower morale might be interpreted less as low morale and more as recognition of, and reaction against, a harsh environment.

IMPLICATIONS FOR SOCIAL POLICY AND SERVICE DELIVERY

These findings illustrate the hazards of either underestimating or overromanticizing the resources of a given minority group. If we assume that older Mexican Americans are content and secure within close family networks, and will neither need nor utilize public resources, we will make a great mistake. If we confuse different issues when we analyze the problems of older blacks, we may perpetuate misunderstandings; our data show middle-aged and older blacks to be deprived, to be sure, but not necessarily depressed. (Of course, in all of this analysis, we need to recognize that we are dealing with self-reports of problems and satisfactions. If an ethnic group has a characteristic pattern of answering survey questions with either complaining about or denying problems, the results are less reliable.)

One implication for social policy comes through clearly from our study. There needs to be more focus on intervention in the earlier years in order to prevent some of the problems of aging. We found that the level of education among the middle-aged and older blacks was substantially lower than that among whites, and that the level of education of Mexican Americans was almost unbelievably low. Among the 65-to-74-year-old Mexican Americans, 71 percent of the men and 86 percent of the women had six or fewer years of education. The problems in educational levels of these two minority groups are drastic even when we count only formal years of schooling and do not consider quality of education; it holds true for the younger cohorts, the 45-year-olds, as well as for the older cohorts, so the gap is not going to be closed for some time. We found low education to be strongly implicated in feelings of unhappiness and low morale. The effects are ramified throughout the life cycle in employment, income, health, nutrition, and quality of life in general. We can do more to make up for poor education during the adult years, and we can especially encourage adequate education in childhood to prevent problems of aging in the future. Other preventive policies involve nutrition, health care, dental care, mental health care, facilitating social interaction, and overcoming racial discrimination.

Some of the differences we observed are indeed racial differences, but many directly reflect poverty and low education rather than race, ethnicity, or culture per se. Poor older blacks may have more in common, relevant to social policy, with poor older whites than with affluent older blacks.

Similarly, we should avoid grouping together different racial and ethnic minorities for consideration. Certainly, the various ethnic minorities within the Asian category have been reminding us of this error. We found that on some factors, such as family arrangement and norms, older blacks were very close to older whites and the older Mexican Americans were distinctive. On other factors, such as attitudes toward aging, blacks were distinctive and Mexican Americans and whites were more similar. Each racial or ethnic category must be considered in itself.

When we follow that principle, however, we may make the error of overgeneralizing within racial groups. To perceive older blacks or older Mexican Americans as relatively homogeneous groups would be an error. We find great variations in living standards, family arrangements, health, attitudes, and morale within groups as well as between groups.

There is a great need for more research with blacks and Mexican Americans and with other minority aging groups. The differences and similarities that are revealed help us to understand our own aging better, as well as to serve the special needs of different populations.

Service to Immigrants in a Multicultural Society

MICHAEL D. BLUM

WORKING WITH PEOPLE who come from another country to live in the United States gives us a unique opportunity to see our society through another person's eyes.[1] The immigrant experience is having a renewed and profound effect upon all of us. Social legislation, policy, and practice, as well as concepts of self-awareness, all are being affected. The lessons we can learn from associating with and serving immigrants offer insights which need to be projected.[2] They are insights which can contribute to a more realistic and healthy reevaluation of the direction, development, and implementation of social welfare policy and practice.

Service to immigrants has broad implications for social welfare that directly relate to program emphasis. Program aspects that should be emphasized are those that encourage individual productivity, responsibility, and a sense of self-worth. As new permanent residents continue to come into our country these goals will remain in clear focus. The design of programs will either aid or undermine the orientation toward achievement, and will either build or tear down the sense of self-worth.

Immigrants enter our country wanting to be productive. In most instances they are prepared to work hard, at whatever job, and to achieve self-sufficiency. They are self-reliant. These same attitudes toward work, self-sufficiency, and self-

MICHAEL D. BLUM is Executive Director, Nationalities Service Center of Philadelphia.
[1] Louis Adamic, *A Nation of Nations* (New York: Harper & Brothers, 1944); Colen Greer, ed., *Divided Society* (New York: Basic Books, Inc., 1974).
[2] William S. Bernard, "Opportunity for America," *Common Ground*, Spring, 1947, pp. 50–52.

reliance are often projected as objectives of contemporary welfare programs. Part of the intent of these programs is that the beneficiaries of service will become contributing members of our society. The managers of these programs hope that society at large, which finances these services, will view them as worthwhile and the beneficiaries as responsible and productive.[3]

Immigration is not a phenomenon of the past. We have experienced a 100 percent increase in the number of immigrants since 1965 (about 400,000 per year) as compared with 1924–65 (about 190,000 per year). In addition, the countries from which immigrants come are not the same ones, resulting in a basic ethnic shift in our immigration, away from Europe and in favor of Latin America and Asia. Pressure for emigration from these areas is intense, with several countries having up to two-year waiting periods for issuance of immigration visas. While immigration policy has formidable restrictions, qualitative as well as quantitative, intended to prevent open migration to this country, our present law incorporates four main goals: family reunification, immigration of individuals with needed skills and abilities, asylum for refugees, and control of visitors.[4]

Immigration, then, is a major factor in the growth and development of the United States. The ethnicity of migrant groups has always been a live and vital element for both the migrant and the host society.[5]

A CHALLENGE TO SOCIAL WELFARE POLICY AND PRACTICE

Those of us, both professionals and lay people, involved in the leadership, advocacy, management, and delivery of services for immigrants should be reviewing our goals, objec-

[3] Alfred J. Kahn, ed., "A Policy Base for Social Work Practice: Societal Perspectives," in *Shaping the New Social Work* (New York: Columbia University Press, 1973), pp. 19–21; Peter Marris and Martin Rein, *Dilemmas of Social Reform* (New York: Atherton Press, 1969) p. 9.

[4] President's Domestic Council Committee on Illegal Aliens, 1976, Preliminary Report (Washington, D.C.), p. 33.

[5] Walter O. Foster, "The Immigrant and the American National Idea," in Greer, *op. cit.*, pp. 67–82.

tives, and work strategies. We should be reviewing these issues because immigration influences our society in many ways. This influence can be seen in such areas as: the undocumented alien and Southeast Asian legislation; the recognition of language in the amended version of the Voting Rights Act; the development of culturally oriented local and national self-help organizations; the federal and state bilingual court actions and legislation; the national and state ethnic studies legislation and grants; and most recently, the controversy surrounding the Bakke case. These are but a few indicators of the direct and indirect impact of immigration, and the efforts of our society to cope with its own heterogeneity.

Our society has accepted the immigrant experience but has not learned effective ways to accept the heterogeneity that comes with it.[6] Part of our history has tried to deny the differences that exist among our people.[7] Today, we are trying to be more open about it, but we have not found an appropriate balance, or an approach to problem-solving vis à vis individuals or groups that meets specific needs within a generally accepted framework.

As an example, legislation and public and private services for Southeast Asians have provided little opportunity or encouragement for them as a group to play a useful role in the processes of resettlement and adjustment. Southeast Asian staff have been hired in some cases, and while important, it is not the same as a group taking some responsibility for itself. We know from the past that where an indigenous cultural network existed, it responded to many of the needs of the new arrivals,[8] and the response took place with little govern-

[6] Carey McWilliam, "How Deep Are the Roots," *Common Ground,* Summer, 1947, pp. 3–11; Otto Feinstein, "American Ethnicity: Moment for Survival" (paper presented at the Nationalities Service Center of Philadelphia and Community College of Philadelphia conference on American Ethnicity: a Movement Toward Justice and Equality, 1975), pp. 1–13.

[7] Audrey Hoan, "Books Make Bigots," *Common Ground,* Spring, 1974, pp. 1–12.

[8] William S. Bernard, "Immigrants and Refugees: Their Similarities, Differences, and Needs," *International Migration,* XIV (1976), 274.

ment intervention. In the case of Southeast Asians an adequate indigenous network did not exist. However, accepting such a status quo avoids the point. The point is not government support *vs.* no support, or established agencies *vs.* indigenous groups, but rather the need to recognize their potential contribution and the role that Southeast Asians could play in attaining self-sufficiency. Let us grant that this situation was somewhat unusual and that an adequate cultural network did not exist. Our legislative and administrative policies did not recognize this aspect as an important part of the resettlement and adjustment process. Our approach currently has not encouraged or explored the place of indigenous involvement. Such an approach[9] is basic to social work, and surely it would be useful, supportive, and healthy in this transition.

Because of the extensive government intervention in the resettlement of Southeast Asians, some of our colleagues see this as an opportunity for initiating new social welfare policy for all immigrants. While there is room for new social policy, caution is needed in determining whether or not the resettlement of Southeast Asians offers the wisest example for building new policies.

Social welfare in the United States evolved historically from a concept of charity to one of rights.[10] In the 1930s, United States social welfare policy changed so as to recognize the rights of individuals, suggesting that institutions do frustrate people regardless of their hard work and good intentions.[11] This sensitivity was not extended in a meaningful way to immigrants. Their adjustment remained the responsibility of family, the private welfare sector, or their own initia-

---

[9] Michael D. Blum and Solomon L. Levy, "A Design for Service Delivery That Reinforces Constructive Tension between a Health Center and Its Consumers and Supports Community Power" (paper presented at the National Association of Social Workers Second Professional Symposium on Human Services and Professional Responsibility, 1968).

[10] Arthur M. Schlesinger, "Immigrants in America," *Common Ground*, Autumn, 1940, pp. 19–28.

[11] The Ad Hoc Committee on Advocacy, "The Social Workers as Advocates, Champion of Social Victims," *Social Work*, XIV, No. 2 (1969), 16–22.

tive and resourcefulness. Only very recently has there been a greater move toward examining the social responsibility of the public sector toward the immigrant and to examine the many profound consequences which grow out of his presence in our society.

While the neglect of the immigrant historically can be considered unfortunate, the lack of government involvement in these past processes might now be viewed as a blessing in disguise. Our governmental programs are having questionable effects. Surely if government intervention reinforces dependency, and rewards unproductivity, we are affecting new populations negatively. Do we want to encourage government intervention if it means that the private sector, family and community, is discouraged from responding to these needs? There is a place for government, but we should move slowly lest we undermine the structures which are essential to self-reliance, responsibility, and self-sufficiency.

Through serving immigrants one becomes immediately cognizant of their drive, resourcefulness, and motivation. One becomes more aware of the commitments and efforts that people make and the risks they take to live in the United States. One soon realizes that in the upheaval of moving from one country to another, people are making sacrifices. These sacrifices are the result of choices, and part of the decision involves accepting the rights and responsibilities of United States citizenship. The conscious decision which takes place at the naturalization ceremony is a covenant, an agreement between the individual and that person's new country.

It should be recognized that not all members of our society have had this type of experience and that our welfare policies must take such differences into account. The basic point remains that citizens in a democracy must make some commitment to the development of that society, if the society is to survive. Our social welfare programs, however, ask very little of their recipients. This relationship in both the short and long run is unhealthy. In our society the general rule has been that no one gets something worthwhile for nothing. Yet, welfare programs lean toward this direction. In our concern for the rights of the individuals within our society, we have forgotten individual responsibility toward that society.

Let me make clear that my concern is with the impact of our social programs. What are they doing to and for people? From a program point of view the issue of demonstrating responsibility toward society needs much creative thought. This concern, however, should not suggest that I support an attitude that would allow the majority society to ignore or avoid those individuals and groups in need.

What I am suggesting is that we in the field of social welfare who serve immigrants have not effectively represented what we know about, and have learned from, the immigrant within the forums of social welfare thinking and planning. In fact, we have been somewhat content to serve immigrants in isolation from the mainstream of social welfare activity.

Social welfare programming might have benefited from reflecting more on the immigrant experience both on a psychological and a social dimension. Our isolation, our lack of involvement in social welfare planning in recent years, meant that the issues of individual initiative, resourcefulness, responsibility, and obligation were not sensitively articulated.

ASSIMILATION VS. INTEGRATION

Our lack of involvement has also meant that the very important issue of language and cultural difference in social welfare planning and programming has been almost completely ignored. Social programs in the public and private sector seldom recognized the old adage "different strokes for different folks." Social work has projected and continues to struggle with the "social" dimension of its profession through its focus on institutional change,[12] and while change is badly

---

[12] Walter R. Dean, Jr., "Back to Activism," *Social Work*, XXII (1977), 369–73.

needed, social workers professionally have paid less attention to the different cultural forces that affect behavior, and by implication influence the design and delivery of services.[13]

Social welfare programming has been dominated by assimilationists; that is, those who support a policy and approach that assume there is a mainstream society to which one must adapt. Rather than developing and implementing welfare programs that responded to the needs of diverse cultural groups, assimilationist programs were implemented. Thus programs sensitive to the needs of cultural and subcultural groups, black, Hispanic, and Asian, have been lacking. The integrationist approach, on the other hand, would establish innovations such as providing Chinese food to elderly Chinese Americans in a multigroup elderly service center or providing bilingual counselors to individuals who are not comfortable with English. These examples represent a sensitivity to cultural implications of service delivery. The integrationist approach coordinates the goals of each cultural group, and allows each group to maintain its culture.[14] We who work with immigrants are aware of diverse value systems and their psychological importance. We who work with immigrants know the value of the integrationist as opposed to the assimilationist approach.[15] What we have learned from our association with immigrants and diverse cultures can certainly make an important contribution that should be utilized in the future formulation of social welfare policy and practice.

[13] Guadalupe Gibson, Ernesto Gomez, and Yolanda Santos, "Bilingual–Bicultural Service for the Barrio," in *The Social Welfare Forum, 1973* (New York: Columbia University Press, 1974), pp. 213–25; Bok-Lim C. Kim, "Immigrants from Asia: a Challenge to Social Work," in *The Social Welfare Forum, 1974* (New York: Columbia University Press, 1975), pp. 135–48; Tsuguo Ikeda, a response to Melvin A. Glasser, "Health as a Right: the Human and Political Dimension," in *The Social Welfare Forum, 1975* (New York: Columbia University Press, 1976), pp. 26–29.

[14] Harry C. Triandis, "The Future of Pluralism," *Journal of Social Issues,* XXXII, No. 4 (1976), 179.

[15] Muriel Webb, "Integration as a Process," in William S. Bernard, ed., *Immigrants and Ethnicity* (New York: American Immigration and Citizenship Conference, 1972), pp. 18–23.

IMPLICATIONS IN NEW INS APPOINTMENT

The Carter Administration has provided an unusual opportunity for those of us who work with immigrants and with
language and cultural differences. President Carter has appointed a social worker of Hispanic background, Leonel J.
Castillo, Commissioner of the Immigration and Naturalization Service (INS). This appointment is a milestone in the
annals of social administration history. Commissioner Castillo
represents a synthesis of professional expertise and cultural
sensitivity. This increases the potential for the development
and implementation of social service programs which can be
more responsive to the diverse cultural and linguistic needs
of the populace.

You will recall that the Nixon/Ford years, with Commissioner Leonard F. Chapman, Jr., were preoccupied with law
enforcement. They were shaped by a political strategy which
reflected the serious personnel shortage at the INS, and presented a limited view of undocumented aliens. Commissioner
Chapman's message to Congress was based on the mentality
of enforcement, and the promise of more jobs for United
States citizens. Unfortunately, this strategy hurt the INS and
delayed service to many.[16]

Commissioner Castillo brings a different perspective and
insight to the field of immigration. He faces many complicated issues legislatively and bureaucratically. While it is not
hard to imagine the resistance he must meet as he tries to set
a new tone within the INS, this is potentially a breakthrough
in INS leadership. Mr. Castillo brings to his job a sensitivity
for the immigrant, for the issues of language and cultural
difference. We need to examine closely the ways in which the
voluntary sector can support his leadership efforts to make

[16] James J. Orlow, "Illegal Alien: Scapegoat or Sinner" (paper presented at the
Nationalities Service Center, Philadelphia, and Association of Immigration and Nationality Lawyers, Philadelphia Chapter conference on Issues in United States Immigration, 1976), pp. 1–14.

more humane and available the delivery and practice of immigration services. Moreover, his success could have an important impact far beyond the offices of the INS, and the social work profession's involvement possibly could help make this so.

NEW DIMENSIONS IN SERVICE

Immigration services will be directly affected by the development of voluntary centers under the auspices of the INS. These are regional centers where volunteers will be trained in aspects of immigration. The program has been designed because

(1) Many aliens are not aware of the immigration laws or benefits they are entitled to under these laws; (2) many aliens lack the necessary education or expertise to fill out immigration petitions and forms; (3) many aliens are reluctant to deal with INS because they have encountered negative experiences with the Service, and rightly or wrongly, they feel the Service will be unresponsive to their needs, or out of fear, they simply will not deal with the Service; and (4) many aliens believe their immigration problems are so complex that they need the service of an expert, and unfortunately, they often fall prey to unscrupulous parties who charge them exorbitant rates for service that the INS provides free.[17]

The voluntary centers, properly organized, will make people more aware of the private nonprofit sector and its potential service role in immigration. They will take some of the mystique and fear out of working with immigration matters and the INS. They may even serve in some small way to bring government processes closer to the people. Usually, engaging people in aspects of service delivery creates understanding, allows for easier accountability, promotes better public relations, and communicates the important message that government is you and me, and we make it work by our volunteer involvement. This involvement encourages the self-reliance we need to preserve.

[17] E. B. Duarte, "Immigration Outreach Program on Action Plan," INS proposal, 1977.

As professionals we know that a variety of complicated issues arises when one involves a volunteer in any aspect of a professional service.[18] Issues such as role, function, accountability, and liability need careful thought. Competition among groups within a community will emerge, and in some cases has already emerged, as a logistical problem in organizing voluntary centers. Volunteers, according to some reports, are misusing their "new" knowledge and relationships. Such problems might be avoided with responsible involvement and cooperation among the private and public sectors.

The private sector has been offered the opportunity to cooperate with INS in this project. Here is an opening for establishing more meaningful programmatic ties on a national and local level. Here is an opening to work, not only on this project, but on related service projects as they affect immigrants. This project will not be an easy one to implement; it will have its rough spots; it will be difficult to maintain. However, the possibilities for greater public and private cooperation, for stimulating greater imagination and creativity in serving people, are so compelling that the potential gains outweigh the risks.

Any part of an over-all effort to improve the availability of services to immigrants requires a closer examination of the legal and social service needs of a particular group of immigrants—the indigent. In some parts of the country this might be less of a problem, but over all I would imagine that the availability of legal and social service assistance to indigent immigrants could be greatly improved.

A project has been initiated in Philadelphia between Community Legal Services (CLS), an agency funded by the Legal Services Corporation passed by Congress, and the Nationalities Service Center of Philadelphia (NSC), a United Way agency. NSC has placed two lawyers in CLS to coordinate legal services to indigent immigrants and to help them to receive needed social services. The project demonstrates an

---

[18] Michael D. Blum, "Citizen Advocacy and the Volunteer" (paper presented at the National Conference on Social Welfare Annual Forum, 1973).

approach for serving the legal needs of indigent immigrants; it encourages further collaboration between the legal and social service professions; and, finally, it offers an approach for responding to the basic personal and social needs of all immigrants. The organization of the project acknowledges the formal legal and social service community structures. Potentially, it opens up a new funding source for legal services to immigrants as well as offering a new advocacy support for meeting their needs.

The special legal service project in Philadelphia is beginning to establish greater expertise in immigration within that agency. The special project lawyers also provide INS, the Lawyers Reference Service, and the members of the Philadelphia Chapter of the Association of Immigration and Nationality Lawyers a focus for service to indigent immigrants. NSC is underwriting the staff costs, while office space and supervision are provided by CLS. While NSC's immigration staff members are accredited, there are under investigation those cases of the type that frequently result in hearings, where NSC believes a lawyer's skills are more appropriate and necessary.

While the project begins to evaluate an appropriate model for serving indigent immigrants, it also opens to investigation the service relationship between lawyers and social workers, so similar to the efforts already made in the field of family and child welfare.[19] When a client's needs suggest that there are other than legal problems, referrals to NSC are encouraged.

This project, however, raises other issues. For example, the section of immigration law which reads, "the alien shall have the privilege of being represented (at no expense to the Government) by such counsel, authorized to practice in such proceedings, as he shall choose"[20] raises a significant question

[19] Jessie E. Peeke, "Counseling Parents in Divorce," in Fred DelliQuadri, ed., *Helping the Family in Urban Society* (New York: Columbia University Press, 1963), pp. 119–32.
[20] Immigration and Nationality Act, 8 U.S.C. 1252.

regarding the *de facto* meaning *vs.* the meaning of the legislation which formed the Legal Services Corporation. The legislation states that the purpose of the Legal Services Corporation is to provide "financial support for legal assistance in noncriminal proceedings or matters to persons financially unable to afford legal assistance."[21]

There are nine limitations under which Legal Services Corporation funds may not be used. None of these appears to include legal services to indigent immigrants. Furthermore, the *Munoz* v. *Bell* (No. CV-77-3765-WPG) decision in the Federal District Court in California provides more support for the rights of indigent immigrants for counsel through federally funded services. As a result of this case the INS has agreed to issue proposed regulations regarding notice to immigrants of the availability of free legal services. Obviously, aspects of this issue will be reviewed in future court actions.

NEW DIMENSIONS IN POLICY

The impact of past and present immigration affects the field of social welfare generally. The impact is being felt as issues of ethnicity[22] gain greater acceptance. Immigration and ethnicity make our society multicultural. This understanding needs to be incorporated still further into the organization and development of social policy, social organization, and social programming. Within a multicultural orientation, the reality that the service industry must be able to deliver its services in a variety of languages is manifest.

Our social welfare literature does not adequately reflect the issues of group difference in service delivery or policymaking. As an example, much of the literature regarding societal groupings confuses ethnicity, race, and language. Our thinking has been influenced by the federal govern-

---

[21] 42 United States Code Annotated 2996 (St. Paul, Minn.: West Publishing Co., 1977), updated supplement, p. 155.
[22] For discussion on the definitions of ethnicity see Michael Novak, *Further Reflections on Ethnicity* (Middletown, Pa.: Jednota Press, 1977).

ment's affirmative action categories. I would hope, rather, that as professionals we would attempt to provide leadership that would point to alternatives, not only in acquiring the necessary group information, but for gathering it in a more accurate manner. Controversy exists politically within some Hispanic communities where certain subgroups feel they are not being acknowledged; also planning and fund-raising bodies understand the concept of minorities in such limited terms that groups are either neglected in the allocation of resources or are not consciously approached for financial contributions. This demonstrates a certain confusion in our social thinking; a confusion which is reflected in fund-raising, social planning, and social service delivery.

The mental health field has done little with language and cultural difference for the treatment of persons under stress. Coping in a new society, or surviving in one that is almost 202 years old, has its stresses and strains. Programs in mental health have been developed as if there were practically no ethnic concerns.[23] Ethnic groups have not been able to avail themselves of mental health services because of inconveniently located facilities and poorly designed outreach programs. The mental health field knows relatively little about the ways in which one ethnic group differs from another. The importance of such delineation has recently been highlighted by Robert E. Alberti.[24] In part he examines assertiveness among Mexican Americans and Asian Americans; additionally, he highlights other multicultural orientations. Shirley Teper states that

ethnicity is a prism through which human behavior is both shaped and perceived. We have paid too little attention to its pervasiveness in determining perceptions, values, attitudes and behavior, as well as its effects on social interaction.[25]

[23] Joseph Giordano, *Ethnicity and Mental Health* (New York: National Project on Ethnic America of the American Jewish Committee, 1973); Richard C. Baron, "Mental Health Services for Ethnic Minorities," *Currents*, III, No. 1 (1978), 1–12.

[24] Robert E. Alberti, *Assertiveness, Innovations, Application, Issues* (San Luis Obispo, Calif.: Impact, 1977).

[25] Shirley Teper, *Ethnicity, Race and Human Development* (New York: Institute on Pluralism and Group Identity, 1977), p. 9.

EDUCATION

One cannot consider social welfare without mentioning the field of education. Schools have become an important intervention point for private and public welfare concerns.[26] There is considerable controversy regarding bilingual education (*Lau* v. *Nichols*, 1974, 414 U.S. 563). California, Massachusetts, and Texas have passed state legislation in this area. Federal dollars for bilingual programs have been inadequate. The programs have been poorly documented and researched.[27] Current bilingual policies appear to be a curious hybrid of pedagogy and politics. As a substantive issue, *Time* reports:

A 1977 nation-wide study of 150 schools and 11,500 students conducted by American Institute for Research in Palo Alto, California, found that bilingual programs helped children learn such subjects as math. But Spanish-speaking children in bilingual programs generally did not improve in English any faster than did foreign speakers in monolingual classrooms.[28]

Dr. Joshua Fishman, a professor of pyscholinguistics at Yeshiva University, states:

It is societies that are conflicted rather than bilingual education as such. If societies can come to accept (value) and optionalize (permit) ethnolinguistic diversity, so that some can treasure it for maintenance purposes, others for enrichment, and others for transitional purposes, I am sure that bilingual education will quickly become what it should be: an internally diversified alternative kind of education for those who want it.[29]

---

[26] Lela B. Costin, "Historical Review of School Social Work," *Social Casework*, X (1969), 439–53; Eugene Litwak and Henry J. Meyer, "The Administrative Style of the School and Organization Tasks," in Fred M. Cox *et al.*, ed., *Strategies of Community Organization* (Itasca, Ill.: F. E. Peacock, 1970), pp. 78–91; Paula A. Meares, "Analysis of the Tasks in School Social Work," *Social Work* XXII (1977), 196–201.

[27] *A Better Chance to Learn Bilingual Bicultural Education* (Washington, D.C.: U.S. Commission on Civil Rights, 1975), pp. 172–74.

[28] *Time*, February 13, 1978, p. 65.

[29] Joshua A. Fishman, *Bilingual Education: Ethnic Perspectives* (paper presented at the Nationalities Service Center of Philadelphia and Community College of Philadelphia conference on Bilingual Education: Ethnic Perspectives, 1977), pp. 1–15 and 47–52.

Part of the confusion also concerns methods and goals. The question asked is: Will the child at the end of his formal education, speak English? While that is an essential question, considering our educational problems, the question could be framed more broadly to inquire what it takes to involve a child in a meaningful educational process. Our educational systems are not succeeding, and it would be too simplistic to blame our educators. Rather, we as a society are not ready to make the changes and commitments necessary to shape a more creative process. For example, if people learn at different rates, why shape a system that requires learning within given periods of time? Surely no one should leave a public education system unable to function at a level defined as acceptable by the society in which he/she lives. If the society accepted this responsibility, and the individuals within it understood and accepted the standard, a whole series of new relationships and economies would be fostered that would support productivity and responsibility. The Quinmester system in Dade County, Florida, and Long Branch, New Jersey, is experimenting with this approach.

Another instance where cultural and language difference has tended to go unnoticed is with the elderly, especially where the group's size in comparison to the larger community is not substantial. While elderly citizens are becoming more outspoken, the non-English-speaking older person is culturally isolated and does not have access to, or feel comfortable with the public forums where needs are presented and discussed. Additionally, in some of the new immigrant/ethnic communities, grandparents serve as babysitters because both parents are working. These grandparents become socially isolated, and the likelihood is that they will become increasingly depressed with their condition. There are also ethnic communities in which the older citizen, due to the effects of aging, either regresses to his/her native language or restricts contacts to the most familiar; they, too, become socially isolated from the community-based resources designed to serve this population.

Within the physical and social planning fields, historically there has been a lack of awareness of language and cultural difference. Urban renewal programs have destroyed neighborhoods which had provided stability for their members. Some of the literature on urbanism expresses regret at having destroyed important cultural forces which unify and give meaning to people's lives and families.[30]

Until recently the focus within intergroup and human relations programs has been on white and black relationships. This view has not reflected the complexity within and between each of these communities.[31] As important as affirmative action programs are for creating opportunity and community consciousness for certain minority groups, these programs are running into policy difficulty, due to charges of reverse discrimination.[32] This state of affairs possibly returns us to where we started. It reflects our inability to describe ourselves accurately, establish acceptable programs, acknowledge the scope of the problem, and order the necessary priorities for coping with it.

Such a public attitude where people are charging discrimination, and countercharging reverse discrimination, suggests a need for more serious community-wide discussions on the issues of ethnicity, social policy, problem-solving, and priorities.[33] Broad representation from diverse segments of our society will allow people to hear and consider views which normally they do not hear or consider. The concern, perspective, and insight of the immigrant/ethnic experience need further projection within our spheres of problem-solving. There is a reality that has been ignored. And continued avoidance contributes to not coping with community-wide

[30] Herbert J. Gans, *The Urban Villagers* (New York: Free Press of Glencoe, 1962).

[31] Nathan Glazer and Daniel P. Moynihan, *Beyond the Melting Pot* (Cambridge, Mass.: M.I.T. Press, 1963).

[32] *Defunis* v. *Odegard* (1974) 416 US 312; *Bakke* v. *Regents of University of California* (1976) 18 C 3d 34; Carl T. Rowan, "Detroit 'Bias' Case Bigger than Bakke," Philadelphia *Evening Bulletin*, March 20, 1978.

[33] For discussion on this issue see papers presented at the Nationalities Service Center and Community College of Philadelphia conference on Affirmative Action: Ethnic Perspectives, 1976.

problems, and further isolates our society's groups from one another. To quote Claude Lévi-Strauss:

All cultural progress depends on a coalition of cultures. The essence of such a coalition is the pooling of the wins which each culture has scored in the course of its historic development . . . the greater the diversity between the cultures, the more fruitful such a coalition will be.[34]

Turning our attention to self-help groups, we find that they provide an interesting opportunity for forming coalitions and broadening the dialogue. Established agencies and self-help groups have many mutual concerns and they need not be threatened by each other's presence. However, there needs to be more reaching out on both sides if this relationship is to become effective. A more careful approach to strategy must be implemented to determine roles, limits, and the value of each other's presence.

Self-help groups provide an important sense of identity, and they represent important forums of advocacy, lobbying, social planning, and service delivery. In some instances, they have greater flexibility than established agencies to move on issues quickly and vigorously. Self-help groups, on the other hand, often do not design effective strategies for involving the established agencies or they are not aware of how to use these institutions appropriately. An agency can be a bridge to other groups and issues, can help to avoid parochialism or extremism, and can offer an opportunity for gaining greater acceptance by others who are unfamiliar with a specific "experience" or "grievance."

Agencies and organizations concerned with immigrants have a unique opportunity to help the society move ahead and make progress in coping with itself. It requires a broad view and it requires a commitment and a conviction that our experience, understanding, and awareness are civilizing. It

[34] Claude Levi-Strauss, "Race and History," in Teper, *op. cit.,* p. 4.

requires a willingness to be part of a much broader scene, a leadership that is searching for and defining the requirements of compromise in a society (and world) made up of diverse individuals and groups.[35]

[35] Ward Shepard, "The Tools for Ethnic Democracy," *Common Ground*, Spring, 1944, pp. 3–17; Brock Chisholm, "Human Relations and World Survival," *Common Ground*, Autumn, 1948, pp. 23–27; Robert L. Heilbroner, *An Inquiry into the Human Prospect* (New York: W. W. Norton, 1974); Alexander Alland, Jr., *The Human Imperative* (New York: Columbia University Press, 1972).

Functional Illiteracy and Social Work

LEONARD SCHNEIDERMAN

To be functionally literate implies a capacity to assign names to objects, people, and relationships in the world in which one lives and to conceive of oneself as an actor in that world. The absence of literacy implies powerlessness and helplessness, the inability to represent one's own world in symbols, to manipulate those symbols effectively, to master the power of language. All of these can leave the nonliterate person unable to define the forces which shape his life, to act on what is undefined, to cope effectively with what appears incomprehensible. Frozen in the present tense by an inability to manipulate the complex symbols of past and future, the illiterate person may find himself unable to comprehend and to communicate effectively in a society where emphasis upon formal communication skill and symbol manipulation is an ever more critical determinant of his life's chances.

Literacy is a subject tied in the most intimate way to place, to social context, to expectations, to man in interaction with his physical environment and with social institutions. Whether as an issue of broad social policy or as a subject for direct remedial intervention, it is necessarily a subject of vital concern to the social work profession. It has a direct impact on issues of basic concern to the profession, issues of justice and inequity. Access to literacy in our society, access to the skills that it implies, matches the problems of access to ade-

LEONARD SCHNEIDERMAN is Dean, School of Social Work, Indiana University, Indianapolis

quate income, to adequate housing, to adequate jobs, to adequate health care. Literacy is another face of the larger issue of social inequity. It seems unlikely to be an issue which can be divorced from our efforts to find solutions to the larger issues of social justice and social equity, so many faces of which engage our professional interests and resources. Literacy, as part of the larger picture of inequity, may be among the strongest of several factors holding some Americans in an underclass from which upward mobility is difficult or impossible.

A startling 56 percent of those with Spanish surnames in the Texas study[1] tested out at the functionally incompetent level. Blacks tested 44 percent functionally incompetent compared with 16 percent for whites. The overrepresentation of minority group members among the functionally incompetent can in good part be traced to lack of schooling. According to the 1970 census, for the first time a majority of all Americans twenty-five years and over were high school graduates. The median for all Americans was 12.1 years of school. The median for whites was 12.2 years. But for blacks and Indians, also over twenty-five years, the median figure was only 9.8 years of school and even less for Puerto Ricans at 8.7 years and for Mexican Americans at 8.1 years. Similarly, more minorities than whites drop out before completing the eighth grade. About one fourth of white adults (26.6 percent) dropped out at that level, but the percentage has swelled to 43.5 percent for Indians, 43.8 percent for blacks, 54.1 percent for Puerto Ricans, and 58.9 percent for Mexican Americans.[2]

To move from nonliteracy to literacy, to promote the acquisition of a skill by adults who lack such knowledge and skill, will almost certainly mean more than remedial education for the imperfectly instructed. It will mean fostering the hope of a new and fuller level of participation in the life of the

---

[1] Norvell Northcutt, *Adult Functional Competency* (Austin, Texas: University of Texas, Adult Performance Level Project, 1975).

[2] *Ibid.*

community. Aspiring to an altered role as actor in community life and nurturing the capability to make this possible necessarily demand an enterprise with profound personal and political meaning for those directly involved and for the community at large.

Two levels of significance are implied for social work:

1. Functional illiteracy is distributed within the total population following a pattern which is similar to the distribution of wealth, income, employment, health care, housing, and opportunities for participation in the social and political life of the country. It is, therefore, part of the broader issue of distributional justice and needs to be approached at the level of corrective social policy intervention.

2. Effective remedial education is needed for the already disadvantaged target population. Efforts must be made to raise the consciousness of, and hence the effectiveness of, social agency programs in coping with this population. It is estimated, for example, that about 75 percent of the United States poverty population possess reading skills at no higher than the eighth-grade level. Yet the procedures and documents of many public welfare agencies require far higher levels of literacy of the clients who receive their written communications. The consequence of this difference between the welfare client's ability to read and the agency's demand for literacy may be significant. One can speculate that it contributes to at least three undesirable program outcomes, namely, (*a*) discouragement of some eligible persons from enrolling for benefits; (*b*) inequities in the distribution_of benefits among enrollees; and (*c*) high rates of administrative error because of clients' inability to participate in correcting information incorrectly transmitted.[3]

Such findings suggest the importance of rewriting documents for maximum comprehension by agency target populations, and the central importance of instructional programs designed to increase the literacy levels of citizens dependent

[3] Marc Bendick, Jr., and Mario G. Cantu, "The Literacy of Welfare Clients," *Social Service Review*, LII, No. 1 (1978), 56–68.

upon legally defined benefits and entitlements. A fully effective instructional methodology has yet to be developed, however. A review of experience to date suggests the role which social workers can and must play in programs designed to offer direct instructional assistance to adult illiterates:

1. The adult learner is most often a part-time learner with heavy responsibilities in other roles, such as adult, spouse, parent, worker, child, sibling, neighbor, and so on, with each of these singly and together influencing motivation and capacity to utilize an instructional program.

2. A "free service" is not a service without cost to the adult participant. Holding the adult learner in an instructional program through maintenance of a favorable balance between client costs and client benefits requires sensitivity to the many costs incurred by the adult learner in time, energy, fear, interruption of relationships, loss of leisure time, and the frustration of the learning task itself. The holding power of any educational program depends upon its sensitivity and responsiveness to the total life situation of the learner.

3. The adult learner is most often in search of knowledge and skills with particular relevance to his life's circumstances. Instructional methods must, therefore, be heavily focused upon life-coping skills rather than upon standardized procedures. This approach requires individualizing the program to achieve a close "fit" to the person's life situation, his particular hopes and aspirations, his sense of threatened well-being, perception of opportunities, and desire for change.

4. To be illiterate is to be a discredited person in our society. A functionally illiterate person is likely to manage information about himself in such a way as to conceal a limitation for which he has been made to feel personal responsibility and shame. In such situations the effort to direct a service to this target population is made difficult by this concealment behavior. One finds a classical encounter between the concealment behavior of the discredited person and the detection behavior of the helping agency. This is a prototypical encounter with which social workers have had a good deal of

experience as they have reached out to persons with discrediting conditions, such as former mental patients, former inmates of the correction system, and so forth.

A practice role for the social worker, based upon these findings, needs to be clearly articulated and aggressively put forward for inclusion in future programs designed to assist this target population. Whatever one's conceptualization of the problem, it seems clear that the social work profession must actively associate itself with efforts to find a solution to a problem so directly linked to its most basic social concerns and commitments. The profession has much to contribute from its understanding of the multiple forces at work in influencing coping behavior. The conception of literacy needs to be significantly broadened to include a range of interventive actions at both the direct remedial level as well as at the level of broad social and educational policy. We need to know much more. We need to know why it is that in a society with a host of educational institutions, each a subject of public policy concern (the schools, the home, the churches, industry, business, and social service organizations), we continue to generate so large a portion of our population without the functional capacity for effective adult performance. We need better analytic tools to understand the consequences of this state of affairs for those directly involved and for the community.

It seems timely for the social work profession to seek out a role in this problem arena, to collaborate with other professional and lay groups interested in the issue. The role needs to include a clear social work presence in adult basic education programs and a clear conceptualization of the link between adult literacy and the broader issues of distributional justice and citizen participation in the political life of the society.

Full Employment in the United States

AUGUSTUS F. HAWKINS

THERE HAS BEEN an unsustainable and almost unholy misinterpretation of the issue of full employment in this country, deliberately managed to lead the people away from their own best welfare.

It is commonplace in our politics to obfuscate the issues in order to shift guilt elsewhere whenever clarity and common sense as well as simple justice would prove one wrong and thereby morally responsible. A deliberate policy that is built on mass involuntary unemployment for whatever reason not only shows contempt for the dignity of the individual person, it is a social and economic waste that is costing us irretrievable human values, the loss of revenues, goods and services, and national pride. It is akin to criminality in that it is both unwarranted and a basic cause of poverty, racial antagonism, illiteracy, murder, family disorganization, suicides, business bankruptcies, and fiscal deficits.

Conservatively estimated, during this quarter century we have lost goods and services worth over $5 trillion, over seventy-two million "man" years in unemployment in excess of full employment (4.1 percent unemployment), and over a trillion dollars in public revenues at all levels. This is the *basic* cause of the other difficulties from which we suffer: the deficiencies in our priority needs as well as the huge deficits in public fiscal budgets.

When Al Capone had Chicago by the throat during the

AUGUSTUS F. HAWKINS is U.S. Representative to Congress from California.

Prohibition era of the 1920s and early 1930s, it was a part of his strategy to blame the city's ills (murder, gang killings, muggings) on "outsiders" and to promote what he called civic pride in "our own home-grown city people." The juxtaposition of the issues of inflation and unemployment by certain economists is akin to this Capone strategy. Which, they would have us select, is the more important: more jobs or less inflation? Clearly, the implication is that more jobs will cause inflation, and the strategy is to make all but the unemployed believe they have nothing to gain by reducing unemployment and would actually lose because that would increase prices.

The double-digit inflation of 1974–75 was blamed on the Arabs and the weather, when the same persons were not blaming it on a "tight labor market" or high wages. We are at least a decade away from a tight labor market. In the meantime, the major causes of inflation relate not to wage demands but to excessive interest, military expenditures, tight money supply, and structural defects. We should understand that while some of these factors are in the national interest, they are inflationary; they, not employment, cause inflation.

In addition, it has become standard to cite "irresponsible and excessive spending" as the root cause of inflation and the high deficits. Federal spending as a percentage of the gross national product has remained constant for several decades in or near the 20 percent–21 percent range. Its composition has changed materially, that is, less defense percentage-wise and more welfare; and precisely as a result of the wrong economic policies that have encouraged low growth, inadequate production, and high unemployment that have necessarily produced more welfare and other income-transfer programs together with recurring recessions.

It is such economic thinking and "flaky" beliefs that have beclouded the fight for full employment and balanced growth in our country—almost to the point where good people in our country (as in Capone's Chicago) have been afraid to speak out and to challenge injustice.

The federal government's concern with human problems

is relatively new since our beginning. Business protection and promotion, in contrast, have always been accepted as part of the federal obligation.

In the 1930s when panic gripped the American people and threatened the infrastructure of our system we were forced into recognition of the commingling of private and public interests that had always been latent in our economy. (Did not business always function through public enforcement of contracts, recording of titles, wise regulation of competition, public roads, and police systems?)

Government concern or "intervention" seems to become distasteful only when it is exercised in behalf of human as opposed to corporate welfare. Society would benefit immeasurably if they were equally recognized, and business would gain greater prestige and profit. Lincoln, in his debate with Douglas, foresaw this dichotomy in our national life in which the people's welfare on the one hand, the "common right of humanity," would be pitted against the elitist doctrine of the "divine right of kings" or the "economic royalists," so to speak, on the other.

Not only our thinking but our action is still colored by this tendency to sublimate that which is attached to property rights as opposed to human rights despite all of our rhetoric to the contrary. One of our ablest economists and most influential public figures, Arthur Burns, is a case in point. His performance—what he actually accomplished in economic terms while with the Federal Reserve Board—has not matched his sterling role of importance and acceptability.

Why is it that persons who serve with equal conviction and perhaps greater fortitude in behalf of human beings enjoy so much less respectability and often have a contemptible image?

To return to full employment and the Employment Act of 1946 which H.R. 50, the Humphrey-Hawkins bill, seeks to update and strengthen:

1. "Full" employment, in the 1946 act, was undefined except in language so broad as to permit a trade-off—

employment subordinate to inflation. In H.R. 50 it is fully defined as an *individual* right, not a percentage of unemployment, and trade-off is prohibited.

2. The President's report was too general and excluded Congressional involvement. The Humphrey-Hawkins bill was specific, and its report must be acted upon by Congress.

3. The act rejected a coordinated and comprehensive approach that included the Federal Reserve Board. Both Congress and the Chief Executive as well as the Federal Reserve Board must address over-all economic policy and goals.

4. Over-all planning with specific goals and timetables.

5. Inflation is not even mentioned in the 1946 act. H.R. 50 includes specific anti-inflation provisions, and price stability is made an objective of the bill and interwoven with that of reducing unemployment.

As to criticism that the bill has been weakened and does not do anything, let me repeat the words of Senator Hubert Humphrey: "Don't listen to those who say this bill is watered down and not worth fighting for." More specifically, none of these main provisions has been weakened:

1. H.R. 50 recommits the federal government to the goal of creating conditions that assure meaningful employment to all who are able, willing, and seeking employment opportunities. The bill mandates interim goals toward this end, and provides for the availability of better jobs, training programs, opportunities for promotion, and better job security.

2. H.R. 50 provides for the comprehensive integration of our fiscal and monetary policies and programs with structural programs to assist disadvantaged groups and reduce inflation.

3. H.R. 50 requires the President to set forth annual anti-inflation goals and to detail the policies and programs needed to reach reasonable price stability and full employment. The bill rejects the discredited trade-off theory which encouraged slowing down the economy to help promote price stability.

4. The bill provides for a coordinated and democratic eco-

nomic policy decision-making process for the federal government. It requires annual and long-term projections to be made by the President and the Federal Reserve Board and reviewed by the Congress. We would no longer have to react to one crisis situation after another (such as energy, food, recessions, and so forth).

5. H.R. 50 specifies an interim numerical target for the reduction of unemployment to 4 percent over all within five years. This replaces the unacceptable notion that 6 percent unemployment, or higher, is "tolerable unemployment."

6. The bill establishes the federal government as the employer of last resort. It is possible that the last-resort jobs may not be needed at all or only in limited amounts if the right policies and programs are undertaken.

7. The bill provides for the bedrock commitment of reducing the high unemployment levels of certain groups in the labor force (youth, minorities, women, elderly, veterans, and the handicapped) to the national average on an equitable and nondiscriminatory basis.

The full employment concept, based on clear unity of purpose and a comprehensive, coordinated, and integrated approach, has broader application and significance than in the context of manpower policy to which it is generally related. We have repeated over and over that the Humphrey-Hawkins bill is not a jobs bill per se and we have stressed its importance in terms of over-all policy formulation and longer-range *democratic* planning.

Most of the country's shortcomings, including deficient economic performance, arise out of these failures: we have no clear-cut, over-all economic policy but a galaxy of fragmented and disjointed policies and we lack any recognizable plan to govern our action as we stumble along from one crisis to another. Consequently, even though we may devise individual programs that seem to offer relief or tangible immediate benefits in terms of public service jobs, an urban policy, energy conservation, welfare reform, tax reduction, affirmative action, youth programs, foreign aid, economic develop-

ment, school assistance, and so on, such policies and programs will continue to be ineffective, divisive, wasteful, and
even contradictory unless they are integrated with each other
and related to long-range goals with targets and timetables
(as H.R. 50 mandates). Implied, of course, is a democratic
planning process whereby annually and as far ahead as possible we will anticipate what is needed to be done to achieve
our publicly stated national objectives and provide accountability in our elected representatives to act responsibly.

As merely one example of such an approach in action, let
me suggest its application to the much-bandied-about issue
of human rights. The Humphrey-Hawkins approach would
move it from international rhetoric to responsible action. Just
as the term "full employment" has been too general to have
practical meaning so the phrase "human rights" has been interpreted to "legalize" almost any conduct or practice desired, or any political system.

We would out of necessity need to spell out standards of
human rights, such as Roosevelt's Bill of Economic Rights,
and make them as applicable to our own conduct in domestic
affairs as to others throughout the world including Houston,
Texas, and Wilmington, North Carolina, where states rights
have prevailed over human rights. We would have to make
our standards apply not only to legal justice but to economic
rights as well and to every phase of our lives, for the words
"life, liberty, and the pursuit of happiness" are meaningless if
one has no opportunity to earn a decent living.

Such an approach would have to touch our total relationships: young and old, the Jewish communities, Hispanics
and blacks, urban and rural and every region, the people of
every continent, the warring factions in the Middle East and
on the continent of Africa, and our Latin American neighbors. Just as we have built a great coalition around H.R. 50,
so would we be encouraged to create a world-wide movement
of understanding and social justice cemented by real human
rights of a recognizable beneficial nature actually applied in
our daily lives. Because it would really mean something, peo-

ple everywhere would follow our leadership, contributing their talents, skills, and know-how.

In the words of H. G. Wells:

A federation of all humanity, together with a sufficient measure of social justice to ensure health, education, and a rough equality of opportunity would mean such a release and increase of human energy as to open a new phase in human history.

Remarks by Governor Edmund G. Brown, Jr.

In May of 1978, the voters of California faced the June 6 balloting on Proposition 13, which would, if passed, effect a sudden and drastic reduction in property taxes and a cut in local governmental services. Because this took precedence over any other local social welfare issue, the Conference scheduled a late evening General Session on May 22 which was addressed by Governor Edmund G. Brown, Jr. On June 6, California voters overwhelmingly passed this Proposition. Local governments and the state government, as well as governments in other states, are speculating about the effects of Proposition 13 and the possible spread of the "taxpayers revolt."

In wide-ranging, informal remarks, Governor Brown touched on many aspects of the relationship between the citizen and government. A major theme was the need to communicate the interdependence of all parts of society, to create a sense of connection between cities and suburbs, aging and youth, all racial groups. "If the city collapses, the suburbs are not far behind; if the aged are shunted aside into nursing homes, the young are adversely affected." In a society which is not homogeneous, where neighborhoods, families, and communities are less tightly knit, and where the media stress individual consumption, voluntary institutions and organizations are essential in developing a feeling for collective responsibility and fostering community goals. The Governor said that bold new ideas come from this source, and that it had been important in fostering the civil rights movement, welfare rights, environmental concerns, the women's movement. Since governmental decisions must reflect a common denominator, there must be stimulation of diverse ideas in the social and cultural field.

Social workers, Governor Brown said, need to communicate to taxpayers a sense of the importance of their work and its human significance.

Governor Brown spoke of the unfinished social agenda, with poverty a major concern. He stressed the rapid technological changes which have resulted in a quarter of the people working in jobs that were not even conceived twenty years ago, and the failure of society to make the linkage between people who want to work and the tasks that are to be done. In an anonymous, competitive world, he said, those who do not "make it" end up needing social services.

As social needs grow and as society must provide what was once provided by families or neighbors, there are greater expectancies from government. Governor Brown, facing the imminent vote on Proposition 13, and the potential of a "wrenching experience," commented on the paradox involved. People look for a lesser tax burden, he said, yet still look to government to pick up medical bills, to help grandparents, neighbors, coworkers. Moreover, as discretionary income might be increased and allow greater private consumption, the social waste would also grow.

Governor Brown said that under Proposition 13, the "property tax limitation initiative," local revenues would decrease from about $12 billion to an estimated $5 billion. He spoke of the damage to local programs and suggested Proposition 8 as an alternative measure. This initiative would reduce taxes somewhat less, and would apply only to owner-occupied dwellings.

Appendix A: Program

GENERAL SESSIONS

OPENING GENERAL SESSION
Speakers: John B. Turner, University of North Carolina, Chapel Hill; President, NCSW
Max W. Fine, Commitee for National Health Insurance, Washington
Panelists: Chauncey A. Alexander, National Association of Social Workers, Washington
Lester Breslow, M.D., University of California, Los Angeles

ALL IN THE FAMILY
Speaker: Peter W. Forsythe, National Commission on Families and Public Policies; Edna McConnell Clark Foundation, New York
Presentation of Report and Recommendations of National Commission on Families and Public Policies, and Summary of Institute Recommendations by Members of the Commission

ISSUES BEFORE CALIFORNIA
Speaker: The Honorable Edmund G. Brown, Jr., Governor, State of California, Sacramento

FULL EMPLOYMENT IN THE UNITED STATES
Speaker: The Honorable Augustus F. Hawkins, U.S. Representative to Congress from California's 29th District, Los Angeles
Panelists: Curtis Aller, Center for Applied Manpower Research, Berkeley, Calif.
Percy Steele, Jr., Bay Area Urban League, San Francisco

WHITNEY M. YOUNG, JR., MEMORIAL LECTURE
Speaker: James Farmer, Coalition of American Public Employees, Washington
Presentation of Social Worker of the Year and Public Citizen of the Year Awards

JOE R. HOFFER MEMORIAL LECTURE
Speaker: The Rev. Jesse L. Jackson, National President, PUSH (People United to Save Humanity), Chicago
Presentation of NCSW Distinguished Service Awards
Presentation of 50-Year Membership Awards

SECTION I: ECONOMIC INDEPENDENCE

FEDERAL POLICY FOR THE AGED
Speakers: Sharon Fujii, Pacific-Asian Elderly Research Project, Los Angeles
Robert Foster, Federal Council on the Aging, Washington

FOLLOW-UP ON GENERAL SESSION ON FULL
EMPLOYMENT—IMPLICATIONS FOR POLICY
Speaker: Curtis Aller, Center for Applied Manpower Research, Berkeley, Calif.

INCOME SUPPORT FOR ONE-PARENT FAMILIES AND
DISPLACED HOMEMAKERS
Panelists: Judith H. Cassetty, University of Texas, Austin
Mary Maschal, San Diego, Calif.

A NEW LOOK AT SOCIAL SECURITY
Speakers: Martha N. Ozawa, Washington University, St. Louis
Larry Thompson, Office of Income Security Policy, Washington

REDLINING: EFFECTS OF LENDING INSTITUTIONS' POLICIES
ON NEIGHBORHOODS
Panelists: Kathleen Connell, City of Los Angeles
Jeffrey Zimsmeyer, Center for Community Change, Washington

SOME DIFFERENT PERSPECTIVES ON WELFARE REFORM
Speakers: Moses Newsome, Jr., Howard University, Washington
Eunice Elton, Mayor's Office of Employment and Training, City and
County of San Francisco, San Francisco
Keith B. Comrie, Los Angeles County Department of Social Services,
El Monte, Calif.

WELFARE REFORM: TO WHAT END?
Speaker: Irwin Garfinkel, University of Wisconsin, Madison
Discussant: Alan D. Wade, California State University, Sacramento

SECTION II: PROBLEMS OF EFFECTIVE FUNCTIONING

ADOLESCENT PREGNANCY: AN INTERPERSONAL SKILL
TRAINING APPROACH TO PREVENTION
Speakers: Steven P. Schinke, University of Washington, Seattle
Lewayne D. Gilchrist, University of Washington, Seattle

BLACK AND WHITE COTHERAPISTS: EFFECTS ON THE
HELPING PROCESS
Speakers: Eugene M. Thomas, Evanston Family Counseling Service,
Evanston, Ill.
Ben Sultz, Evanston Family Counseling Service, Evanston, Ill.

CHILD SUPPORT ENFORCEMENT: FEDERAL AND STATE
PERSPECTIVES ON POLICY AND OPERATIONS
Speakers: Louis B. Hays, HEW, Washington
David L. Bailey, Michigan Department of Social Services, Lansing

THE CONTRACT IN HUMAN SERVICES: HOPE OR HOAX?
Speakers: Pallassana Balgopal, University of Houston, Houston, Texas
Carlton E. Munson, University of Houston, Houston, Texas

CRISIS IN THE FAMILY? A NATIONAL DEBATE
Speaker: A. Kenton Williams, HEW, Kansas City, Mo.

DAY CARE AS A SOCIAL WORK CAUSE: THIRTY-FIVE
MILLION CHILDREN—OUR MOST IGNORED CHILD
POPULATION
Speakers: Louise L. Sally Brown, Wayne State University, Detroit
Elizabeth Prescott, Pacific Oaks College, Pasadena, Calif.

DOMESTIC VIOLENCE, POLICE SOCIAL WORK, AND POLITICS:
A MODEL FOR CHANGE
Speaker: Maryann Mahaffey, Wayne State University, Detroit

EFFECTIVE PROGRAMMING IN FAMILY TREATMENT OF
ALCOHOLISM
Speaker: Curtis Janzen, University of Maryland, Baltimore

EMPLOYEE ASSISTANCE PROGRAM IN INDUSTRY: BECHTEL
CORPORATION, A MODEL
Speakers: Roger K. Good, Bechtel Corporation, San Francisco
Beth A. Tozer, Bechtel Corporation, San Francisco
John Turner, M.D., Bechtel Corporation, San Francisco

ERRONEOUS USE OF ECONOMIC AND CULTURAL FACTORS IN
FAMILY THERAPY
Speakers: George S. Greenberg, Louisiana State Medical School, New
Orleans
Luciano A. Santa Cruz, University of Arkansas, Little Rock
William S. Van Veen, M.D., Louisiana State Medical School, New Or-
leans

EVALUATING SOCIAL WORK PRACTICE: A CONCEPTUAL
MODEL AND CASE EXAMPLE
Speakers: Steven P. Schinke, University of Washington, Seattle
Betty J. Blythe, University of Washington, Seattle
Howard J. Doueck, University of Washington, Seattle

FACTORS RELATED TO STABILITY IN UPWARDLY MOBILE
BLACK FAMILIES
Speaker: Harriette Pipes McAdoo, Howard University Washington

FAMILIES, SOCIAL SERVICES, AND SOCIAL POLICY
Speakers: Robert W. Moroney, University of North Carolina, Chapel
Hill
Mary Lystad, National Institute of Mental Health, Rockville, Md.

FINDINGS AND IMPLICATIONS FROM AN IN-SERVICE
CASEWORK TRAINING PROGRAM FOR PARAPROFESSIONALS
Speakers: Bruce C. McQuaker, Travelers Aid Society, Chicago
Henry H. Ebihara, Travelers Aid Society, Chicago

INTEGRATING STAFF AND RESIDENT GROUP PROCESSES IN
ADOLESCENT GROUP HOMES
Speakers: Carlton E. Munson, University of Houston, Houston, Texas
Chris Anlauf Sabatino, Fairfax Public Schools, Springfield, Va.

MAJOR LEGISLATIVE AND POLICY ISSUES AFFECTING FAMILIES, CHILDREN, AND YOUTH
Speaker: Harold Washington, University of Kansas, Lawrence

THE MOTHER-CENTERED FAMILY: A RESPONSE TO A SOCIOECONOMIC REALITY
Speaker: Elvira Craig De Silva, University of Wisconsin, Milwaukee

PLIGHT OF THE BLACK CHILD IN THE 1970s; SUGGESTIONS FOR THE 1980s
Speaker: Bob Jones, Niles Children's Home, Kansas City, Mo.

RECRUITING BLACK HOMES FOR BLACK CHILDREN—CONCEPTS AND TECHNIQUES
Speaker: Jacqueline Hampton, Black Adoption Programs and Services, Kansas City, Kans.

TRANSACTIONAL ANALYSIS IN PARENT COUNSELING AND EDUCATION
Speaker: Rebecca F. Griffin, Montgomery County Public Schools, Silver Spring, Md.

UTAH: THE FIRST STATE TO REMOVE STATUS OFFENSES FROM JUVENILE CODE-PROGRESS REPORT
Speakers: Willard Malstrom, Utah Department of Social Services, Salt Lake City
James P. Wheeler, Utah Department of Social Services, Salt Lake City

SECTION III: SOCIAL ASPECTS OF HEALTH

ADOLESCENT PARENTS—SERVICES AND POLICIES
Speakers: Mrs. Caroline Gaston, New Futures School, Albuquerque, N.Mex.
Susan H. Fischman, University of Maryland, Baltimore

A COMMUNITY DEVELOPMENT APPROACH TO AN ALTERNATIVE AFTERCARE PROGRAM FOR DISCHARGED MENTAL PATIENTS
Speakers: Stephen M. Rose, State University of New York, Stony Brook
Donna L. Chaglasian, State University of New York, Stony Brook

COST CONTAINMENT IN PRIMARY HEALTH CARE: AN INTERDISCIPLINARY APPROACH
Speakers: Roger Manela, Health Care Institute, Detroit
Harold Gardner, M.D., Health Care Institute, Detroit
Discussant: Rosalie A. Kane, University of California, Los Angeles

THE EFFECTS OF NEW MENTAL HEALTH LAWS ON CHILDREN'S SERVICES
Speakers: Anita Bryce, St. Francis Hospital, Pittsburgh
Suzanne Stenzel, University of Pittsburgh, Pittsburgh
Judge Leopoldo G. Sanchez, Superior Court of Los Angeles County, Los Angeles
Stephen J. Morse, University of Southern California, Los Angeles

ETHICAL AND LEGAL ISSUES IN THE CARE OF DEFECTIVE
NEWBORNS
Panelists: Betty Bernard, M.D., University of Southern California
Charlotte C. Green, University of California Medical Center, San
Francisco
William J. Winslade, University of California, Los Angeles

EXPANDED ROLES FOR SOCIAL WORKERS
Speakers: Lucie Benedikt, New York State Department of Health, New
York
Wilma Rose, Nassau County Medical Center, East Meadow, N.Y.
Shirley Komoto, Charles R. Drew Medical School. Los Angeles
Susumu Yokoyama, University of Southern California Medical Center,
Los Angeles

FOLLOW-UP ON OPENING GENERAL SESSION ON HEALTH
INSURANCE—IMPLICATIONS FOR PRACTICE
Speakers: Harold Hambrick, Western Association of Neighborhood
Health Centers, Los Angeles
Milton I. Roemer, M.D., University of California, Los Angeles

FREE CLINIC CONCEPT AND HOW THE CLINICS FUNCTION
Speakers: Miriam West, Los Angeles
Eugene Lokey, Northern California Council of Free and Community
Clinics
Castulo de La Rocha, La Clinica Familiar Del Barrio Free Clinic, Los
Angeles
Estelle Tuvman, Senior Citizens Screening Clinic, Santa Monica, Calif.
Helene K. Cohen, Association of Free and Community Clinics, Los
Angeles County, Los Angeles

GROUP SERVICES FOR CANCER PATIENTS AND THEIR
RELATIVES
Speakers: Sona Euster, Memorial Sloan-Kettering Cancer Center, New
York
Lucie Benedikt, New York State Department of Health, New York

AN INNOVATIVE HEALTH CARE PROGRAM FOR SERVING
AND INVOLVING THE ELDERLY
Speakers: Jordan I. Kosberg, Case Western Reserve University, Cleve-
land
Fran L. Thoms, Cleveland State University, Cleveland

MINORITY PARTICIPATION IN DEVELOPMENTAL
DISABILITIES PROGRAMS: A PRELIMINARY REPORT OF A
NATIONWIDE STUDY
Speakers: Mrs. Naomi T. Gray, New Dimensions in Community Ser-
vice, San Francisco
Beverley J. Morgan, New Dimensions in Community Service, San
Francisco

THE MULTIDISCIPLINARY GERONTOLOGY CENTER: A RICH
RESOURCE FOR THE DEVELOPMENT OF SERVICES WITH AND
IN BEHALF OF OLDER ADULTS
Panelists: Margaret E. Hartford, University of Southern California,
Los Angeles
Steven Zarit, University of Southern California, Los Angeles
Robert Wiswell, University of Southern California, Los Angeles
Pauline Ragan, University of Southern California, Los Angeles
Mary M. Seguin, University of California, Los Angeles

THE NEWBORN AS A CITIZEN WHOSE BEHAVIOR MAKES A
DIFFERENCE
Speaker: Lewis P. Lipsitt, Brown University, Providence, R.I.

AN OVERVIEW OF HOLISTIC HEALTH CARE
Speaker: Patricia Phillips, Holistic Health Center, Beverly Hills, Calif.

PRERETIREMENT PROGRAMS
Speakers: Joanne Muir Behm, Community College of Philadephia
Ceane Rabada, Montgomery County Office on Older Adults, Norris-
town, Pa.
Vickie E. Brewer, Mental Health/Mental Retardation of Southeast
Texas, Beaumont
Karen Coller, Gulf Coast Community Services Association, Houston,
Texas
Reactor: Ted Ellsworth, Los Angeles County Federation of Labor, Los
Angeles

PSYCHOSOCIAL ISSUES IN THE CARE OF PEOPLE WITH
CHRONIC DISEASES
Panelists: Kris Ferguson, University of Michigan Arthritis Center, Ann
Arbor
Barbara Figley, University of Michigan Arthritis Center, Ann Arbor
Barbara Bradley, Rancho Los Amigos, Downey, Calif.
John J. Wood, National Multiple Sclerosis Society, New York
Respondents: Carol Doss, Nancy Kennedy, and Steve Long

QUALITY ASSURANCE SYSTEMS FOR THE LARGE HOSPITAL OR
LARGE SOCIAL WORK DEPARTMENT
Speakers: Tessie S. Cleveland, Martin Luther King, Jr., General Hospi-
tal, Los Angeles
Claudia J. Coulton, University Hospitals, Cleveland

QUALITY ASSURANCE SYSTEMS FOR THE SMALL HOSPITAL OR
SMALL SOCIAL WORK DEPARTMENT
Speakers: Mona Stone, Stamford Hospital, Stamford, Conn.
Lois Portnoff, Suburban General Hospital, Norristown, Pa.

REHABILITATION SERVICES TO CANCER AMPUTEES—AN
INTERAGENCY PROGRAM
Panelists: Catherine Cordoba, American Cancer Society, Los Angeles
Linda Nishinaka, Orthopaedic Hospital, Los Angeles
Patricia Heidelberger, Sarcoma Consultative Network, Los Angeles

RURAL HEALTH CARE: MEETING HEALTH NEEDS IN THE
AREAS OF PHYSICAL AND MENTAL HEALTH, HEALTH SERVICE
PLANNING, AND MANPOWER
Speaker: Darrell Burkland, St. Luke's Hospital, Fargo, N.Dak.
Reactor: Milton I. Roemer, M.D., University of California, Los Angeles

SOCIAL WORK AND EMERGENCY SERVICES—IMPLICATIONS
FOR PRACTICE
Speakers: Edith Groner, Northridge Hospital Foundation, Northridge,
Calif.
Tessie S. Cleveland, Martin Luther King, Jr., General Hospital, Los
Angeles
Charles Wilt, St. Paul-Ramsey Hospital and Medical Center, St. Paul;
Janet Polley, University of Minnesota, Minneapolis; and V. B. Tuason,
M.D., St. Paul-Ramsey Hospital and Medical Center, St. Paul (coauthors)

SOCIAL WORK SERVICES IN SEPARATION, DIVORCE, AND
DEATH
Speakers: Janet Winn Korpela, University of Rochester, Rochester,
N.Y.
Hal Lipton, Children's Hospital National Medical Center, Washington

THE THEORY AND PRACTICE OF ETHNIC MEDICINE: ETHNIC
FACTORS AND THE DISCREPANCIES BETWEEN PATIENTS' AND
DOCTORS' PROBLEM LISTS
Speaker: Sydney G. Margolin, M.D., Denver Department of Health and
Hospitals, Denver
Discussant: Hector F. Myers, Charles Drew Postgraduate Medical Cen-
ter, Los Angeles

URBAN AND RESERVATION NATIVE AMERICAN ALCOHOLISM
PROGRAMS—NEEDS OF THE RECIPIENTS AND SERVICES
OFFERED
Speakers: Sarge Campbell, Flathead Reservation Comprehensive Alco-
hol Program, Ronan, Mont.
Darrel Whitebear, Native American Alcoholism and Drug Abuse Pro-
gram, Oakland, Calif.

VICTIMS OF RAPE
Speaker: Gail Abarbanel, Santa Monica Hospital Medical Center, Santa
Monica, Calif.

SECTION IV: LEISURE-TIME NEEDS

INFORMAL EDUCATION AND RECREATION—PART OF TOTAL
DEVELOPMENT
Speakers: Anne Freidus, Girl Scouts of the USA, New York
Glenn Martin, Torrance-South Bay YMCA, Torrance, Calif.

INTEGRATED PLANNING—VOLUNTARY AND PUBLIC
RECREATION AND LEISURE-SERVING AGENCIES
Panelists: James Hadaway, Los Angeles City Recreation and Park De-
partment

Joseph Halper, Los Angeles County Department of Parks and Recreation, Los Angeles
Marilyn A. Jensen, California State University, Long Beach
Gordon Trigg, Los Angeles United School District
David Friesen, United Way, Los Angeles

LEISURE—WHAT IS IT FOR THE AGING?
Panelists: Marion Marshall, California Department of Education, Sacramento
Herbert Nalibow, Department of Human Resources, Long Beach, Calif.
Domingo Delgado, Los Angeles County Department of Parks and Recreation, Los Angeles

NEW LEGISLATIVE PROPOSAL FOR THE RENEWAL OF VOLUNTARY AGENCIES' FACILITIES
Speaker: Peter L. Kohnstamm, YMCA of Greater New York, New York

VOLUNTEER CAREER: HOW HIGH IS UP? HOW BROAD IS WIDE?
Panelists: Ann Shaw, National Center for Voluntary Action, Los Angeles
Betty Kozasa, Asian American Voluntary Action Center, Los Angeles
Edward Piper, United Airlines, Los Angeles
Dean Porter, Association of Junior Leagues, Long Beach, Calif.
Leta G. Reynolds, County Department of Health Services, Los Angeles

VOLUNTEERISM—NOW AND IN THE FUTURE
Speaker: Eva Schindler-Rainman, Los Angeles

SECTION V: PROVISION AND MANAGEMENT OF SOCIAL SERVICES

CASE COORDINATION AND SERVICE INTEGRATION PROJECTS: CLIENT IMPACT, PROGRAM SURVIVAL, AND RESEARCH PRIORITIES
Speakers: Raymond M. Steinberg, University of Southern California, Los Angeles
Genevieve W. Carter, University of Southern California, Los Angeles
Eunice B. Evans, Pennsylvania Department of Public Welfare, Wilkes-Barre
Jerry Turem, HEW, Washington

CONSUMERS' PERSPECTIVES ON HUMAN SERVICES
Speakers: Chuck Richardson, Northeast Ohio Areawide Coordinating Agency, Cleveland
Arnold Perkins, Youth Advocates of San Francisco, Sausalito, Calif.
Dolores Arenas, National Latin American Federation, Cheyenne, Wyo.
Carol Turner, Urban League of San Diego, San Diego

COORDINATION OF SOCIAL SERVICES IN PUBLIC AND
PRIVATE ARENAS
  Speaker: Wilbur Finch, University of Southern California, Los Angeles
  Joav Gozali, Jewish Vocational Service, Milwaukee

DO WE NEED SERVICE INTEGRATION?
  Speaker: Steven A. Minter, Cleveland Foundation, Cleveland

IMPACT OF SEPARATION OF SERVICES FROM INCOME
MAINTENANCE
  Speaker: Irving Piliavin, University of Wisconsin, Madison
  Discussant: Jon Van Til, Rutgers University, Camden, N.J.

MOBILIZING SUPPORT FOR SOCIAL SERVICES
  Speakers: Michio Suzuki, HEW, Washington
  John Conway, United Way of America, Alexandria, Va.
  George M. Nishinaka, Special Service for Groups, Los Angeles

OUTCOME ASSESSMENT AND NEEDS ASSESSMENT IN HUMAN
SERVICES
  Speakers: Edmund H. Armentrout, Research Group, Atlanta
  Jon L. Bushnel, University of Wisconsin, Milwaukee
  Allan L. Service, University of Wisconsin, Milwaukee

THE PERSONAL SOCIAL SERVICES SYSTEM—AN APPROACH
TO INTEGRATED SERVICES DELIVERY
  Speakers: John A. Yankey, Case Western Reserve University, Cleveland
  Steven A. Minter, Cleveland Foundation, Cleveland

THE ROLE OF DATA IN DECISION-MAKING BY SOCIAL
WORKERS
  Speakers: Deborah Bass, HEW, Washington
  Discussants: George Rold, HEW, Denver
  Robert Lewis, Utah Unification Project, Salt Lake City
  John Hiland, Montgomery County Department of Social Services,
  Rockville, Md.

VOLUNTEER CITIZEN PARTICIPATION IN RURAL AND URBAN
SOCIAL SERVICES
  Speakers: Susan Beard, West Virginia Department of Welfare, Charles-
  ton
  Kathleen Hill, Howard University, Washington
  Discussant: Jon Van Til, Rutgers University, Camden, N.J.

SECTION VI: SOCIETAL PROBLEMS

COMMUNITY-BASED PROGRAMS AND POSTRELEASE
ADJUSTMENT OF YOUTH FROM CORRECTIONAL PROGRAMS
  Speakers: William H. Barton, University of Michigan, Ann Arbor
  Charles Wolfson, University of Michigan, Ann Arbor

COMMUNITY-RELATED ALTERNATIVES TO JUVENILE
DELINQUENCY
Panelists: Mrs. Betty G. Adams, Department of Institutions and Social
Rehabilitation Services, Oklahoma City
Marian Opala, Oklahoma State Industrial Court, Oklahoma City
Bill Stephens, Smith-Stephens Associates, Oklahoma City
George Howard, California Youth Authority, Sacramento, Calif.
Judge Alan J. Couch, Cleveland County, Oklahoma
Dan Broughton, Department of Institutions and Social Rehabilitation
Services, Oklahoma City
Doug Gibson, Youth Criminal Center for Oklahoma County, Oklahoma City

ENVIRONMENTAL CONSIDERATIONS IN SOCIAL WELFARE
AND/OR ECOLOGICAL PRINCIPLES IN SOCIAL WELFARE
Speaker: Hunter Sheldon, California Conservation Project, Los
Angeles

HELPING RAPE VICTIMS IN RURAL AREAS
Speakers: Judith Davenport, Mississippi State University, State College,
Miss.
Joseph Davenport III, Mississippi State University, State College, Miss.
Vickie Stasth, Rape Crisis Center, Visalia, Calif.

IMMIGRATION: CURRENT ISSUES AND IMPLICATIONS FOR
SOCIAL WELFARE
Speaker: Leonel J. Castillo, U.S. Immigration and Naturalization Service, Washington

LEGALLY FREED—THEIR ONLY CHANCE
Panelists: Virginia Hayes Sibbison, Welfare Research, Albany, N.Y.
Joseph J. O'Hara, Welfare Research, Albany, N.Y.
Discussants: Helaine Kerfoot, California State Department of Health,
Sacramento
Richard O. Pancost, Children's Home Society of California, Los
Angeles

SCHOOL DESEGREGATION—HOW CITIZENS AND COMMUNITY
AGENCIES CAN HELP IT WORK
Speakers: Sam Ethridge, National Education Association, Washington
Zane Meckler, Community Network Integration Fact Line, Los
Angeles
Discussant: Harry Kitano, University of California, Los Angeles

SOCIAL WORK ON WHEELS
Speakers: Harris Chaiklin, University of Maryland, Baltimore
Shlomo Sharlin, Haifa University, Haifa, Israel
Discussant: Norman V. Lourie, Pennsylvania Department of Public
Welfare, Harrisburg

TRENDS IN INSTITUTIONALIZATION OF JUVENILE
DELINQUENTS IN THE UNITED STATES, COLONIAL TIMES
TO 1970
Speaker: Mike Sherraden, University of Michigan, Ann Arbor
Discussant: Brian F. Cahill, California Association of Children's Residential Centers, Sacramento

WITHOUT READIN' YOU AIN'T NOTHIN' (GETTING
FUNCTIONAL ILLITERACY ON THE SOCIAL WORK AGENDA)
Speakers: Leonard Schneiderman, Indiana University, Indianapolis
Paula Schneiderman, Indiana University, Indianapolis

WOMEN AND WORK
Speaker: Kathleen Riordan, U.S. Department of Labor, Philadelphia
Discussants: Jane Moody, U.S. Department of Labor, San Francisco

WORK IN AMERICA—THE FUTURE
Speakers: Wil J. Smith, West Virginia University, Morgantown
Frederick A. Zeller, West Virginia University, Morgantown
Robert Bykowski, University of Michigan, Ann Arbor

WORK IN AMERICA—PAST AND PRESENT
Speakers: Wil J. Smith, West Virginia University, Morgantown
Frederick A. Zeller, West Virginia University, Morgantown

AUTHORS' FORUM

ADMINISTRATION: STAFF DEVELOPMENT
Speakers: George Hoshino, University of Minnesota, Minneapolis
Dorothy Van Soest, Ramsey County-University of Minnesota Training
Project, Minneapolis
Nancy Wilson, Ramsey County-University of Minnesota Training Project, Minneapolis
Jerome Seliger, California State University, Northridge, Calif.

ADMINISTRATION: STAFF RESOURCES
Speakers: Morley D. Glicken, University of Kansas, Lawrence
David Jeffreys, Winthrop College, Rock Hill, S.C.
Larky Worth, Social Action Workshop, Philadelphia

THE CARING FUNCTION IN SOCIAL WORK
Speakers: Paul Abels, Case Western Reserve University, Cleveland, and
Sonia Abels, Cleveland State University, Cleveland (coauthors)
Frederick W. Massey and Ronnie Fishman, County of Los Angeles/Harbor General Hospital, Torrance, Calif. (coauthors)

EVALUATION OF AGENCY SERVICES
Speakers: John S. Wodarski, University of Maryland, Baltimore
Barbara K. Shore, University of Pittsburgh, Pittsburgh, and Hobart
Harris, Allegheny County Mental Health/Mental Retardation Programs, Pittsburgh (coauthors)

INTEGRATION OF SERVICES
Speakers: Roland G. Meinert, University of Missouri, Columbia
Kenneth Schuman, Lower East Side Family Union, New York
John R. Seaman and Pallassana Balgopal, University of Houston, Houston, Texas (coauthors)

MENTAL HEALTH
Speakers: Lambert Maguire, University of Michigan, Ann Arbor
Steven P. Segal, University of California, Berkeley
Arthur J. Cox, Florida State University, Tallahassee

SOCIAL WORK PRACTICE IN DIFFERENT SETTINGS
Speakers: Dan Rubenstein and Richard E. Mundy, Syracuse University, Syracuse, N.Y., and Mary Louise Rubenstein, Onadaga County Child Care Council, Syracuse, N.Y. (coauthors)
Joseph R. Steiner, Syracuse University, Syracuse, N.Y., and Esther C. C. Borst, Hoogovens Ijmuiden B. V., Alkmaar, Netherlands (coauthors)
Carlton E. Munson, University of Houston, Houston, Texas, and Carole Malin and Roderick Wagner, Homewood Retirement Centers, Hagerstown, Md. (coauthors)

VALUES UNDERLYING PRACTICE BEHAVIOR
Speakers: Joseph R. Steiner, Syracuse University, Syracuse, N.Y.
J. M. Kapoor and Sudarshan K. Singh, Indiana University, Indianapolis (coauthors)

Cordell H. Thomas, The Road, Philadelphia

CONTINUING EDUCATION UNITS

CASE MANAGEMENT: RESPONDING TO THE WHOLE PERSON, PROVIDING ACCESS TO THE WHOLE SYSTEM
Workshop leaders: Ray M. Steinberg, University of Southern California, Los Angeles
Rachel Downing, University of Southern California, Los Angeles

CHANGING TRENDS IN THE VOLUNTEER WORLD
Workshop leader: Eva Schindler-Rainman, Los Angeles

CHILD ABUSE
Workshop leader: Jeanne Giovannoni, University of California, Los Angeles

COMPREHENSIVE/ADMINISTRATIVE MANAGEMENT PLANNING
Workshop leader: Alex J. Norman, University of California, Los Angeles

EFFECTIVE PUBLIC RELATIONS: ESTABLISHING AND ACHIEVING SPECIFIC GOALS
Workshop leader: Frances J. Hynds, University of Southern California, Los Angeles
Guest resource speaker: Don Bates, Public Relations Society of America, New York

UNDERSTANDING AND WORKING WITH SELF-HELP
ORGANIZATIONS
Workshop leader: Alfred H. Katz, University of California, Los Angeles

THE HOSPICE AS A SOCIAL HEALTH CARE INSTITUTION
Developed with the assistance of the Hillhaven Foundation, Tacoma,
Wash.
Speakers: Esther Lucile Brown, San Francisco
William C. Farr, M.D., Hillhaven Hospice, Tucson
Sister Teresa Marie McIntier, CSJ, Hillhaven Hospice, Tucson
Mary A. Cummings, Kaiser Foundation Health Plan, Los Angeles
Theodore H. Koff, University of Arizona, Tucson
Mrs. Marion Lupu, Pima Council on Aging, Pima, Ariz.
Stephen Shanfield, M.D., University of Arizona Medical Center, Tucson

INSTITUTES

NATIONAL SPEAK-OUT ON FAMILIES
Partially supported by the Office of Human Development Services, HEW

COMMISSION MEMBERS
Chairman: Mrs. Cynthia Wedel, American National Red Cross, Washington
Vice-chairman: Peter W. Forsythe, Edna McConnell Clark Foundation,
New York
Members: Lydia Rios Aguirre, University of Texas, El Paso; Scott Briar,
University of Washington, Seattle; Andrew Brown, United Auto
Workers, Detroit; Wallace Fulton, Equitable Life Assurance Society of
the United States, New York; Jack Hansan, American Public Welfare
Association, Washington; Alfred J. Kahn, Columbia University, New
York; Stanley Kruger, U.S. Office of Education, Washington; Judge
Jean L. Lewis, National Council of Juvenile Court Judges, Portland,
Oreg.; Helena Z. Lopata, Loyola University, Chicago; Norman V.
Lourie, Pennsylvania Department of Public Welfare, Harrisburg; Robert M. Rice, Family Service Association of America, New York; Sidney
Spector, National Council on the Aging, Cleveland; Dana F. Tracy,
Coalition for Children and Youth, Washington; John B. Turner, University of North Carolina, Chapel Hill; Eloise Whitten, Detroit;
George T. Wolff, Moses H. Cone Memorial Hospital, Greensboro,
N.C.

WHAT IS THE FEDERAL GOVERNMENT DOING ABOUT
REORGANIZING SOCIAL SERVICES?
Partially supported by the Office of Human Development Services, HEW
Speakers: Robert Morris, Brandeis University, Waltham, Mass.
C. David St. John, President's Reorganization Project, Washington
Jerry S. Turem, HEW, Washington

NATIONAL CONFERENCE ON SOCIAL WELFARE

THE EMERGING ROLE OF HISPANIC WOMEN
Panelists: Carmelo LaCayo, National Association for Spanish-speaking Elderly, Los Angeles
Alicia Madrid, Office of Migrant Services, Sacramento, Calif.
Gracia Molina Pick, Secondary Education Commission, La Jolla, Calif.

REPORT OF THE PRESIDENT'S COMMISSION ON MENTAL HEALTH
Speaker: Beverly Benson Long, President's Commission on Mental Health

SERVICES TO VIETNAMESE REFUGEES—CONCEPTS AND PROBLEMS
Panelists: Tran Ninh Tung, M.D., George Washington University Medical School Hospital, Washington
Elena S. H. Yu, University of Victoria, Victoria, B.C., Canada
Anthony Ishisaka, University of Washington, Seattle
Mrs. Le Thi Naga, Illinois Department of Public Aid, Chicago

NCSW PUBLIC RELATIONS COMMITTEE

THE EDITORIAL DECISION—WHERE AND HOW DO SOCIAL WELFARE AGENCIES FIT?
Panelists: Peter Noyes, KNBC News Center 4, Los Angeles
Arthur Schreiber, Commuter Computer, Inc., Los Angeles

VIDEO THEATER

CHICANO CONTENT FOR COMMUNITY PRACTICE PRESENTATION
Discussion leader: Clayton T. Shorkey, University of Texas, Austin

CHILD DEVELOPMENT
Discussion leaders: Mario Tonti, Case Western Reserve University, Cleveland
Clayton T. Shorkey, University of Texas, Austin

CHILD DEVELOPMENT AND DEVELOPMENTAL HANDICAPS
Discussion leader: David Katz, Washington University, St. Louis

LIVE DEMONSTRATION: MAKING A VIDEOTAPE
Session leaders: Dorothy Van Soest, Ramsey County-University of Minnesota Training Project, Minneapolis
Maura Zunt, Ramsey County-University of Minnesota Training Project, Minneapolis
Nancy Wilson, Ramsey County-University of Minnesota Training Project, Minneapolis

REGARDING OURSELVES: THE HISTORY OF WOMEN IN SOCIAL WORK
Discussion leaders: Sondra Match, National Association of Social Workers, Washington
Betty Johnson, National Association of Social Workers, Los Angeles

SOCIAL WORK EDUCATION AND PRACTICE IN CHILE TODAY:
AN EYEWITNESS REPORT
Speaker: Maryann Mahaffey, Wayne State University, Detroit

VANTAGE POINT: VIDEO-ASSISTED TRAINING FOR CHILD
PROTECTIVE SERVICE
Workshop leader: C. Thomas Cruthirds, University of Tennessee, Nashville

VOLUNTEER ADMINISTRATION FOR SOCIAL HUMAN
SERVICES
Discussion leader: Mrs. Harriet H. Naylor, HEW, Washington

ASSOCIATE GROUPS

ALLIANCE OF INFORMATION AND REFERRAL SERVICES

GAO REPORT: IMPROVED FEDERAL INVOLVEMENT IN
INFORMATION AND REFERRAL SERVICE
Speakers: William Henderson, U.S. General Accounting Office, Seattle
Henry Tomlinson, U.S. General Accounting Office, Seattle

INFORMATION AND REFERRAL SYSTEM IN THE LIBRARY
Speakers: Terry Crowley, California State University, Chico
Myles Martin, University of Toledo, Toledo

NETWORK CONCEPT: INTERAGENCY COOPERATION IN
INFORMATION AND REFERRAL
Speakers: Jackie Dehner, Information and Referral Service, Portland,
Oreg.
Harold Edelston, United Way of America, Alexandria, Va.
Steve Fox, Los Angeles County Department of Public Social Services,
El Monte, Calif.
Caroline Sullivan, Area Agency on Aging, Portland, Oreg.

NEW TECHNOLOGY IN INFORMATION AND REFERRAL
Speakers: Henry L. Mayers, Michigan Department of Social Services,
Lansing
Thomas Deahl, Health and Welfare Council, Philadelphia

UNIFORM CLASSIFICATION SYSTEMS IN INFORMATION AND
REFERRAL
Speaker: Robert Galloway, National Assembly, New York

USE OF INFORMATION AND REFERRAL DATA IN SOCIAL
SERVICE PLANNING AND ADMINISTRATION
Speakers: Shirley Lee Zimmerman and Richard Sterne, University of
Minnesota, Minneapolis (coauthors)
Reactor: Michael Goodroad, South Dakota Tie-Line, Pierre, S.Dak.

VOLUNTEERS IN INFORMATION AND REFERRAL:
RECRUITMENT, SELECTION, RETENTION
Speakers: Arlene Schindler, National Center for Voluntary Action,
Washington
Yvonne Cooper, Voluntary Action Center, Las Vegas, Nev.

AMERICAN COUNCIL FOR NATIONALITIES SERVICE

SERVICES TO IMMIGRANTS: IMPLICATIONS FOR SOCIAL WELFARE POLICY IN A MULTICULTURAL SOCIETY

Speaker: Michael D. Blum, Nationalities Service Center of Philadelphia
Discussants: Sister Susan Kam, Los Angeles County Indochese Social Service Demonstration Project, Los Angeles
Elisa Riesgo, El Centro de Salud Mental, Oakland, Calif.
Joseph H. Solis, University of California, Berkeley

AMERICAN PUBLIC WELFARE ASSOCIATION

MANPOWER DEVELOPMENT AND TRAINING FOR THE HUMAN SERVICES: TWO STATES' EXPERIENCES UNDER TITLE XX

Speakers: L. G. Ferguson, Texas Department of Human Resources, Austin
Anthony W. Mitchell, Utah Department of Social Services, Salt Lake City

PUBLIC AND PRIVATE ROLES IN THE DELIVERY OF HUMAN SERVICES

Speakers: Samuel P. Berman, Vista del Mar Child Care Service and Reiss-Davis Child Study Center, Los Angeles
Merle E. Springer, Texas Department of Human Resources, Austin

WELFARE REFORM: JOBS AND WORK REQUIREMENTS

Speakers: Joseph Corbett, U.S. Department of Labor, Washington
Keith Comrie, Los Angeles County Department of Public Social Services, El Monte, Calif.

ASIAN AMERICAN SOCIAL WORKERS

SERVICE DELIVERY TO SELECTIVE GROUPS—ALTERNATIVE MODELS

Speakers: Jocelyn G. Yap, Pacific/Asian Mental Health Clinic, Los Angeles
Sister Susan Kam, Los Angeles County Indochinese Social Service Demonstration Project, Los Angeles
Sam Chan, Children's Hospital of Los Angeles
Discussant: Seico Hayashi, Asian Rehabilitation Services, Los Angeles

ASSOCIATION OF JUNIOR LEAGUES

VOLUNTEERS WORKING AS PARAPROFESSIONALS IN THE JUVENILE JUSTICE FIELD: SUCCESSES AND CONCERNS

Panelists: Sylvia Pizzini, Department of Social Services, Los Angeles
Mrs. Lydia Kelly, Florence Crittenton Home, Los Angeles
Marcina Buck, Los Angeles
Discussants: Joanna Knopinski, Los Angeles
K. C. Law, Los Angeles
Judy Baron, Los Angeles

CHILD WELFARE LEAGUE

THE COUNCIL ON ACCREDITATION OF SERVICES FOR FAMILIES AND CHILDREN: WHAT WILL IT MEAN FOR AGENCIES?

Speaker: Jeffrey Hantover, Council on Accrediation of Services for Families and Children, New York

FOSTER PARENTING AN ADOLESCENT

Speaker: Joseph Moore, Child Welfare League of America, New York

ORGANIZING A STATEWIDE VOLUNTEER PROGRAM IN A VOLUNTARY AGENCY

Panelists: Mrs. Eloise Segebartt, Children's Home Society of California, Los Angeles

PARENTING PLUS: AN INTRODUCTION TO FOSTER PARENTING

Speaker: Jeanne Hunzeker, Child Welfare League of America, New York

PURCHASE OF SERVICES: TITLE XX CONTRACTING FOR CHILDREN'S SERVICES

Panelists: Eileen Wolff, HEW, Washington
Robert Lippert, Boys' and Girls' Aid Society of San Diego, Calif.
Candace Mueller, Child Welfare League of America, Washington

TURNING THEM LOOSE: COMMUNITY AGENCIES RESPONSE TO STATUS OFFENDERS

Panelists: Jane Martin, Los Angeles County Probation Department, Downey, Calif.
Frank Jameson, Jr., Police Department, Pasadena, Calif.

THE USE OF TRAINED VOLUNTEERS AND EDUCATIONAL FILM DISCUSSION LEADERS

Panelists: Mrs. Eloise Segebartt, Children's Home Society of California, Los Angeles
Mrs. Charlotte De Armond, Children's Home Society of California, Los Angeles

VALUES CLARIFICATION IN ASSESSMENT OF ADOPTIVE AND FOSTER FAMILIES

Speaker: Julius R. Ballew, University of Michigan, Ann Arbor
Discussant: Carla Overberger, Children's Home Society of California, San Francisco

COUNCIL ON SOCIAL WORK EDUCATION

DEVELOPMENT IN EDUCATION AND PRACTICE FOR SOCIAL WORK IN AN INDUSTRIAL SETTING

Speakers: Myles Johnson, Project on Social Work in an Industrial Setting, Washington
Carvel U. Taylor, CNA Insurance Company, Chicago
Mario D'Angeli, San Francisco State University, San Francisco

WOMEN AS SOCIAL SERVICE MANAGERS
Speakers: Mary Ann Quaranta, Fordham University, New York
Naomi Gottlieb, University of Washington, Seattle

FAMILY SERVICE ASSOCIATION OF AMERICA

FINDINGS OF THE FAMILY SERVICE ASSOCIATION OF
AMERICA ETHNICITY PROJECT: MODEL MENTAL HEALTH
DELIVERY SYSTEMS TO BLACK AND PUERTO RICAN
COMMUNITIES
Speaker: Emelicia Mizio, Family Service Association of America, New
York

ADVOCACY PROGRAMS: AWARD WINNING MODELS
Panelists: Judy Bretz, Family and Child Services, Birmingham, Ala.
Mrs. Eleanor D. Taylor, Family and Children's Service of Lancaster
County, Lancaster, Pa.
Ronald Yoder, Metropolitan Family Service, Portland, Oreg.

HIAS

THE NEWLY ARRIVED SOVIET JEWISH IMMIGRANTS:
CHARACTERISTICS; ADJUSTMENT; NATURE OF SETTLEMENT
ASSISTANCE BY COOPERATING JEWISH COMMUNAL SERVICES
Speaker: Gaynor I. Jacobson, HIAS, New York
Discussants: Mel Roth, Jewish Family Service, Los Angeles
Doris Hirsch, Jewish Vocational Service, Los Angeles
Ludmila Goldman, West Side Jewish Community Center, Los Angeles

NATIONAL ASSEMBLY

CAN VOLUNTARY AGENCIES COLLABORATE TO SERVICE
STATUS OFFENDERS? THE EXPERIENCE OF THE NATIONAL
JUVENILE JUSTICE PROGRAM COLLABORATION
Panelists: Martha Bernstein, National Council of Jewish Women, New
York
Marjorie Bigsby, National Board of YWCA, New York
Marianna Page Glidden, National Juvenile Justice Program Collabo-
ration, New York
Bill Burns, Interagency Collaboration Effort, Oakland, Calif.

NATIONAL ASSOCIATION FOR STATEWIDE HEALTH AND WELFARE

FUNDING STATE CONFERENCES AND CITIZEN ACTION
ORGANIZATIONS
Speaker: Rowland Bishop, National Association for Statewide Health
and Welfare, and National Conference on Social Welfare, Columbus,
Ohio

INFLUENCING STATE LEGISLATION FOR HUMAN SERVICES
Speaker: James W. Wimberly, Texas United Community Services, Austin

NATIONAL ASSOCIATION OF SOCIAL WORKERS

THE CARTER ADMINISTRATION AND AMERICAN FAMILIES: A
PROFESSIONAL SOCIAL WORK PERSPECTIVE
Panelists: Stephen Antler, Boston University, Boston
T. James Parham, HEW, Washington
Robert Hill, Urban League, Washington

CETA AND SOCIAL WELFARE
Panelists: Al Gonzales, National Association of Social Workers, Washington
Nancey ReMine, National Association of Counties, Washington
Kate Jesberg, National Rural Center, Washington

DEINSTITUTIONALIZATION: WHAT DOES THE PRESIDENT'S
COMMISSION ON MENTAL HEALTH SAY?
Panelists: Georgia L. McMurray, Community Service Society, New
York
Stuart A. Kirk, University of Wisconsin, Milwaukee
Norman V. Lourie, Pennsylvania Department of Public Welfare, Harrisburg

IMPLICATIONS FOR THE SOCIAL WORK PROFESSION: RECENT
DEVELOPMENTS IN SOCIAL SERVICE DELIVERY
Speaker: Arthur Katz, University of Kansas, Lawrence

PERSPECTIVES ON LONG-TERM CARE NEEDS OF MINORITY
AGED
Panelists: Alejandro Garcia, Brandeis University, Waltham, Mass.
Barbara Solomon, University of Southern California, Los Angeles
Frances Kobata, University of Southern California, Los Angeles

THE PURSUIT OF PEACE IN A VIOLENT SOCIETY: OPTIONS,
OBSTACLES, AND OPPORTUNITIES
Panelist: Barbara Star, University of Southern California, Los Angeles

VALIDATING SOCIAL WORK
Panelists: Marie Keeling, California Department of Health, Sacramento
Betty Pollack, Los Angeles
Marcia Stapleton, Reno, Nev.

WHY AREN'T MORE WOMEN SOCIAL WORK
ADMINISTRATORS?
Speakers: Ellen Dunbar, Eastern Washington State College, Cheney
Mary Flanagan, University of Houston, Houston, Texas

NATIONAL COUNCIL ON ALCOHOLISM

FAMILY TREATMENT FOR ALCOHOLISM
Speakers: Lorraine Hinkle, Coordinating Office for Drug and Alcohol
Abuse Programs, Philadelphia

Katherine Pike, National Council on Alcoholism, Los Angeles
Patricia Tate, California Black Commission on Alcoholism, Los Angeles

NATIONAL COUNCIL ON THE AGING

ELIMINATING MANDATORY RETIREMENT: IMPLICATIONS
FOR SOCIAL WELFARE ORGANIZATIONS AND FOR PRACTICE
Speaker: Jack Ossofsky, National Council on the Aging, Washington

EXPERIENCES IN THE USE OF OLDER PARAPROFESSIONALS
IN THE DELIVERY OF SOCIAL AND HUMAN SERVICES
Panelists: Rev. Leuma Maluia, Greater Los Angeles Community Action
Agency, Los Angeles
Leon Harper, Los Angeles County Department of Senior Citizens Af-
fairs, Los Angeles
Vicente Pichardo, Los Angeles United School District

MODELS FOR ASSURING CONTINUUM OF SERVICES FOR
OLDER PERSONS
Speakers: Lucile S. Costello, Senior Services, Cincinnati
Barbara Sklar, Mt. Zion Hospital and Geriatric Services, San Francisco

NEW ROLES FOR THE VOLUNTARY SECTOR: PROMOTING
AND MAINTAINING INDEPENDENT LIVING OF OLDER
PERSONS
Panelists: Martin Sicker, Administration on Aging, Washington
Hadley Hall, San Francisco Home Health Service, San Francisco

SELF-DISCOVERY THROUGH THE HUMANITIES: AN
INNOVATIVE PROGRAM FOR OLDER PERSONS IN GROUP
SETTINGS
Panelists: Velma Krauch, Senior Center Humanities Program, Vaca-
ville, Calif.
Rhea Rubin, Oregon State Library, Salem

NATIONAL INSTITUTE OF MENTAL HEALTH

DEINSTITUTIONALIZATION—A CRITICAL ASSESSMENT
Speakers: Stephen M. Rose, State University of New York, Stony Brook
William Tenhoor, National Institute of Mental Health, Rockville, Md.

REVISING SOCIAL WORK EDUCATION: TOWARD A NEW
AGENDA FOR MENTAL HEALTH TRAINING
Workshop leaders: Stephen M. Rose, State University of New York,
Stony Brook
Donna Chaglasian, State University of New York, Stony Brook
Marta Sotomayor, National Institute of Mental Health, Rockville, Md.

NATIONAL MULTIPLE SCLEROSIS SOCIETY

THE MULTIPLE SCLEROSIS HOME CARE COURSE—A
NATIONAL COLLABORATION
Speaker: John F. Larberg, National Multiple Sclerosis Society, New
York

Discussants: Mrs. Marie Fuess, Los Angeles Chapter of American National Red Cross

Jacquelyn Becker, Southern California Chapter of National Multiple Sclerosis Society, Burbank

NATIONAL RETIRED TEACHERS ASSOCIATION/AMERICAN ASSOCIATION OF RETIRED PERSONS

GOVERNMENT AND PRIVATE ORGANIZATIONS COOPERATE IN PROVIDING SERVICES TO THE ELDERLY. HERE'S HOW!!!

Panelists: Mary Ahern, American Red Cross, Los Angeles

Janet Levy, California Department on Aging, Sacramento

William Patberg, American Association of Retired Persons, Santa Barbara

Leon Harper, National Association Area Agencies on Aging/Senior Citizens Affairs, Los Angeles

PLANNED PARENTHOOD–WORLD POPULATION

ABORTION—WHAT'S NEW?

Panelists: Jill Jakes, Esq., American Civil Liberties Union, Los Angeles

J. Hugh Anwyl, Planned Parenthood of Los Angeles

Irvin Cushner, M.D., University of California, Los Angeles

NEW APPROACHES TO AN OLD ISSUE—TEEN SEXUALITY

Speakers: Linda Wilson, Planned Parenthood of Los Angeles

Francie Young, Planned Parenthood of Los Angeles

Farrell Freeman, Planned Parenthood of Los Angeles

Monica Mizrahi, Planned Parenthood of Los Angeles

Susan Kendall, Planned Parenthood of Los Angeles

Jeff Williams, Planned Parenthood of Los Angeles

RURAL SOCIAL WORK CAUCUS

RURAL SOCIAL WORK CAUCUS MEETING

Chairman: Lynn Hulen, California State University, Fresno

SALVATION ARMY

RESIDENTIAL TREATMENT FOR ABUSED WOMEN AND CHILDREN

Speaker: Dorothy Deering, Salvation Army, Seattle

VETERANS ADMINISTRATION

A MODEL FOR INTERAGENCY COLLABORATION IN HUMAN SERVICES

Panelists: Norma Donigan, Veterans Administration, Southern California

Janet Erickson, Veterans Administration, Southern California

Tadashi Kowta, Veterans Administration, Southern California

Tony Winkowski, Veterans Administration, Southern Caliornia

U.S. COMMITTEE ICSW

GOING TO JERUSALEM—PLANS FOR THE ICSW CONFERENCE
   Speaker: Werner Boehm, Rutgers University, New Brunswick, N.J.

HUMAN SERVICE MANPOWER IN THE DEVELOPING
WORLD—IMPLICATIONS FOR AMERICAN INSTITUTIONS
   Speaker: James Goodman, Agency for Internaional Development,
   Washington

INTERNATIONAL PERSPECTIVE IN COMMUNITY
DEVELOPMENT: AMERICAN AND CANADIAN INDIANS
   Panelists: Emmett Dawson Sarracino, American Indian Free Clinic,
   Compton, Calif.
   Herbert Patrick Joe, Chilliwak Area Indian Council, Sardis, B.C., Can-
   ada
   Discussant: James Goodman, Agency for International Development,
   Washington

Appendix B: Organization of the Conference for 1978

OFFICERS

President: John B. Turner, Chapel Hill, N.C.
First Vice-president: Bertram M. Beck, New York
Second Vice-president: Bernard J. Coughlin, S.J., Spokane, Wash.
Third Vice-president: Tsuguo Ikeda, Seattle
Secretary: Dorothy Hollingsworth, Seattle
Treasurer: Frederick M. Isaac, Columbus, Ohio
Past President: David Jacobson, San Antonio
President-elect: Mitchell I. Ginsberg, New York
Executive Director: Margaret E. Berry, New York and Columbus, Ohio

NATIONAL BOARD
(Includes officers listed above)

Term expires 1978: Robert A. Anderson, Ottawa, Kans.; Curtis L. Decker, Baltimore; Charlotte Dunmore, Pittsburgh; Jane Edwards, New York; J. Julian Rivera, Brooklyn, N.Y.; Sidney Spector, Cleveland; Paul Unger, Cleveland
Term expires 1979: Mrs. Charles Bedford, Fort Worth, Texas; Lloyd H. Bell, Pittsburgh; Mrs. E. Rew Bixby, Los Angeles; Phillip Fellin, Ann Arbor, Mich.; William D. Ginn, Cleveland; Mrs. Patricia Miller, Indianapolis; Mrs. Sara-Alyce P. Wright, New York
Term expires 1980: Mrs. Dale Bumpers, Bethesda, Md.; Peter W. Forsythe, New York; Mrs. Edward L. Hughes, Salem, Oreg.; Eleanor M. Hynes, Atlanta; Pearl Mitchell, St. Paul; John Ramey, Akron, Ohio; Harold R. Withe, Morgantown, W.Va.
Representative from NCSW Committee on Public Relations: Donald F. Bates, New York
Representative from National Association for Statewide Health and Welfare: John M. Wilson, Richmond, Va.
Chairman, U.S. Committee of ICSW: John B. Turner, Chapel Hill, N.C.
Chairman, Combined Associate Groups: Lt. Col. Mary E. Verner, New York
Legal Consultant: Rudolph Janata, Columbus, Ohio

COMMITTEE ON NOMINATIONS

Chairman: Dee Morgan Kilpatrick, Ann Arbor, Mich.
Vice-chairman: Mrs. Ruth Casey, Topeka, Kans.

, *Term expires 1978:* Andrew W. L. Brown, Detroit; Mrs. Margery P. Carpenter, Washington; Mrs. Ruth Casey, Topeka; Hayward H. Coburn, Philadelphia; Neil P. Fallon, Boston; Dee Morgan Kilpatrick, Ann Arbor, Mich.; Kiyo Yoshimura, Chicago
Term expires 1979: Sara Lee Berkman, New York; Mrs. Guadalupe Gibson, San Antonio; Betty K. Hamberger, Baltimore; Hubert E. Jones, Cambridge, Mass.; Ann McCarty, Winnetka, Ill.; Murray B. Meld, Hartford, Conn.; Jerome Page, Seattle
Term expires 1980: Glenn Allison, Washington; L. Diane Bernard, Tallahassee, Fla.; Corezon Esteva Doyle, Phoenix; Mrs. Mary K. Lazarus, Columbus, Ohio; Marian H. Miller, Chicago; Mrs. Harriet H. Ruggles, Dallas, Pa.; Morton I. Teicher, Chapel Hill, N.C.

COMMITTEE ON PUBLIC RELATIONS

Chairman: Donald F. Bates, New York
Vice-chairman: Mrs. Adele Braude, New York
Term expires 1978: Ronald Kozusko, New York; Mrs. Betty Leslie Lund, Southbury, Conn.; Joe A. Pisarro, New York; Mrs. Elly Robbins, New York; Susan Roberts, New York
Term expires 1979: Marshall Boyd, New York; Herbert S. Fowler, Washington; Rae M. Hamilton, Washington; Mrs. Barbara Wallace, Washington; James D. Williams, New York
Term expires 1980: Farida Burtis, New York; Mrs. Elma Phillipson Cole, New York; Ronald E. McMillen, Washington; Mrs. Mary Jane O'Neill, New York; Guichard Parris, New York; Saul Richman, New York; Fred Schnaue, New York; Mrs. Ida Sloan Snyder, New York; Frank Strauss, New York; Owen T. Wilkerson, New York

TELLERS COMMITTEE

Chairman: John Behling, Columbus, Ohio

EDITORIAL COMMITTEE

Chairman: James Huddleston, Washington
Members: H. Frederick Brown, Chicago; John J. Cardwell, New York; Lela Costin, Urbana, Ill.; Bernice Harper, Washington; Mrs. Patricia W. Soyka, New York

U.S. COMMITTEE OF ICSW

Chairman: John B. Turner, Chapel Hill, N.C.
Vice-chairman: Morton I. Teicher, Chapel Hill, N.C.
Secretary: Maurine Didier, Albany, N.Y.
Treasurer: John D. Twiname, New York
Representatives of National Organizations: American Public Welfare Association, Edward T. Weaver, Washington; Council of International Programs, Paul A. Unger, Cleveland; Council on Social Work Education, James R. Dumpson, New York; HEW, Arabella Martinez, Washington; National Assembly of Voluntary Health and Social Welfare Organizations, Mrs. Michael Harris, New York; National Association of Social Workers, Jacqueline Fassett, Baltimore

Members-at-Large: Mrs. Evelyn Blanchard, Portland, Oreg.; Mrs. Margery Carpenter, Washington; Catherine S. Chilman, Milwaukee; Mrs. Edith Coliver, San Francisco; Bernard J. Coughlin, S.J., Spokane; Thomas A. Dine, Washington; Mrs. Guadalupe Gibson, San Antonio; Shelton B. Granger, Philadelphia; Mrs. Margaret Hickey, Tucson; Mrs. Carolyn Hubbard, Brooklyn, N.Y.; Kenji Murase, San Francisco; Gardner Munro, Providence, R.I.; Patrick Okura, Rockville, Md., Makunda Rao, United Nations; Mrs. Virginia Smyth, Atlanta; Jerry A. Schroeder, New York; Samuel J. Silberman, New York; Michio Suzuki, Washington; Terushi Tomita, Staten Island, N.Y.; Eloise Waite, Washington

Liaison:
NASW European Unit: Major Peter J. McNelis, Europe, APO, New York
New England Committee: Pearl M. Steinmetz, Cambridge, Mass.
NCSW Program Committee: Phyllis Harewood, Brooklyn, N.Y.
NCSW National Board: Bernard Schiffman, New York
Subcommittee Chairmen:
Membership Committee: Ellen Winston, Raleigh, N.C.
Nominating Committee: Bernard Nash, Washington
U.S. Program Participants: Virginia M. Smyth, Atlanta; Nelson Jackson, Pelham, N.Y.
Future Role and Resource Development: Bernard Schiffman, New York
Cooperative International Projects: Mitchell I. Ginsberg, New York.
Inter-American Conference: Mary Catherine Jennings, Washington
Members of Committee of Representatives, ICSW: Norman V. Lourie, Harrisburg, Pa.; John B. Turner, Chapel Hill, N.C.
Officers of ICSW (residing in the U.S.): Dorothy Lally, Vice-president, Washington; Mrs. Florence Hutner Rosechan, Assistant Treasurer General, Miami; Charles I. Schottland, Immediate Past President, Waltham, Mass.; Mrs. Kate Katzki, Secretary General, New York

COMMITTEE ON PROGRAM FOR THE 105TH ANNUAL FORUM

President and Chairman: John B. Turner, Chapel Hill, N.C.
Past President: David B. Jacobson, San Antonio
President-elect: Mitchell I. Ginsberg, New York
Members-at-Large: Mrs. Carmely Baca, Los Angeles; Awilda Castro, Brooklyn, N.Y.; Dan Edwards, Salt Lake City; Yvonne Lopez, Pueblo, Colo.; Robert McGarra, Washington; Dorothy M. Pearson, Washington; Rudolfo Sanchez, Washington
Representatives of National Social Welfare Organizations: American Public Welfare Association, Edward T. Weaver, Washington; Council on Social Work Education, Nancy Coleman, New York; National Assembly of National Voluntary Health and Welfare Organizations, Vernon Goetcheus, New York; National Association for Statewide Health and Welfare, Marilyn Schiff, New York; National Association of Social Workers, Mrs. Ernestine B. Lincoln, Silver Spring, Md.; National Health Council, Mrs. Pauline Miles, New York
Liaison Members: HEW, Jerry Silverman, Washington; Los Angeles Sponsoring Committee, Mrs. Jean Endicott, Encino, Calif.; NCSW Combined

Associate Groups Committee, Lt. Col. Mary Verner, New York, and Emelicia Mizio, New York; NCSW National Board, Sidney Spector, Cleveland; NCSW Public Relations Committee, Mrs. Elma Phillipson Cole, New York; U.S. Committee of International Council on Social Welfare, Phyllis Harewood, Brooklyn, N.Y.

NCSW SECTIONS

SECTION I: ECONOMIC INDEPENDENCE
Chairman: Raymond C. Munts, Madison, Wis.
Vice-chairman: Sidney E. Zimbalist, Chicago
Members: Sharon Fujii, Los Angeles; James Lowery, Los Angeles

SECTION II: PROBLEMS OF EFFECTIVE FUNCTIONING
Chairman: Leon W. Chestang, Chicago
Vice-chairman: Francis M. Moynihan, Detroit
Members: Mrs. Patricia Miller, Indianapolis; James Mitchell, Chicago; Mrs. Dorothy Nayles, Little Rock, Ark.; Kenton Williams, Kansas City, Mo.

SECTION III: SOCIAL ASPECTS OF HEALTH
Chairman: Jane Collins, Denver
Vice-chairman: Stanley J. Sterling, Lawrence, Kans.
Members: Amy Barnard, Denver; Ruth Breslin, New Haven, Conn.; Capt. Carol Bryant, Chicago; Darrel Burkland, Fargo, N.Dak.; George Dixon, Denver; Alicia Fairley, Washington; Nettie Fisher, M.D., Denver; Theodore Koff, Tucson; Bonnie Orkow, Denver; Ernestine Player, Columbia, S.C.: Betty Reichert, San Diego; Pablo Santistevan, Las Cruces, N. Mex.; Edith Sherman, Denver; Jack Snyder, Denver; Major Mary A. White, St. Paul; Mrs. Dale Bumpers, Bethesda, Md.

SECTION IV: LEISURE-TIME NEEDS
Chairman: Helen I. Brady, New York
Vice-chairman: Joyce Leanse, Washington
Members: Ruth March, Los Angeles; Dorothy Meyer, Los Angeles; John H. Ramey, Akron, Ohio

SECTION V: PROVISION AND MANAGEMENT OF SOCIAL SERVICES
Chairman: Merl C. Hokenstad, Jr., Cleveland
Vice-chairman: Harriet H. Naylor, Washington
Members: Charles Berman, Harrisburg, Pa.; William D. Ginn, Cleveland; Steven Minter, Cleveland; Gregory O'Brien, Milwaukee; Nancy Randolph, Cambridge, Mass.; Gabriel T. Russo, Rochester, N.Y.; Paul Unger, Cleveland; John A. Yankey, Cleveland

SECTION VI: SOCIETAL PROBLEMS
Chairman: Leon H. Ginsberg, Charleston, W. Va.
Vice-chairman: John J. McManus, Washington
Members: Betty Adams, Oklahoma City; Natalie Duany, Castleton, Vt.; Jacquelyne A. Gallop, Tallahassee, Fla.; Karen Harper, University Center, Mich.; James Huggins, Pittsburgh; John Blair Hunter, Fairmont, W.Va.;

Louis Levitt, New York; Nancy J. Norman, Charleston, W.Va.; James Painter, Pittsburgh; Kathleen Riordan, Philadelphia; Daved R. Rosser, Pittsburgh; Margo Swain, Mississippi State, Miss.; Harold R. White, Morgantown, W. Va.

COMBINED ASSOCIATE GROUPS

Chairman: Lt. Col. Mary E. Verner, New York
Vice-chairman: Emelicia Mizio, New York

ASSOCIATE GROUPS AND PROGRAM CHAIRMEN

AFL-CIO Department of Community Services: John J. McManus
Alliance of Information and Referral Services: Risha Levinson
American Association of Workers for Children: Martha Innes
American Council for Nationalities Service: Sidney Talisman
American Foundation for the Blind: Dorothy Demby
American Home Economics Association: Alice Stewart
American Jewish Committee: Mrs. Ann G. Wolfe
American National Red Cross: Dorothy C. Rose
American Public Welfare Association: Bruce Gross
Association for Voluntary Sterilization: Mrs. Betty Gonzalez
Association of American Indian Social Workers: John Mackey
Association of Asian American Social Workers: Rosalind Tanishita
Association of Junior Leagues: Jeweldean Jones Londa
Association of Puerto Rican Social Service Workers: Irma Serrano
Association of Volunteer Bureaus: Albert J. Page
Child Welfare League of America: Maxine Phillips
Council of Jewish Federations and Welfare Funds: Stephen Lecker
Council on Social Work Education: Nancy Coleman
Executive Council of the Episcopal Church: Woodrow W. Carter
Family Service Association of America: Emelicia Mizio
Foster Parents Plan: Reinhart B. Gutman
HIAS: Joseph Edelman
International Social Service of America: Mrs. Lemina Williams
International Union, United Automobile, Aerospace and Agricultural Implement Workers of America, UAW: Andrew W. L. Brown
The Menninger Foundation: Anthony J. Tangeri
National Assembly of National Voluntary Health and Social Welfare Organizations: Vernon Goetcheus
National Association for Statewide Health and Welfare: Lawrence A. LaMotte
National Association of Housing and Redevelopment Officials: Judy Morris
National Association of Social Workers: Lelia V. Whiting
National Board, YWCA of the U.S.A.: Vivian L. Grove
National Child Labor Committee: Jeffrey Newman
National Conference of Jewish Communal Service: Ted Kanner
National Council for Homemaker–Home Health Aide Services: Mrs. Mary G. Walsh

National Council of Jewish Women: Florence M. Bernstein
National Council of Senior Citizens: William R. Hutton
National Council on Alcoholism: Juanita Palmer
National Council on the Aging: Marjorie Collins
National Easter Seal Society for Crippled Children and Adults: Mrs. Rhoda Gellman
National Federation of Settlements and Neighborhood Centers: Walter L. Smart
National Federation of Student Social Workers: Sandy Reynolds
National Health Council: Madeline Kerman
National Jewish Welfare Board: Albert Dobrof
National Multiple Sclerosis Society: John Larberg
National Retired Teachers Association/American Association of Retired Persons: Wayne Moulder
National Urban League: Edward Pitt
Planned Parenthood–World Population: Lelia V. Hall
The Salvation Army: Lt. Col. Mary E. Verner
Trabajadores de LaRaza: Gloria Lopez McKnight
United Cerebral Palsy Associations: Ethel S. Undersood
United Methodist Church, Board of Global Ministries: Lulu M. Garrett
United Presbyterian Church, Health, Education and Social Justice: Ty Shin
United Seamen's Service: Edward J. Sette
United Service Organizations: Sheila Sturdivant
United Way of America: Hamp Coley
Veterans Administration, Central Office: Robert Siegfeld
The Volunteers of America: Lt. Col. Belle Leach

Index